Understanding Offending
Behaviour

Other titles from Longman include:

NSPCC: *Child Sexual Abuse: Listening, Hearing and Validating the Experience of Children* by Corinne Wattam, John Hughes and Harry Blagg

NSPCC: *Listening to Children: The Professional Response to Hearing the Abused Child* edited by Anne Bannister, Kevin Barrett and Eileen Shearer

NSPCC: *From Hearing to Healing: Working with the Aftermath of Child Sexual Abuse* edited by Anne Bannister

NSPCC: *Making a Case in Child Protection* by Corinne Wattam

NSPCC: *Key Issues in Child Protection for Health Visitors and Nurses* edited by Christopher Cloke and Jane Naish

NSPCC: *Children Speak: Children, Trauma and Social Work* by Ian Butler and Howard Williamson

NSPCC: *Participation and Empowerment in Child Protection* edited by Christopher Cloke and Murray Davis

Making Sense of the Children Act (2nd edition) by Nick Allen

Female Sexual Abuse of Children: The Ultimate Taboo edited by Michele Elliott

Looking After Young People in the Care System by Pat Goodall, Tony Laughland, Simon Biggs and Fergus Smith

Getting Started with NVQ: Tackling the Integrated Care Awards by Barry Meteyard

Young People and Drugs: A Multi-Disciplinary Training Manual by Mike Carr and Rosie Higgins

Answers: A Handbook for Residential and Foster Carers Looking After Young People Aged 11–13 Years by Ann Wheal and Ann Buchanan

Management and Delivery of Social Care by Max Taylor and Christine Vigars

Diversion from Custody for Mentally Disordered Offenders by Catherine Staite, Neill Martin, Michael Bingham and Rannoch Daly

Child Care Law for Practitioners in Social Work, Health and Education edited by Nick Allen

Competence in Youth Work for Part-Time Youth Workers by Mark Price and Rosemary Napper

Competence in Youth Work for Managers and Trainers by Mark Price and Rosemary Napper

Social Services Training Manuals

First Line Management: Staff by Kevin Ford and Sarah Hargreaves

Effective Use of Teambuilding by Alan Dearling

Manual on Elder Abuse by Chris Phillipson and Simon Biggs

Developing Training Skills by Tim Pickles and Howie Armstrong

Training for Mental Health by Thurstine Basset and Elaine Burrel

Monitoring and Evaluation in the Social Services by David and Suzanne Thorpe

Quest for Equality by Errol John and Barbara Deering

Care Sector Quality: A Training Manual Incorporating BS5750 by Steve Casson and Clive George

Understanding Offending Behaviour

by

John Stewart,
David Smith
and
Gill Stewart

with
Cedric Fullwood

Published by Longman Information and Reference,
Longman Group Limited, 6th Floor, Westgate House, The High,
Harlow, Essex CM20 1YR, England and Associated Companies
throughout the world.

A catalogue record for this book is available from The British
Library

ISBN 0–582–23432–8

Typeset by The Midlands Book Typesetting Company, Loughborough

Printed in Great Britain by BPC Wheatons Ltd, Exeter

To the Probation Officers of Britain

Contents

List of figures and tables

Acknowledgements

The authors wish to thank the Social Policy (Steering) Group of the Association of Chief Officers of Probation, which was responsible for initiating and guiding the survey on which this book is based. The first chair of the Group was John King (CPO East Sussex, now retired) who provided invaluable encouragement, enthusiasm and support in the early days of the project. He was followed by Roger Statham, CPO Cleveland, who steered our research project to a satisfactory conclusion. The membership of the Group changed over the years, but we recall with particular affection for their unstinting support and advice: Sheila Leathley, Debts and Benefit Adviser, West Yorkshire PS; Stephen Stanley, Intelligence Officer, Inner London PS; David Stephenson, Senior Probation Officer, West Midlands PS and NAPO representative.

We wish to thank Cedric Fullwood (CPO Greater Manchester Probation Service) for his kindness in agreeing to contribute a chapter to this book.

Our small research team of Dr Moira Peelo, Ann Prior and our secretary Kate Hewer ensured that the survey construction, administration, processing and analysis were undertaken to the highest academic standards.

Out 'in the field' there are seven people whom we shall remember for their hard work, thoroughness, patience and skill in administering the questionnaires and conducting or organising the interviewing: Helen Davies (West Midlands PS); Marc Ghosh (Durham); Una Mulrenan (Nottinghamshire); Alan Peggie (Northumbria); Shirley Phillips (Avon); Dr Philip Whitehead (Cleveland); John Wilkinson (Inner London).

We do not know their names and so cannot acknowledge each personally, but around the country hundreds of probation officers took the time to complete our questionnaires – thoughtfully. It is an inadequate mark of our appreciation for that work, but we thank them most warmly and, with the rest of their colleagues in the probation service, dedicate this book to them.

Gill Stewart, John Stewart
David Smith
Lancaster, June 1994.

List of abbreviations

ABH	actual bodily harm
ACOP	Association of Chief Officers of Probation
CHE	community home with education (residential child care)
CPO	chief probation officer
CSO	community service order
DSS	Department of Social Security
ET	employment training
ILPS	Inner London Probation Service
MPSO	money payment supervision order
NACRO	National Association for the Care and Resettlement of Offenders
NAPO	National Association of Probation Officers
PS	probation service
pw	per week
RTA	road traffic act (offences)
SIR	social inquiry report
TWOC	taking (a vehicle) without the owner's consent (hence *twocer, twoc'ing* etc.)
WRVS	Women's Royal Voluntary Service
YOI	young offender institution
YTS YT	youth training scheme

1 The study in context

Introduction

As probation officers try to make sense of the experience of those with whom they work, they constantly stress its sheer complexity, and the impossibility of identifying a single clear cause of crime. This book will, therefore, be discouraging to those in search of simple answers to the questions of what causes crime and what should be done about it.

The bulk of the book consists of the presentation and analysis of data on the offending behaviour of young offenders in contact with the English probation service in January 1991. It offers a typology of offending based on the accounts given by the probation officers involved, of how they understood the problems of these young people and what they had tried or would try to do about them. From these accounts there emerges a vivid sense of the difficulties many young offenders face in managing their lives, and the difficulties probation officers face in trying to help them. The background is often one of poverty (with little hope of relief), disrupted and unhappy early experience, substance dependency and stressed relationships, within a local environment which offers plentiful opportunities and even encouragement for criminal involvement. A recurring theme is the way in which economic pressures and problems of social and personal adjustment interact to produce the circumstances in which offending becomes a possible, even a likely, outcome. The typology of offending behaviour is an attempt, necessarily an untidy one, to impose an intelligible structure on a mass of data which has the rawness and immediacy of front line practice with society's most troubled and troublesome young people.

The process of constructing the typology and its results are discussed in Chapter 2. The aim of the present chapter is to describe the policy context in which the probation officers in the study were working. Clearly all social work practice has a policy context — in the case of probation, the most immediately relevant policy area is that of criminal justice. But criminal justice policy is formed within a wider context of policy which largely determines the room for manoeuvre which probation officers have, as well as having an impact on the lives of offenders and the choices open to them. Thus, for example, changes in housing policy will affect the ability of probation officers to help offenders find suitable, stable and when necessary supported accommodation, and in January 1991 their capacity was widely felt to have been reduced by cuts in the public sector and in the availability of supported lodgings schemes (Paylor, 1992). Changes in social security policy in the 1980s had the effect of greatly increasing the likelihood of severe poverty among young people, with dramatic results for the young offenders in this study (and see Stewart et al., 1989).

Probation officers and managers are thus liable to feel that while they will do their best to follow the Home Office's prescriptions for good practice their ability to deliver this effectively is often undermined by policy developments in other fields which make their work more difficult, a point illustrated by Cedric Fullwood in this book's concluding chapter. The Home Office's frequent injunctions to the probation service and other criminal justice agencies to co-operate and communicate with each other more effectively would carry more credibility if there were evidence of co-operation and communication between central government departments (Smith, 1994). Thus, while for reasons of space the focus of the following discussion is on criminal justice policy and its impact on the probation service, it should be remembered that policy on social security and housing (and indeed on education and training, urban renewal, and transport, to name no more) also influences both the lives of offenders and what probation officers can do to help them — a point returned to in the conclusion of the chapter.

Criminal justice policy and probation practice

As Downes and Morgan (1994) have shown, criminal justice policy has, at least since 1979, been more vulnerable than other policy areas to sudden shifts in the prevailing political wind, the revival of an openly punitive style among Home Office ministers in 1993–4 providing a dramatic recent example. In early 1991, however, the main policy expectations of the probation service were fairly clear, and it was possible to trace a pattern of coherent development back to the early 1980s and perhaps beyond. The general line was set by the *Statement of National Objectives and Priorities* (Home Office,

1984), which established the service's first priority as diversion of offenders from custody. What were then still called social inquiry reports were to be selectively targeted on relatively serious offenders for whom the courts might consider custodial sentences; resources for supervision in the community were to be established and maintained at a level which would command credibility with courts as an alternative to custody — meaning that they should provide guarantees of substantial amounts of contact with offenders, and that the content of work should be specific and relevant. Other aspects of the service's work — through-care and after-care, civil work, and the vaguely defined 'wider work in the community' — were to be subordinated in terms of effort and resources to work which directly served the government's aim of reducing the prison population.

The theme that the probation service should work with more serious offenders (rather than with minor offenders who might have problems but were not at risk of custody) was not new (Blagg and Smith, 1989; Cavadino and Dignan, 1992). What was new was, first, the interest of the Home Office in setting *national* objectives for a locally organised service, and in trying to ensure that these were actively pursued by the requirement that each service should produce statements of local objectives and priorities within the framework of the national objectives. A more active and strategic style of local management was to develop, within a context of enhanced accountability and performance measurement (Humphrey and Pease, 1992). Secondly, the Home Office became increasingly prescriptive about the content of work with offenders. This was largely defined in terms of 'tackling offending behaviour' (Home Office, 1988a; 1988b). The probation service was being asked to shift its practice from the provision of generic help and support to offenders to a much more specific focus on offending as the target for change.

It would be wrong to see this change of emphasis as an attempt by a repressive government to change the balance of practice from 'care' to 'control', although this is how it was interpreted by some, notably the probation officers' union NAPO (Blagg and Smith, 1989). To see it in this way is to over-simplify the policy processes at work. The idea that social work with offenders could sensibly concentrate on the reason why the 'client' had become a client in the first place — that he or she had offended — emerged from juvenile justice practice before it became a theme of Home Office policy (Thorpe et al., 1980). It was not, therefore, as alien to social work practice as was sometimes claimed, nor as unwelcome to probation officers struggling to define a rationale for their work in the gloomy atmosphere created by the prevalent (but mistaken) belief that 'nothing works' (Raynor et al., 1994). It is, however, important to locate the emphasis on offending behaviour as *the* target for probation intervention within the context of this penological pessimism and the criminological thinking associated with it. The material presented in following chapters supports our contention that a focus on offending behaviour runs the risk of neglecting the personal and social context in which that behaviour occurs.

Offending behaviour as the target for change

The 1984 statement of objectives defined them in terms of changes in the criminal justice system, rather than in individuals. It was in this way very much a product of the period in which the orthodox view among policy makers, criminologists and practitioners was that it was probably impossible to help individual offenders to change in a positive direction. In an effort to make sense of the presence of social work within criminal justice, practitioners came to agree with academic commentators that its best justification was diversion from custody. 'Low tariff' intervention was seen as more likely to harm (by drawing offenders unnecessarily into the system) than to help (Pitts, 1988). Intervention should therefore be reserved for those at risk of joining the prison population. But, if nothing worked, what should the content of work be? There were those who argued that it did not matter; the important thing was that whatever was done should be 'credible' with courts, for instance by emphasising the supervisory element of work rather than any helping element. Others, more optimistic, argued that while the 'treatment model' in which offending was viewed as the symptom of underlying personal ills was certainly discredited (Bottoms and McWilliams, 1979), a relevant focus for work could still be found in offending itself and in the personal and social circumstances associated with it (Denman, 1982; Priestley and McGuire, 1985).

Social work was thus able to promise that it would concentrate on the offending of those placed under its supervision, although it was to be some time before it could make any promises about whether this would be more effective than what it had been doing before. The promise was timely, because it fitted the government's policy agenda, that more — and more serious — offenders should be supervised in the community. There was also a fit between the cognitive approach to work advocated by practitioners who made offending their focus and the kind of criminology which became influential in the Home Office in the 'nothing works' period (roughly, 1975–1990). From the early view that crime might be understood mainly as a product of opportunity (Mayhew et al.,

1976) emerged the image of the 'reasoning criminal' (Cornish and Clarke, 1986), a rational calculator who weighed up costs and benefits before embarking on a criminal act. The traditional enterprise of criminology, seeking understandings of crime in offenders' personal histories or social circumstances, could for all practical purposes be abandoned. Situational crime prevention measures, involving increased surveillance and 'target–hardening', were the most — or only — promising approach to crime reduction.

There is a good deal of evidence to support the idea that much offending is the product of some process of reasoning — for example, when would-be burglars ponder on the most attractive targets (Bennett and Wright, 1984). It is also true that there is much in the concept of crime as reasoned action which can make it appealing to social workers. Social work after all requires that its clients be capable of rational discourse, that they be open to argument and persuasion. If they are not, they become someone else's responsibility, a psychiatrist's, for instance (Philp, 1979). On empirical, practical and theoretical grounds, it is preferable for social workers to think of offending as willed action rather than as the result of a sudden surfacing of irresistible urges from the depths of the unconscious mind. But there is an important limitation to the kind of pre-social scientific classicism which presents us all, offenders or not, as rationally self-interested economic actors. As Braithwaite (1989) has noted, most of us never reach the point of wondering which house we are going to burgle next; we have never considered the possibility of burglary, let alone of more serious offences. We do not refrain from murder or armed robbery because of lack of opportunity; the thought of committing such acts never crosses our minds.

The reasons why some people not only have such thoughts but act upon them have been the main topic of criminology since the discipline assumed something like its modern form towards the end of the nineteenth century, and in the next chapter we discuss what kinds of answers make most sense in the light of the data from the probation survey. Our point now is that the image of crime as reasoned action should not mean that we detach crime and our understanding of it from the structural, cultural and biographical circumstances of offenders (for a suggestion of how probation officers can use these different levels of explanation in understanding offenders and offending, see Raynor, 1980). Crime — or at least the predatory and violent 'street' crime with which criminal courts are chiefly concerned — is far from randomly distributed in the population. It is, for example, predominantly a male and youthful activity, and predominantly urban; young people with strong attachments to their parents or their school, and high educational or occupational aspirations, are less likely than others to offend; and crime is associated with economic and social marginalisation (Braithwaite, 1989).

Probation officers cannot help being interested in the way such factors operate and interact as causes of crime beyond the immediate reasoning process which precedes a criminal act; they cannot be concerned with the abstract and decontextualised 'offending behaviour' alone. Furthermore, there is evidence that work which might be excluded or given a lower priority by a narrow focus on the offender as the target for change may well be important in reducing the likelihood of further offending. Haines (1990), for example, shows that the after-care literature strongly suggests that the prisoners who do best on release are those with strong sources of social support (and for the importance of kinship networks see Paylor and Smith (1994)). Unless this is remembered, work which may well be important for the longer term prospects of reoffending is liable to be seen as an optional 'welfare' extra — for example, work to support the female partners of prisoners (Peelo et al., 1991). We are not, in summary, opposed to making offending the main focus of probation work; but we do insist, and the data which follow show, that probation officers are unlikely to get very far unless they also attend to the social and economic circumstances of this behaviour, and are allowed to work within offenders' social networks as well as with offenders themselves. Cedric Fullwood's final chapter suggests, encouragingly, that this message is beginning to be heard in policy-making circles in the Home Office.

Towards punishment in the community

The reasoning criminal, provided by the abandonment of criminological interest in the wider causes of crime, was a convenient figure for a government committed to denying that poverty and unemployment had anything to do with offending rates (despite evidence to the contrary from within the camp — see Field (1990); Downes (1993). The criminal did not suffer from economic marginalisation but from wickedness; social causes were admitted only if they could be located well away from the government's door, in the parental laxity of the 1960s' generation or the 'trendy' ideas of primary school teachers. The proper response to offending was punishment; offenders should get their 'just deserts' (or 'desserts', as the Home Office (1990a) quaintly put it). But this could not mean prison alone, since prison was 'an expensive way of making bad people worse' (Home Office, 1990a, para.2.7). The probation service had already been warned that if it failed to adopt the more rigorous styles of supervision supposedly embraced by the voluntary sector then it might find aspects of its work hived off to more compliant agencies (Home Office, 1988a; Blagg and Smith, 1989). It had been told to tackle offending and to target the young adults who were its main perpetrators by developing packages of intensive supervision (Home Office, 1988b). In 1990 the Home Office published White and Green Papers (Home Office, 1990a; 1990b) which respectively foreshadowed the sentencing provisions of the 1991 Criminal Justice Act and outlined proposals for the effective implementation of what were to be 'community penalties' — ways of punishing offenders by restricting their liberty, but doing so in the community rather than in prison. The Green Paper also discussed various options, including the amalgamation of probation services, which would make central control and standardisation of practice more certain.

This was the policy context in which the probation officers whose accounts are used in this book found themselves in January 1991. The Criminal Justice Act was twenty-one months away from implementation, but its main features were known, and probation officrs were about to start to be trained in such skills as assessing the seriousness of offences and abiding by the national standards for practice which were to be introduced along with the Act's sentencing framework. Probation was about to be redefined as a sentence in its own right — as punishment in the community; the length and intensity of supervision were to be determined not (primarily) by an offender's needs or problems but by the seriousness of his or her offence. Some probation areas might cease to exist as the Home Office sought greater central control and economies of scale. Although the basic statutory duties of preparing court reports and supervising offenders were to remain the responsibility of probation officers, other aspects of practice might be entrusted to 'independent sector' agencies in partnership with probation, leaving probation officers to enforce court orders, while others provided the help (Home Office, 1990c).

While the worst (from a probation point of view) has not happened at the time of writing (the spring of 1994), it was inevitable in early 1991 that many probation officers should feel anxious about the future shape of their service and their work, and resentful that the Home Office, whose policies depended heavily on probation for their implementation, should appear more critical than supportive of their efforts. The rhetoric of the White Paper — of just deserts, restriction of liberty, the need for community penalties to be 'demanding' and predictable, rather than individualised according to need — was inevitably alienating to probation officers. But the intentions behind the White Paper were consistent with the policy which had been developed since 1984. Prison was to be reserved for the most serious offenders, particularly those convicted of crimes of violence or sexual offences; property offenders were whenever possible to be punished in the community. The probation service was to implement the punishment by ensuring that the conditions of orders were fulfilled, but nothing in the White Paper implied that they should themselves behave punitively. While offence seriousness was to determine the sentencing band (custody, community penalties, or nominal and monetary penalties), the 'suitability' of one community measure over another was to be judged on the basis of an assessment of individual needs, problems and interests. The White Paper did not promise, and the Act did not introduce, a rigid system of just deserts sentencing from which individual considerations were excluded.

There were, therefore, grounds for optimism about the part the probation service would continue to play in the criminal justice system; indeed, the service was said to have a chance to 'move centre stage'. Some officers in early 1991 might also have begun to be aware of the findings of research which suggested that the 'nothing works' message had been exaggerated. Raynor (1988) and Roberts (1989) reported better results from probation projects than from prison, and McIvor's (1990) review of research both supported a cautious optimism about the results of work with offenders in the community and gave a strong hint of what kinds of approach were likely to work better than others. If the hint was not exactly what probation officers most wanted to hear, it was certainly not what some Home Office ministers might have preferred either. McIvor argued that work with serious or persistent offenders required a substantial amount of worker–client contact to be effective (something like two two-hour groupwork sessions a week), but that beyond this level nothing was gained, and something might be lost, by increasing the intensity of supervision. The kind of practice which was most likely to work was cognitively based, focused on offending and related problems (defined as such by the offenders and not just by the workers), and well structured and predictable within a planned programme; it should provide for choices between methods of work and an element of community integration. The most punitive forms of practice, 'shock probation' and 'scared straight' programmes, were found to be counter-productive.

The outcome of the most thorough and authoritative review of research available was thus broadly encouraging for probation officers interested in developing the kind of practice which already existed in probation day centres. While supporting a focus on offending, it also showed the need to work on related problems.

It argued against coercive and punitive approaches and in favour of open, contractual styles of work within a structure which provided for more than perfunctory contact but avoided increasing the intensity of supervision for its own sake, without regard to the risk posed by the offender. While one should not expect the results of research to be quickly or directly reflected in practice (Smith, 1987), it would be reasonable to expect some sign in probation officers' practice of a general awareness that this was the direction in which research pointed. And the probation officers whose accounts are presented from Chapter 3 on do often, though not by any means always, describe their work in terms of trying to help offenders change their cognitive processes, the ways in which they think and make sense of the world, in so far as these are relevant to their offending. But again and again the stronger sense is of the difficulty of doing this effectively and consistently with people whose lives are chaotic and disrupted, or who are so preoccupied with immediate problems of getting through their days that even if they saw the point of a structured and coherent programme of work requiring their regular participation over a period of six months or so they would find it very difficult to sustain motivation and commitment. While their reasoning processes might well improve, nothing else in their lives would.

Conclusions: with hindsight

Looking back to early 1991 from the vantage point of 1994, the policy context of probation practice has in some ways turned out better from a probation perspective than might have been expected, and in some ways worse. The better than expected developments include the emergence of a strategy for partnerships that has been more measured and careful than some of the early rhetoric suggested (Smith et al., 1993) and the continuation of a form of national organisation which allows for local accountability and diversity. The Criminal Justice Act 1991 showed in its early months that it could produce the pattern of sentencing which was intended, away from custody and towards community sentences and fines (Home Office, 1993); and NAPO (National Association of Probation Officers), among others, discovered its virtues just as these were being legislated out of existence by hasty amendment and undermined by powerful criticism (Feaver and Smith, 1994). Research began to produce more encouraging and convincing results (Raynor et al., 1994), and to suggest that even in conditions of severe social and economic deprivation it was possible for probation officers, adequately resourced, trained and supported, to engage the interest of offenders in the kind of structured and offence-focused programme described above.

On the other hand, a remarkable volte-face in policy led to a massive rise (of about 8,000) in the prison population in 1993 and early 1994, and created confusion and doubt not only in the probation service but in other criminal justice agencies which had tried to take seriously the reasonably consistent policy direction of the previous ten years (Faulkner, 1993). In the wake of the Home Secretary's declaration in October 1993 that 'prison works' came suggestions that the probation service might become the Corrections Agency, that it was time to put probation officers into uniform, and, with the announcement of a review of qualifying training, that officers should perhaps be trained as something other than social workers. New legislation in the pipeline was liable to criminalise social groups disapproved of by the government and its supporters, such as 'new age' travellers, hunt saboteurs, squatters and environmental protesters, and allowed for the establishment of 'secure training centres' for 12 to 14-year-olds convicted of three imprisonable offences. The government announced that it would repeat the ill-starred experiment in electronic 'tagging' of a few years previously.

The justification for all this punitive enthusiasm, when justification in terms of something other than political advantage was thought to be required, was said to be incapacitation and deterrence; the guilty would be locked up, and the potentially guilty dissuaded from crime by the frightful consequences of conviction. It is perhaps worth stating the obvious: that to argue thus is grossly to over-estimate the ability of changes in the workings of the formal criminal justice system to affect crime rates. For one thing, only 3 per cent of all crimes lead to the identification of an offender available to the system (Barclay, 1993). For another, while it is clear that the existence of some system of law enforcement and criminal justice has a broad deterrent effect, increases in the severity of actual punishments (within imaginable limits) add very little to this effect (Cavadino and Dignan, 1992, Chapter 2); and there is some evidence that offenders in any case over-estimate the likely severity of penalties (Light et al., 1993). Thirdly, Brody and Tarling (1980) estimated for the Home Office that massive increases in incarceration would be needed to produce even a modest reduction in the crime rate, while if the prison population were to be reduced substantially the increase in crime would be small — their estimate was that if the numbers in prison were reduced by 40 per cent the increase in crime would be 1.6 per cent.

Our conclusion is that while changes in criminal justice policy can certainly have an important impact on probation officers' practice their general effect on offending and offenders is likely to be minimal. This is not to say that what happens to individual offenders is unimportant; of course it matters whether someone is sent to prison, what the length of a prison sentence is, and whether offenders on probation are helped effectively and conscientiously. But none of these variables will affect the overall crime rate to any appreciable extent. Policy in other fields will — in housing, education and training, provision of resources for young people, social security, child care, and regional regeneration and support for investment. Not all of the factors associated with high crime rates are within any government's control; changes in local labour markets and employment opportunities, for example, are usually the result of international shifts in economic power and productive capacity which are beyond the reach of social (but not necessarily economic) policy. Some factors, however, *are* within the ambit of social policy, and many of the accounts from practice which follow show clearly how the position of young offenders (that is, young people who have been convicted — or are about to be convicted — of an offence) has been made more difficult and stressful as a result of policy decisions, most often in social security and housing. We are therefore sympathetic to the argument of 'republican' criminologists (Braithwaite and Pettit, 1990) that the aims of criminal justice policy should be linked with those of social policy in other fields, and indeed to some conception of what would count as a good society. We think that probation officers should be actively concerned with the effects of policies outside their immediate sphere of operation — and the study shows that many of them are. An individualised approach to offending behaviour is not enough, and probation officers cannot indefinitely endure the moral discomfort of telling poor and disadvantaged people that 'it is they who must change, and not their social circumstances, even when these circumstances may appear to make crime a rationally self-interested option' (Raynor et al., 1994, p.108).

2 A typology of offending behaviour

The main aims of this chapter are to describe the typology of offending behaviour which structures the remainder of the book and to discuss how it was produced. This discussion is framed, however, by a brief account of the research from which the typology was derived, an explanation of some methodological issues, and, finally, an attempt to set the findings of the study and the typology within a broader criminological framework.

The survey and the sample

The survey was commissioned by the Association of Chief Officers of Probation (ACOP) and was conducted in January 1991 (full details are given in Stewart and Stewart, 1993a). A sample of offices in seven probation areas, selected to provide a 10 per cent national sample and to cover a range of social and economic environments, was sent a questionnaire which sought information on 17-, 20- and 23-year-olds under some form of statutory probation supervision (excluding community service) or the subject of court reports during that month. Two small neighbouring areas, Cleveland and Durham, were treated as one for purposes of area analysis. The other areas covered were Avon, Inner London, Northumbria, Nottinghamshire and the West Midlands. The focus on younger offenders reflected the policy priority given to this group by the Home Office, as discussed in Chapter 1.

The questionnaire asked for factual crime-related details of offenders such as their legal status and current offence, and previous convictions. It also sought information about their personal histories, their present household circumstances, their material situation, what probation officers thought were the major issues in the offenders' lives, and what the offenders themselves would say the major issues were. Officers were asked for an overview of the young people's offending behaviour and for their views on the influence of their social backgrounds. They were also asked what the objectives of supervision were or would be if an order were made, and what their aims and hopes were in working with these young people. The questionnaire allowed for extended comment and description as well as strictly factual answers, thus providing qualitative as well as quantitative data. Most of this book is concerned with the qualitative material, but it will be useful initially to give a broad idea of the sample's characteristics. It is worth noting that while the method employed was similar to that of Davies (1969) the scope of the present survey is broader, since it covers the range of types of supervision, not just probation. Criminological comparisons would therefore not be valid, but where it is possible to make valid and illuminating comparisons between the two samples this has been done.

A total of 1,389 questionnaires was returned, an average of 231 from each area, with most (292) from Nottinghamshire and fewest (198) from the West Midlands. (Not all questionnaires contained usable information on all topics.) Of the sample, 11 per cent of the sample were women, and 12 per cent were from minority ethnic groups. The largest age group was the 20-year-olds (638 or 46 per cent of the total); 23-year-olds accounted for 31 per cent (427) and 17-year-olds for 23 per cent (324). Overall 24 per cent of the sample were in custody at the time of the census, 19 per cent under sentence and 5 per cent on remand. Cases which involved the preparation of a court report rather than ongoing supervision were 8 per cent. Almost half (666 or 48 per cent) were on probation. As was to be expected from the nature of the sample, most had previous convictions, as shown in Table 2.1.

Over half (54 per cent) were said never to have been sentenced to custody; 21 per cent had served one custodial sentence, 9 per cent two, 10 per cent three or four, and 5 per cent, five or more. The majority of their offences were of dishonesty, although in 27 per cent of cases at least one of the current offences involved violence or sex.

Turning to their personal histories, many of these young people (a fifth of the total and over one-third of the 23-year-olds) had already been through a marriage or a comparable close relationship. Just over a quarter had at least one child, but only 41 per cent of male offenders who were fathers were currently living with their child(ren), compared with 78 per cent of the mothers in the sample. (The 1991 National Prison Survey (Dodd and Hunter, 1992) revealed a similar pattern.) The suggestion of irregular or disrupted patterns of living was borne out by other findings. For

Table 2.1: Previous convictions

% of age groups	17	20	23	all ages	
none	17	8	6	131	9%
1 to 3	47	29	20	425	31%
4–5	16	23	14	257	19%
6–10	16	25	29	336	24%
11 plus	2	10	24	172	12%
unspecified/					
multiple	1	3	4	40	3%
not known	1	2	3	28	2%
Total	324	638	427	1389	

example, while 46 per cent of the sample were living with their parents or intended to do so on release from custody only 17 per cent had lived with their parents all their lives. The most common reasons for leaving home were conflict within the family and the young person's own behaviour. Of the sample, 26 per cent were known to have spent some time in local authority care (comparable with the prison population but dramatically out of line with the population as a whole, of whom 2 per cent have been in care (Dodd and Hunter, 1992)). Of these young people, 22 per cent were said to be chronically incapacitated through physical disability, illness or addiction.

These personal and social difficulties were exacerbated for many by current poverty. Only 20 per cent were said to be in paid work; another 9 per cent were on some kind of training scheme; 7 per cent were full-time carers; and 64 per cent were unemployed. Davies (1969) found that in 1964–5 59 per cent of his sample of probationers were in paid employment, and was able to conclude that, since young people on probation had on the whole shared in the growth of affluence in the 1950s and early 1960s, the problems experienced by young people on probation were not (apart from a few cases of hardship) material ones. No-one could draw the same conclusion from the 1991 findings. Table 2.2 shows the weekly income of offenders in the present sample and compares it with Davies's findings converted to 1990–91 rates (for the basis of the conversion see Stewart and Stewart (1993a), p.24).

Although only 13 per cent of the sample were said to have been always unemployed, very few had the educational or vocational qualifications which might enable them to compete effectively in the job market (disregarding the disadvantages of having a criminal record). 80 per cent had left school with no qualifications at all, compared with about 8 per cent of all school leavers in 1989–90 (Stewart and Stewart, 1993a, p.29). 16 per cent had effectively

Table 2.2:   Weekly income, 1991 and 1964–5

	1991			1964–5	
Income	N	%	Income		%
Nil	110	13	Nil		3
£1–£19	41	5	under £36.40		12
£20–£29	306	37	up to £72.80		33
£30–£39	99	12	up to £109.20		32
£40–£59	58	7	up to £145.60		14
£60–£79	70	8	up to £182		3
£80–£99	56	7	over £182		2
over £100	86	10			
Total	826			N = 461	

left school before the minimum legal age. As Downes (1993) has argued, the link between unemployment and crime is complicated by the finding that, for offenders in their early 20s, and beginning to acquire financial responsibility for others, merely having a job is not a predictor of desistance from crime; the quality of the job, its present wage and its future prospects, also matters. Very few of this sample were in a position to aspire realistically to this kind of employment, even if it were available (and there were regional variations in the expected direction, with lower levels of unemployment in the southern areas) in their locality.

In summary, the sample of offenders with whom this book deals differed from the general population along other dimensions than offending. All the comparisons are to the disadvantage of the sample; they were far more likely than average to come from disrupted family backgrounds, and to be leading irregular and unstable lives, with little security in relationships or in housing. They were far less likely to have educational qualifications and far more likely to be unemployed. Distressingly for a sample of young people, over one-fifth suffered from some chronic disability — a source of difficulty and potential discrimination which is often disregarded in discussions of social work with offenders, where race and gender are usually assumed to be the major sources of discrimination. The disabilities of young offenders may make them especially vulnerable to stigma and moralistic judgements because they are seen as their own fault — the product of substance abuse, of crime, or at least of recklessness.

None of this should come as any surprise. As Cedric Fullwood notes in his concluding chapter, the caseload of the probation service is characterised by a higher incidence of social and personal problems than that of any other agency. And the findings are along the lines which criminological control theory predicts. The factors which stop most of us from being serious or persistent offenders

— the bonds of attachment, commitment to and involvement in conventional behaviour, and belief in its value and rightness — are weak or absent in the lives of most of these offenders (Hirschi, 1969). Even when some elements are present which ought to be protective against crime, such as a valued relationship or the responsibilities of parenthood, they may be insufficient to counteract the influences of subcultural involvement (Braithwaite, 1989) with its associated experience of stigma and marginalisation, or of the despair and nihilism which result from social and economic exclusion without hope of change (Campbell, 1993).

How the typology was produced

The typology is an attempt to make coherent sense of a mass of data provided by people in a good position to make informed and sympathetic assessments of the reasons why the young people in the sample had become and remained offenders — probation officers. Our knowledge is their knowledge: the survey required that they be regarded as authoritative and informed sources of ideas and explanations of offending, and of what might be done about it. Readers will judge how convincing the accounts of the probation offfficers are; we have largely refrained from critical comment on them. The probation officers knew the offenders and their circumstances; we did not. Only occasionally, when it seemed that an explanatory account was at variance with the facts as stated, or when some other explanation seemed more helpful, have we remarked on the probation officers' interpretation of events. For example, we have sometimes suggested that a more social and contemporary explanation is possible, when the probation officer has stressed psychological factors rooted in the offender's early experiences. If we have been surprised by anything in probation officers' ways of understanding offending, it is by the persistence of psychodynamic ideas about the origins of a tendency to offend. While the sociological accounts of more recent criminology are also to be found, they have taken their place alongside, rather than supplanted, psychodynamic thinking. Having noted our surprise, we should also say that it is understandable that an approach which stresses the importance of early experience should have seemed useful to probation officers in many cases, since the early life of many of these young people was spectacularly disrupted and (by reasonable inference) unhappy. And there is convincing evidence (which does not need to be interpreted psychodynamically) that serious and persistent offending can be predicted with reasonable accuracy from the age of 8–11 (Farrington, 1990).

The typology is a way of analysing and categorising the accounts given by probation officers of offending behaviour and its motivation. It is not an analysis by type of offence, although some offences are more often found in one category than in others. The actual offence which gave rise to the current involvement of the probation service was often described by probation officers as incidental to the overall *pattern* of offending. It is these patterns — as seen by probation officers — which the typology seeks to isolate and describe. It is a typology of offending within a social context which reflects the reported experience of probation practice. Inevitably, the categorisation of cases to one type of offending behaviour rather than another is often disputable. Other analysts might have come up with somewhat different results, and quantitative statements based on the typology should, therefore, be treated with caution. Some of the cases discussed later illustrate the difficulty of assigning offending behaviour confidently to one type rather than another. These marginal decisions may sometimes seem arbitrary (the reader can judge), but we are confident that the typology as a whole is not arbitrary, but reflects real distinctions in probation officers' interpretations of offending behaviour. A further point to bear in mind is that the explanation of an individual's offending behaviour can vary over time. Past offending may be explained differently from present offending. For instance, offending as a social activity can slide into offending as a social norm (the drift into subcultural involvement familiar to criminology (Braithwaite, 1989)); or offending as self-expression can lead to offending as part of a 'life-style', when substance use becomes dependence. The point of the typology is not to obscure such complexities but to make them available for systematic description and analysis.

A typology of offending behaviour

The great majority of the reported offending, past or present, fell into one of the following categories, presented here in order of increasing commitment to offending behaviour, and less exactly of offence seriousness.

Self-expression: offending as a response to frustration or resentment; a reaction to stress; the expression of anti-authority feelings; a product of mental health problems. No predominant type of offence, but offences, whether against property or against persons, are generally non-utilitarian (i.e. not obviously committed for material gain). Probation officers' aims are most often expressed in terms of improving offenders' self-esteem or self-image, through supportive counselling.

Self-expression — frustration, reaction to stress, resentment, anti-authority, mental health. 32% of cases.

Social activity — mainly within peer groups and influenced by peer group pressures. 29% of cases.

Social norm — condoned/supported within the family; or by the 'community' of a geographically definable area. 16% of cases.

Coping — in reaction to poverty and financial pressures; 'survival' thefts. 19% of cases.

Life-style — substance abuse related; heavy drinking and drug abuse; involving homelessness, squatting. 29% of cases.

Professionalism — a means of earning a living — a form of 'work'. 28% of cases.

(Cases are multiple response to the typology categories and hence percentages total more than 100)

Figure 2.1   Typology of offending behaviour

Social activity: offending as a peer group activity, in which the individual is influenced by peer pressures. Types of offence vary according to the interests of the subculture to which the group is loosely or strongly affiliated. Since subcultures provide for the satisfaction of a range of interests (Braithwaite, 1989) offending can involve (for example) car theft, criminal damage, drugs, and racist violence. Probation officers are more likely to engage in or envisage groupwork focused on offending behaviour with this category of offenders than with others.

Social norm: offending is not sanctioned or supported merely within a particular group, but within a whole neighbourhood or community; or, in some cases, the young person's offending is seen as continuing a family tradition. The norms favourable to offending may be those of relatively stable and organised 'criminal areas' (Foster, 1990) or, more often, of neighbourhoods where the population is transient but new recruits to criminal involvement are readily supplied (Foster and Hope, 1993). Offences are generally more serious, more organised and more utilitarian than in the previous categories. Probation officers are more likely to be pessimistic about bringing about change in individuals; no set of aims for work emerges clearly as predominant, and there is little evidence of probation involvement in neighbourhood development or crime prevention efforts (of the kind described, for example, by Geraghty (1991)).

Coping: offending is a response to poverty and severe financial pressure; sometimes described in terms of survival, it is a utilitarian reaction to an immediate situation which would otherwise be intolerable. The characteristic offences are against property — various forms of theft. The offenders in this group are more likely than others to be in the youngest group, and more likely to be women. Some are homeless; all are materially insecure. Probation officers' aims reflect these perceptions by concentrating on supportive work on the problems arising from poverty and its associated stresses; they try to help with budgeting, to secure welfare entitlements, and to ease the pressure of immediate crises.

Life-style: offending is intimately bound up with other aspects of an individual's life, which sometimes may entail illegality (drug use, squatting); all the illustrative cases include some form of substance (mis)use. The actual offences cover a wide range, including property crime to get money for drugs and violence when under the influence of alcohol. Probation officers' aims generally focus on problems associated with substance use or dependence: with alcohol problems, help is provided or proposed from within the service; for other drug problems, other agencies are or will be used.

Professional: offending as a means of earning a living, a form of work; this may mean serious property offences, but it includes the important subgroup of 'offenders' whose professional crime is that they work as prostitutes. Offending in this category is seen as rational, utilitarian, consciously chosen as a feasible way of life. Apart from prostitution, it consists of serious or persistent crime against property or other potentially lucrative criminal activity, such as drug dealing. With most of these offenders probation officers' aims are unclear, and they doubt the possibility of using rational persuasion against a rationally chosen option. Victim empathy is sometimes mentioned as an aim. The exception is work with women convicted of soliciting, when probation officers see the offending as an intelligible and even valid choice in difficult circumstances, make no negative moral evaluation of the offender, and see their task as protecting her from the rigours of the criminal justice system and, if possible, the risks of her work.

The typology as originally presented (Stewart and Stewart, 1993a) included a seventh category: 'within the family'. Only a small number of cases (44 — under 4 per cent of the total of 1,216 cases for which codeable responses were given) could be categorised under this head, however, and it has been excluded from the analysis given here. Its apparent minority status, however, should not be allowed to obscure two important points. First, some of the 'within the family' offending was very serious: it included 'domestic violence', violence against children, and child sexual abuse. There is no doubt that official figures (including the data on offence types given above) grossly underestimate the extent of these crimes (Finkelhor, 1984; Smith, 1989). Secondly, many of the cases described in the following chapters show that young offenders have often themselves been victims — sometimes of actual abuse and violence, often of parental neglect, dislike, rejection and cruelty (on offenders as victims, see Peelo et al., 1992). Probation officers are right to identify what has happened in the family lives of young offenders as important in understanding the roots of at least some kinds of offending.

Over the total sample, the type of offending behaviour most often identified from probation officers' accounts was self-expression. The three categories of social activity, life-style and professional offending followed closely behind, each being mentioned at least once in about 30 per cent of all questionnaires. Coping, the most specialised category in terms of offence type (since it relates almost entirely to various kinds of stealing), and social norm offending were each mentioned in about one sixth of questionnaires. There were, however, important variations in the frequency of each type between the age groups. Self-expression, social activity, social norm and (as mentioned above) coping offending were types more often found among the youngest group (the 17-year-olds), and self-expression in particular was by some way the most common type in relation to past offending behaviour. Life-style and professional offending, by contrast, were more likely to be the favoured explanations for the 20- and 23-year-olds.

Probation officers thus move from explanations that are individualistic and psychological (self-expression), or based on the influence of an immediate peer group (social activity), to explanations in terms of professional commitment to offending or substance misuse and dependence (life-style) as they seek to understand the older offenders. They have the support of recent criminological theory: since the 20- and 23-year-olds have by definition not desisted from offending in their late teens, the trend is exactly that predicted by Braithwaite (1989) — increasing subcultural involvement and increasingly serious offending as the original failure of social controls to protect against offending is amplified by stigmatising, labelling and social exclusion, and by the accessibility of criminal subcultures offering a variety of attractive options.

Other variations in the frequency with which different types of explanation appeared were found between probation areas and, importantly, between male and female, and White and Black, offenders. The area differences could reflect different habits of thought between areas or real variations in the prevalence of different types of offending among young people in contact with the probation service. The first possibility loses some credibility in the light of Macdonald's (1994) finding that favoured explanations of offending can differ widely among officers in a single team. It seems likely, therefore, that (for example) the less frequent appearance of explanations in terms of professional offending in Cleveland, Durham and Nottinghamshire than in the other areas (especially Inner London) reflects real differences in the pattern of offending, and, behind this, in the nature and organisation of criminal subcultures. On the other hand, the influence of local organisational cultures (perhaps associated with concentrations of officers from one or two training courses) seems plausible as at least a partial explanation of the low level of social norm accounts and the high level of coping accounts in Nottinghamshire (a probation area with a distinctive identity and management style). The data do not allow us to decide the issue with any conviction; but overall the consistency of accounts across the areas is more impressive than the variation.

In relation to gender differences, there are important discrepancies in the kind of accounts given of offending, very much in the direction predicted by criminological work in this field (e.g. Gelsthorpe, 1989). We found, without surprise, that the offending of women was more likely than that of men to be explained as self-expression or as coping, and less likely to be explained in terms of social activity, life-style, or professionalism. But this should not be understood as meaning that probation officers unthinkingly attach gendered stereotypes to women offenders; rather, as later chapters will show, they give different accounts of male and female offending because women's offending is distinctive. It is more likely than that of men to be the product of desperate economic circumstances or of an unbearable personal situation (remember that the women in the sample were much more likely than the men to be responsible for the care of children); it is less likely to be the pastime of a peer group or the result of immersion in a subculture of professional crime or substance dependence. Women do not have equal access to these networks which support and organise criminal activity; moreover, as a criminological truism, women's offending is overall less serious and less persistent than men's (Heidensohn, 1988).

This is not to say that women do not engage in organised criminal activity of a very professional kind, as in the case of large scale planned shoplifting. They do; but those who do are not typical of the population of women offenders.

When we compared the explanations of offending given for Whites and Blacks in the sample, we found that overall the distribution of types was similar, with one striking exception. Black people in the sample were seen by probation officers as having much the same problems as Whites, and their motivation for offending was generally understood in similar ways. The exception is that Black people were less likely to be described as lifestyle offenders than Whites, and more likely to be described as professionals. Again, there are two possibilities: that the difference reflects a real distinction in patterns of offending, and that it is a product of probation officers' different ways of understanding the offending of Black people. Research from the early 1980s suggested that probation officers did tend to view Black people's offending differently from that of Whites, and that this was reflected in the accounts offered in reports to courts. More recent work, however, has found less evidence to support the view that probation officers contribute directly to what are undoubtedly discriminatory outcomes for Black people within the criminal justice process (Waters, 1988; Hood, 1992).

There is evidence later in this book that probation officers are sensitive to the ways in which racism may have an effect on young Black people which can increase the risk of offending — that is, they may view Blacks' offending differently, but the difference arises from the Black experience of racism, not from an imputed pathological quality in Black offenders. It is still possible, however, that probation officers are more likely to miss or ignore problems of substance dependence in Black people, and to assume that they have access to an organised or 'professional' drug-based subculture which is peculiar to Blacks. The alternative explanation is that such subcultural networks actually do exist, and, if they are organised around cannabis rather than more damaging drugs such as heroin, that they provide opportunities for professional criminal careers without serious risk of drug-induced harm to the people involved. Again, the data do not allow us to reach a firm conclusion.

We have tried here to indicate some of the questions which were raised for us in the construction of the typology, and which will no doubt occur to the reader. Clearly, there were variations in the quality of the accounts given by probation officers of the social context of offending behaviour and of their aims in supervision — quality being assessed in terms of clarity, consistency, coherence and the like. But we reiterate the point that the probation officers were well placed to give informed assessments of the problems the young people in the sample experienced and how these related to their offending behaviour. With the provisos we have noted, we were encouraged in developing the typology by the fact that identifiable themes and issues recurred time and again in accounts from different areas. We are confident, therefore, that the typology does help in understanding the range of difficulties probation officers encounter, and the various ways in which they try to help young offenders. Moreover, while the typology emerged from close engagement with the survey data rather than as an attempt to impose a pre-set theoretical framework derived from criminology, the different patterns of offending behaviour it reveals, and the light it sheds on how these change and develop over time, are encouragingly in line with the kind of criminological theory which has most empirical support from elsewhere. The final section of this chapter discusses how our data can (and, we think, should) be interpreted criminologically.

Control theory, labelling and subcultures

Control theory in criminology starts by asking not just why some people offend but why many people do not (Hirschi, 1969). Conformity is treated as requiring explanation as much as deviance. The answer, in very broad terms, is that we refrain from offending in so far as we are bound to the conventional order. The elements of the bond are given by Hirschi as attachment to others, commitment to and involvement in conventional lines of behaviour, and belief in the rightness of conformity and the wrongness of offending. But, as critics of Hirschi's version of control theory have objected, we do not conform simply out of fear of what would happen if we did not — not merely formal punishment, but the loss of the respect of those whose good opinion we value and of other goods such as a job or a career, or a loving relationship (Braithwaite, 1989). We refrain from serious offending because it does not occur to us to do otherwise; we have an inbuilt conscience which makes some acts literally unthinkable, and others abhorrent, to our sense of duty, obligation and care towards others.

While minor offending in adolescence is common, serious and persistent offending is relatively rare. The young offenders in this study belong to this minority. While there is endless room for argument about the precise processes at work, there is an overwhelming consensus in criminology that early experiences are important in shaping a disposition to offend or to conform — in building a conscience. Children who grow up with loving parents who exercise fair and consistent discipline are strongly protected against offending, and will, other things being equal, be strongly committed to conventional definitions of good and right behaviour. Time and again in the material which follows, the reader will encounter stories of children who did not enjoy these early advantages. In childhood, these young offenders typically experienced not consistent love and care but disturbance, inconsistency, neglect and abuse.

The early years, then, are crucial for the development of the bonds of attachment and commitment to law-abiding behaviour. But control does not come from the family alone. Attachment to school teachers and belief in the value of education are consistently associated with lower levels of offending (Braithwaite, 1989). The young people in this study failed at school, or school failed them. As a result they were at a disadvantage in the labour market; and many, unable to find legitimate work yielding a decent wage, were deprived of another potential source of commitment to conformity. And while many had entered relationships of what Braithwaite calls 'interdependence' — with partners and with children — these, even when reasonably happy and stable, were for many not sufficient to provide the basis for a bond to conventional behaviour.

Of course the sample consists, in the older age groups, of those who had continued to offend, usually more seriously, after the traditional point of desistance in the late teens. Others who were offenders at 17 do become law-abiding at 20, as the bonds of family relationships and commitments begin to take effect. But we believe that the survey suggests that personal relationships are insufficient in the lives of many young offenders to provide a bond to conformity when other elements are missing and there seems to be no prospect of their being acquired. Personal relationships are, so to speak, being asked to achieve more, to do more work, than can reasonably be expected of them in a context of long term economic deprivation and poverty. Downes (1993) draws on American research to argue that long term local unemployment is associated with higher rates of crime because it weakens informal community controls and provides an environment in which drug use can spread (Pearson, 1987); and, as mentioned above, he suggests that the type of jobs available also matters: stable jobs providing a reasonable income and some prospects are strongly protective against offending. Our data are entirely consistent with this argument.

In Chapter 1 we argued that the idea that crime is reasoned action was compatible with a concern with offenders' social and personal circumstances. This position is also that of control theory. Offenders make choices when they offend; but they choose within constraints, internal and external, which limit the range of choices practically available to them. The limits to choice are set not only by their own biographies and the economic environment but by the consequences of their involvement in the formal criminal justice system. Braithwaite (1989) argues that the typical experience of offenders who become enmeshed in this system is of stigmatising labelling which leads to social marginalisation and the risk of movement into a milieu of subcultural criminality. A number of the accounts which follow refer specifically to the destructive effects of labelling in making a law-abiding life more difficult to achieve, and to the processes by which a variety of subcultures provide support, opportunities and encouragement for further and more serious offending. Control theory cannot explain the diverse phenomenon of 'crime' unaided; ideas from labelling theory and subcultural theory are also required, as the probation officers in this study are often well aware, to make sense of serious and persistent offending, and offending which is closely tied to particular ways of life.

No single theory can sensibly be expected to explain all types of crime; indeed, one of the messages we draw from the typology is the sheer variety of offending behaviour which probation officers have to confront. Generally, however, we think that the data are best explained by the type of theory outlined above, in which the initial offending is viewed in terms of the weakness of the bond to conventional behaviour, and its persistence in terms of labelling and the consequent attractions of subcultural involvement. Readers may feel, like some of the probation officers, that another explanation is sometimes equally plausible; for example, self-expressive offending could be fitted neatly into the negative strain theory suggested by Agnew (1985), in which the strain arises not, as in traditional strain theory, from failure to achieve some desired good but from failure to escape from an environment experienced as destructive or frustrating. A specific example where alternative explanations are possible is the influence of time spent in local authority care on subsequent offending. We have been struck by the frequency with which probation officers mention care as an important starting-point for offending careers. Should this be understood as the product of learning and social support within a 'subculture' of care (as we think on the whole it should) or as negative strain which produces an angry response to a restrictive environment? The answer (whether one of these or another) could only emerge from further research. But, as we said at the start of Chapter 1, this is not a book for those who like simple answers; and we hope that the complex answers we have tried to give will be found reasonably convincing — or, if not, that they will provide material for fruitful disagreement.

3 Self-expression

Intelligent, alienated, unqualified young male seeks excitement through crime, and reacts against violent alcoholic father and overprotective mum (Avon).

Introduction

It may be argued that, as self-expression is our most complex type covering many circumstances which involve offending, it is to be expected that the type will be large, but that does not mean it is little more than a portmanteau for offending which does not fit the other categories. In explaining what each offender under supervision had done and their objectives, the probation officers most often used the language of personal, psychological explanations: being frustrated; reacting to personal stress; resentment against their family — and more vaguely against 'society'. Two other kinds of explanatory circumstances within self-expression could be construed as constituting residual, or even separate groups: anti-authority behaviour and mental health. Because the language which probation officers used in describing these two is personal and psychological, there is more justification for placing them within self-expression than anywhere else.

We are aware that psychiatric conditions could be thought to warrant a separate type. In placing mental conditions within self-expression we are taking a conscious decision to avoid a medical model. By a completely different line of reasoning, anti-authority behaviour may be seen by others as ideologically motivated, even political and hence socially structured. We shall be exploring these possibilities in the following discussion. It has also to be admitted that much of the anti-authority behaviour we shall be describing seems like, or may be associated with, peer group activities.

Leaving home and mobility

Adolescence is a transition and may be expressed by moving away from parents. For the general population, in 1987 27 per cent of females and 15 per cent of males aged 19-years-old had left home (Roll, 1990). In our study of offenders under the supervision of the probation service only 17 per cent had lived with their parents continuously throughout childhood and adolescence and were still doing so, although 46 per cent were with their parents at the time of the survey. That appearance of stability at the time of the study concealed mobility earlier in their lives. But it is important to stress the degree to which mobility characterises the age group in general these days. The General Household Survey and local studies have revealed how young people from working-class backgrounds often make several attempts to leave home before settling permanently on their own (Jones 1987; the spread of evidence is reviewed in Stewart and Stewart 1993b, ch.2). However, our group of offenders made their first move earlier than average, even for their social class, with 16 being the peak age for leaving home, but a third had been younger than that when they first left. It was the young women in our study who were more likely than men to have left home, and to have done so at an earlier age. The activity is at a higher level, though consistent with national data and the local studies cited above.

What may give rise to the greatest concern here is that all the mobility noted in our study tended to be the result of conflict and poor relationships within the parental home *and* was positively associated with the onset of offending. For both males and females the reason for leaving the parental home in half the cases was either overt conflict within the original 'natural' family, abuse by a family member or being thrown out. Other reasons were hardly less negative — divorce, re-marriage, step-parent trouble, death of parent: about a quarter of the sample. It is a commonplace that the modern family is subject to relationship breakdowns and re-formations of a highly complex nature, but if the resident children believe they have to leave home because of those changes it must be because those changes were perceived as negative. Only 6 per cent of these leavers did so for more positive passages to adulthood such as seeking work and travelling. Of course the high rate of mobility was not restricted to people categorised as Self-expressive offenders, although most Self-expressive offenders were also highly likely to have left home and moved around in the way we have described. That being probable, leaving the parental home, moving around a lot, even drifting, are particularly relevant social background to the theory of social control which underpins our typology in general and Self-expression in particular.

Control and strain

If offending behaviour as a social activity has an explanation in theories of subcultural deviance, our classification of Self-expression looks to control and strain theories for explication. Indeed we have argued that offending behaviour is best explained by control theory, in conjunction with a weak version of subcultural theory; our point being that strain and subcultural theories seek to explain situations which develop in the absence of adequate, appropriate social controls.

Without controls people will explore a range of behaviour much of which may be labelled as deviant (Box, 1981, p.132). Delinquency is controlled through social bonding, typically: attachment to other people; commitment to those relationships giving one a share in conformity; involvement in ordinary, generally approved activities; and a belief in the value of following the rules (after the formulation of Hirschi, 1969, ch. 2). The social institutions of bonding are said to be the family, school and, more rarely at the end of the 20th century, religion. Within the family the significant attachment is to parents, or one of the parents. There is considerable debate currently as to whether parental relationship breakdown and actual separation is, or is not, crucial of itself in either failure to bond or absence of social controls (Wilson and Herrnstein, 1985, pp.246–53). What appears to militate strongly against social bonding with parents is a relationship, whether breaking-down or not, which is fraught with arguments and violent behaviour. Following from that, the research evidence shows the predictor of later offending to be not so much the separation of adult partners, but the family conflicts, tension and aggression worked-out, particularly between step-parents, in the presence of children (several surveys are reviewed by Utting et al., 1993, pp.19–22). But new evidence reported by Cockett and Tripp (1994) suggests the children of families 're-ordered' by separation or divorce were more likely than children from intact families to have encountered health problems, need extra help at school and suffer low self-esteem. Probation officers certainly identify low self-esteem to be amongst their probationers' most significant problems. In contradiction to the conclusion of Utting, Cockett and Tripp assert that, although severe marital conflict was associated with a negative outcome for the children, it was the family reorganisations themselves which adversely affected children's lives. Where parents remained together, their children themselves said they felt better than those where the adults had separated, whatever the level of conflict involved (Cockett and Tripp, 1994). Whichever explanation proves to be the more relevant predisposing condition, conflict or separation, both are important to our analysis based on social control theory, because time and again probation officers report either or both to be significant factors in offenders' backgrounds.

The evidence of a negative relation between offending and bonding to school is even more dramatic. Poor school performance and lack of attachment to school and teachers is a predictive indicator of offending behaviour (evidence reviewed by Braithwaite, 1989, pp.28–9). In our survey, 'Most of the young people . . . were early school leavers with no qualifications. . . . Little esteem was accorded to teachers, nor the qualifications of which the education system is the custodian' (Stewart and Stewart, 1993a, pp.29, 32).

Social control acquires common-sense acceptance through daily repetition and traditional communication. The 1993 Nobel literature laureate, Toni Morrison, chants a litany of social control for ordinary lives:

> *Where's your daddy? Your mama know you out here in the street?*
> *Put something on your head. You gonna catch you death a cold.*
> *Ain't you hot? Ain't you cold? Ain't you scared you gonna get*
> *wet? Uncross your legs. Pull up your socks. I thought you was*
> *goin to the Junior Choir. Your slip is showin. Your hem is out.*
> *Come back in here and iron that collar. Hush your mouth. Comb*
> *your head. Get up from there and make that bed. Put on the*
> *meat. Take out the trash. Vaseline get rid of that ash.* (Morrison, 1978, p.307)

Control theory may be thought to have a problem in explaining to what it is people are supposedly attached and may seem only to account for 'less serious, comparatively trivial, forms of delinquent behaviour . . . (which people) dip into and out of' (Box, 1981, p.153). But on the latter point, most offending behaviour is in any case like that and subcultural theory can account for *attachment to crime* in a serious and entrenched manner without undermining the primacy of control theory.

It is strain theory which helps explain the first problem: 'conformity to what?' Material success is a widely shared goal, achieved conventionally through educational qualifications and well-paid employment. Indeed it is easy to develop an argument showing how the social controls which parents actually exercise on children are directly geared to pursuing this material success by the conventional routes. Strain theorists argue that, if the route to the accepted goal is barred, the person will adopt illegal means to achieve it (the classical statement is in Merton, 1957). So far, in the abstract, the argument would seem to explain Professional offending behaviour for material gain in a calculated manner, but it does not take into account cross-cultural differences. British evidence indicates that delinquents have low and conventional aspirations. The horizons of young offenders are no higher or wider than the similarly limited aspirations of the much larger social group of which they are a part (Downes, 1966; Willis, 1977). However, strain points us towards the stress, anxiety and tension which offending behaviour may resolve emotionally for a young person unable to achieve legitimately the rather ordinary goals of conventional society: house, partner, job, car and so on. Often one notes that the actual offences have relatively little to do with material gain, in which cases one can suggest a notion of *negative* aspirations, mirror-imaging the positive goal of worldly success. The young person's opportunity to escape some home-centred problem has been blocked. Strain arises from a failure to escape bad conditions rather than achieve good ones. The result is frustrated, resentful, anti-authority actions, some of which are offences (Agnew, 1985).

Our Self-expressive type of offending behaviour tends to contradict the blocked opportunities view of crime favoured, in its exemplary exposition, by Cloward and Ohlin (1960), where, if legitimate routes to the achievement of a goal are blocked, then the illegitimate ones must be open and available for delinquent behaviour to develop. 'Thus having either legitimate paths to success goals open or illegitimate paths closed may be enough to prevent an adolescent from becoming delinquent' (Braithwaite, 1989. p.32). Even that tentative conclusion may be rather premature. Young adults can do all manner of illegal things to themselves, others and property which express frustration at their failure to achieve a goal or escape from a bad situation without travelling a 'path' to anywhere. There are obvious strictures on property crimes (there have to be cars around for the *opportunity* to steal them to exist), but given the ubiquitous nature of 'offences', when are there not opportunities for crime: hitting people, burning stuff, defacing something?

We will demonstrate that much offending behaviour of this kind takes as its social and cultural references the family and authority organisations (such as the police). One pre-disposing factor for this to happen has often been the absence or inappropriate application of social controls. We find persuasive the theory of offending underlying the majority of our probation officers' Self-expressive explanations which links offending with people's experience in terms of blocked opportunities and failures, associated by probation officers with their clients' bad, erratic or poor parenting and their experiences of formal institutions such as schools, police and residential child care.

Relations with parents

From the questionnaires in our study we often read a bald statement like this: *'Inadequate parenting resulting in lack of appropriate controls and guidance during his developmental years.'* This 17-year-old had been *'Ejected from the family home due to behavioural problems; stayed with a local family temporarily and then returned home.'* But with 20-year-old **Colin** the probation officer supervising his throughcare (prison for burglary of dwelling, motoring, breach of parole) gives a fuller account: *'Records indicate that as the youngest of five he was shielded by his mother from a punitive father — a relationship was not created. Members of the family have rejected him because of his delinquency. Colin has strong feelings against his father who cohabited and then married a woman a year older than his eldest son. Stepmother has two children by Colin's father causing him to reject Colin.'* His mother died when he was fifteen: *'Colin has an immature understanding of the situation and since the loss of his mother does not care.'* The probation officer suggests that socialising controls are absent due to a failure of bonding with the father, which had been aggravated by the appearance of a stepmother. The death of Colin's mother presumably precipitated the offending behaviour (the dates tally) and Colin's father would seem to have made only negative attempts to exercise control, though research indicates that by then it was too late anyway (Farrington, 1990).

The root failure in Colin's case may be presented as a disagreement between mother and father about how to exercise control. But the pressures which underlie Self-expressive offending can lead to young people drifting into subcultures which provide social support for further offending, as we discuss next. **Bert** is a racist member of a peer group which beats up Asians in the north east. The probation officer supervising Bert's YOI licence also judges that inconsistent and inappropriate parenting and controls lie, somewhere, behind the current offending behaviour which was: *'Often in partial response to an over-punitive father and overprotective mother, who used Bert as a scapegoat for their marital problems'.* It is not suggested that the gang get excitement out of racist attacks as a social activity by breaking adult norms, but rather there was something amiss with the socialising of controls: *'Family background pertinent to client's personality development and offending. There are strong entrenched gender roles within the family.'* Before rejecting a connection between the actual offending behaviour here and parental rôles, and controls, one must consider how this learned racism might be addressed. Maybe helping Bert to understand that his racism fronts an essentially negative and ultimately destructive version of patriarchy might be fruitful. Bert's probation officer points us to a difficulty in control theory. It cannot predict the ways people in different circumstances are drawn to one offence rather than another. The psychological explanation of learned gender rôles offered by Bert's probation officer actually aids our understanding of that particular issue.

Exploring further the bonding of the child–parent(s) theme and the rôle of stepparents, consider the 20-year-old **Paul**, homeless in Nottinghamshire, of whom the SIR writer stated: '*He is extremely angry with his mother and the fact that she married his stepfather when Paul was small. There is also some suggestion that the way he was brought-up aggravated the situation as he was frequently smacked for punishment. I do not think housing, employment or finance has been a particular problem for this family.*' Which was crucial for Paul, the relationship breakdown, the new partner, or lone parenting itself as claimed next with **Alan**? '*One parent family, lack of parental control.*' However Alan's 'parenting' after the age of 14 came from the local authority '*Care system [which] left him ill-prepared for adulthood.*' Substitute child care received much criticism from our probation officers. One example was of a 23-year-old man from Northumbria in prison for robbery who would be homeless on release: '*No parental support or "rôle models". Gravitated through a variety of homes whilst in institutional care* [from the age of eight — also he had two children of his own in Aberdeen]. *The impersonal environment of homes and the fact that it seems no one really cared a great deal about him, has perhaps led to him not caring too much about himself. Also lacks skills to create worthwhile lifestyle for himself.*' That a sizable minority of offenders under supervision have been in residential child care (a quarter in our study) and the probation officers believe it to be significant in offending behaviour merits an explanation. We deal with the issue in various contexts, but principally as an aspect of Coping (p. 115) because of the association with survival thefts whilst on-the-run. Here, it is worth considering **Tristan** who had suffered parental rejection and residential child care, but the outcome was positive because of his self-determination.

At the time of the survey Tristan was 20, living on £28.50 Income Support and £2.90 per hour part-time at a supermarket three days a week. He lived on his own in a housing association tenancy in Birmingham after his discharge from residential child care at 18. He had £5 electricity direct and £4 rent direct. There were debts of fine, rent, electricity and bus pass. The current offence for which Tristan was on probation was theft and breach. He had started at 14 with burglary and had four convictions with one custodial sentence: '*Latest offence in my view committed under the influence of alcohol and on the spur of the moment. The earlier offences perhaps as a result of deprived childhood and no family support. Unemployment a factor too.'* Tristan had been in *'various childrens' homes'* since the age of three: *'He had no contact with his father or stepmother since then. He has no knowledge of his natural mother and no family support of any kind since then.'* He had done a YTS motor mechanic course for six months. The probation officer set out the objectives, but it was Tristan's will-power which achieved the positive results: *'Regular employment; discourage drinking habits; minimise loneliness by encouraging social involvement which he did because he became involved with a youth centre adventure playground all on his own; help with budgeting, especially encouraging him to regularly pay-off fines and rent arrears. These objectives have not been achieved by me as his supervising officer since client has been completely unco-operative in reporting. . . . This self-determination and progress has saved Tristran from breach proceedings.'* Somehow a very unpromising start seemed to have been turned-round. The probation officer was clearly convinced that absence of parental social controls and residential child care had played a negative rôle.

'Female explanations'

The majority of control explanations contextualised by parental psycho-dynamics were offered for females and this may suggest another kind of interpretation: gendered explanations for women clients. Consider **Mandy,** whose first offence at 17 was arson and who is currently on probation for being carried in a vehicle she knew to be stolen: *'Both offences have occurred when she has been drunk and seem to have been testing-out her parents and authority generally, as well as attention-seeking. There are no obvious links* (with social background) *as the parents seem to have done everything "right" and have sought the advice of experts for a number of years in coping with first, "difficult" behaviour, and now offending. Mandy has had a lot of advantages in life, but has not been spoilt.'* Mandy lived in what may have been a *ménage à trois* with her boyfriend and his wife. The medical condition from which she had suffered was dormant and although it prevented her working outdoors in bad weather, she had easily obtained and lost eight different jobs in two years despite having just two GCSEs. Mandy herself stated she was: *'sometimes worried about her lack of control and drinking. She thought her offending was a way of 'getting back' at parents'.*

We have shown (see p. 21–2) that female offenders under supervision are more likely than males to be judged Self-expressive. In what ways do comparisons between the questionnaire texts of men and women show the explanations to be gendered?

Amy was a 23-year-old mother of two children who lived with her in a housing association tenancy in Nottinghamshire. *'All my client's ABHs are on other young women, generally her partner's lovers. It is a case of misplaced anger on impulse. . . . Client's childhood was dominated by her abusive and alcohol-dependent father. She seems caught "in a trap" of successive relationships with abusive men and her ABHs are a direct response to this.'* The probation officer deals fully with a range of practice issues, the most important of which was: *'Single parent with two young and demanding children — issue of child care and parenting and child care provision (lack of it!).'* Amy states as one of her concerns: *'No break from childcare.'* Nor are Amy's material concerns ignored (with £62.50 per week Income Support she has serious arrears of rent, poll tax, a commercial loan debt and a Social Fund loan repayment of £10.38 per week) as the probation officer wrote: *'All Amy's other offences [thefts etc.] are a direct result of her desperate financial situation and based on rational decisions.'*

If there is a gendered explanation here, and one in common with the accounts for other female offenders, it rests on references to the men who were currently in their lives as being the occasion for Self-expressive offending in a stressful context of some kind. There was usually a dual stressful context of child care responsibilities and a failure of the aspiration to escape from financial stress, which is of course itself strain-producing. Here, with Amy, that stressful context was the infidelity of her partner. The probation officer notes the partner's infidelities, but was more concerned with *'breaking the cycle of stress-related offending by exploiting alternative models'.* Although some probation officers might attempt joint counselling, Amy's partner was in prison and in any case the focus of Home Office advice via National Standards is on the crimes of the offender under supervision rather than the broader context. The probation officer may have been doing little more than responding to the requirements to 'tackle offending behaviour'. The attention to child care issues has more to do with structured gender rôles than matters for which probation officers and the service may be responsible.

Gendered explanations — anxious women victims of men

Jill was a 23-year-old woman lodging in Gateshead, under supervision for her usual crimes of fraud and deception. It is worth remembering in the words of Jill's supervising probation officer that her crimes were *'mainly reactive to financial stress and mismanagement of finances resulting in relatively minor offences of deception of the DSS or similar'.* The explanation revolves around Jill's vulnerability to unreliable men. *'The client seeks security and love in successive* *relationships with the opposite sex which seem to reinforce her insecurity and isolation. Her circumstances can easily be subordinated by her to this quest and whatever demands her partner places on her. This tends to leave her especially vulnerable to change, negative partnerships and the potential consequences of rapidly changing sexual partners.'* The pressures which the partners have applied concerned influencing her to offend. So far the stereotype of a woman vulnerable to dominant males in her life who cause stress leading to offending behaviour is maintained. However, we also learn of the same absence of early controls that seems to apply to most of the men too: *'Unhappy, insecure upbringing followed by premature independence at 17, which followed lack of parental support, their divorce and then friction with the new step-father. Then she followed a somewhat nomadic lifestyle doing casual work. Jill then became a single parent and financial stress seems to have been the temptation or pressure to offend.'* The offences, at least those for which there were convictions, were not a stress reaction to either the relationship breakdown of her parents or Jill's friction with her stepfather, as the convictions did not start until three years later. But it does seem to be viewed as a stress reaction to bringing-up a baby on her own. Coping would have served as an explanation, but perhaps because she later had the two babies taken into Care and then adopted, her continuing frauds were more difficult to explain as Coping. Hence it becomes Jill's current relations with men which furnish the overall explanation of her offending behaviour.

'Anxiety' was often mentioned in explaining the offending of female probationers. Living in Lewisham with her mother, **Nancy** was 20 and working part-time for £60 per week (no children, no debts): *'No pattern to her offences* [motoring, affray], *both of which were committed under slight pressure from peers and at times of over-anxiety. Her home circumstances have contributed largely to her state of mind and anxious state and lack of confidence.'* The probation officer was referring to Nancy's agoraphobic mother as the source of anxiety at home. Nancy also had a hormonal problem requiring medical treatment. Consistent with such an assessment, the aims and objectives were to *'give general counselling and reduce the level of anxiety by helping with any practical issues at home and to encourage her to develop work and interests to improve Nancy's self-esteem, overall appearance and aid relaxation'.* If readers were wondering whether probation officers concern themselves with the appearance of male offenders: they do. There is no particular mention of the lone parenting within which Nancy had grown up, but the Self-expressive offending behaviour is related to stress with a female parent — none of which is inconsistent with explanations offered for men.

Gendered accounts – male offenders and their children

For 20-year-old *John* motoring offences started when he was 16, '*just prior to leaving home and his girlfriend becoming pregnant. Offending represents inability to deal with responsibilities and desire to drive cars* (he's never taken a driving test). *Social problems and stresses lead to offending.*' He lived with his girl friend and young child in a council tenancy in London. He is '*an immature man with unsettled family background having difficulty in coping with his new responsibilities of family life. Mad about cars, which he steals for joy rides especially in times of stress. John has immature attitudes towards women*'. The probation officer had an idea of how to tackle the car obsession, by gaining him a place a specialist motor project, which '*addresses attitudes towards cars*'. Attitudes towards women are perhaps a little different from cars and so the probation officer was to: '*discuss how he handles relationships especially in family/with women*'. There are at least two points: first and somewhat undermining our surmise, John's Self-expressive stress offending relates directly to a woman currently in his life, rather than parents in the past, but child care is not an issue for John's probation officer as it had been for probation officers in the female cases. The issue of attitudes towards women and John's immaturity was seen as being with his partner, although he has a four-year-old daughter. Sixteen is a likely age to start appearing before the courts, but not to have children and set up home. A regular partner, children, a home: these are often claimed to be the very stuff of attachment and commitment by which young adults are bonded to the norms of society. However, John is at one and the same time also supposed to be exercising that social control himself as father, and presumably head-of-household.

In support of our thesis, the probation officer supervising 23-year-old *Beesty* has no doubt what led to his ten court appearances for assault, indecent assault, theft, Twoc and so on since he was 17: '*No offences prior to his parents' marital breakdown. Most, if not all, of the young people I deal with come from broken homes. This young man is no exception. Difficult to enlarge upon this as they usually deny offending is connected to marital breakdown, or are reluctant to discuss it.*' The explanation for all the offending behaviour relates to Beesty's failure to get on with his stepfather at 16. Beesty lived with his girlfriend and their six-month-old baby in a council tenancy in Nottinghamshire. As with John, the probation officer did not mention child care when it might be expected. The denial of 'relationships' as a problem for young men, which *may* relate to their offending behaviour, could be the truly significant finding here. And if that case is a stereotype for the devil-may-care leader of the pack who, '*always took the view that people whom he had hit deserved it'*, the female parallel lies in the woman as 'victim' — Jill.

We would not be justified in drawing any strict distinctions between the way male and females explanations for offending behaviour are presented. True there appears to be a different vocabulary — anxiety rather than stress for example; and a tendency to play up the current rôle of male partners. For the rest the distinctions rest on structured gender inequalities (full-time wages), rôles (child care responsibilities) and stereotypes (non-aggressive behaviour; nurturing) which probation officers and the service may reproduce, but certainly have not created. What may be more illuminating and interesting is whether probation officers are able to address those gender issues in their practice, and that will be discussed later.

Reacting to stress

Committing offences in reaction to a stressful situation is not so nebulous as might be supposed. We can distinguish particular circumstances which have much in common with the concept of 'significant life events': loss and change in a person's life such as bereavement, redundancy, relationship breakdown; altered sexual identity; onset of disabilities; psychiatric conditions. In an earlier study we have shown how the arrival or departure of people from a household — including of course births or deaths, entails immense financial difficulties for those households most vulnerable to income loss (Stewart and Stewart, 1991, pp.28–30: only a quarter of probationers in that survey had not experienced such a recent 'life event'). But in the present context the reaction to such pressures is not the Coping strategy to be considered in Chapter 16, because in these cases of Self-expressive offending behaviour there is rarely a material link between what has been lost or changed and the crimes which result.

Loss of relatives

It may be claimed in the literature that bereavement is not particularly significant in the background circumstances of offenders (Utting et al., 1993, p.19) but for 20-year-old **Mo** the death of his mother was of great significance. *'Records indicate that he went to pieces when his mother died four years previously. Mo stayed out all the time, the armed robbery being the climax of delinquent behaviour with* *his peer group.'* His three court appearances began at age 14 and the four-year prison term started when he was 18. The probation officer supervising Mo's throughcare comments that the influence of his social background was: *'Substantial. Asian family with high expectations — mother's death affected him and he drifted with peers — drinking and playing machines.'* On release from prison he will be able to return to the family home and business: *'He has a good supportive family. He has a job in his family's shop'*; although we are also told of his drug abuse, drink problem, low morale in prison and his two abscondings from custody. Rejection by one's mother may function in a similar way to bereavement: the loss of a significant instrument of social control is clearly a factor. **Tom's** probation officer believed social background was of: *'Major significance* [in terms of] *unsettled parental history and divorce and the rejection of Tom, plus placement into care* [at 16] *has damaged his personality.'* The offences were *'Petty, impulsive, arising from an unsettled personal and family history, low self-worth, and no interest in forward planning.'*

So far we have only considered the stress resulting from loss of parents, which is realistic in terms of both their reported significance and the people in any person's life who are most likely to exercise and engender effective social control. From our study other family members have been crucial in that respect too. For 23-year-old **Russell,** a private tenant living in Bristol on his own after a relationship: *'His parents separated when he was young and he remembers being unhappy at home when his mother re-married and he lost contact with his father. Family links are very important to him and the only consistent relationship in his life has been with his older brother. During a temporary breakdown in their relationship he began to offend.'* Fitting in with the kind of offending we have identified, Russell committed several criminal damage offences for a year. But later, perhaps *'as a consequence of an unsettled life'*, he started committing violence offences which *'would seem to be out of character'*. Russell was on a YOI licence and the focus of the supervising probation officer's work was *'to monitor and support his decision to reduce his drinking'* which it was believed had adversely affected past relationships, not least with his brother. Russell had been thrown out of the family home when he was 18 and though it is difficult to distinguish between significant events, that was both when he began offending and lost contact with his brother. We may not be able to say what 'caused' someone to offend, but in an important sense that is not the point. How had Russell seen his life disintegrating into offending and what relationships were of value to him? Research in which one of the present authors has been engaged revealed that many prisoners had close family members who were irresponsible and so tended to rely for help on a wider network of kin and friends (Paylor and Smith, 1994).

Reacting to unemployment and poverty

For those people who have been used to regular full-time employment its loss is a major life event. As unemployment continues into a chronic state those affected must accommodate to the losses and changes it brings or be overwhelmed (Fagin and Little, 1984, review the evidence). Most of the people in our study, young though they were, had an intimate acquaintance with unemployment, for although only 13 per cent had never worked at all, only 4 per cent had been continuously employed or on a training scheme. As for the rest it was a mixture of work, schemes and unemployment, but the duration of those spells of regular employment was extremely short. Among those who had ever held waged work, 47 per cent had had only one job: 53 per cent of that group spent just six months or less as the longest time in any one job. In such circumstances, the experience of being unemployed has to be different from the unemployment of those workers whose experiences were reviewed by Fagin and Little, because never having worked, our unemployed young men lacked that route to maturity and self-esteem (see Campbell, 1993; Willis, 1977). However, one should guard against accepting stereotypes and instead examine how offending behaviour is explained and here we have a problem. Can redundancy-related stress be distingusihed from Coping? With difficulty, as the distinction rests on instrumentality and intention.

Noel started offending as a: '*direct response to being isolated and without adequate financial support subsequent to redundancy. He was also made homeless on account of redundancy*'. Noel had left home at 18 mainly because his parents were then retired and living in Spain. They had owned a garage in Nottingham, through which Noel '*had gained considerable mechanical skills but no formal qualifications*' after leaving school at 18 with six GCE 'O' levels.

The redundancy came about after Noel had: '*Worked for a year as a forklift driver for a local Nottingham company. He was made redundant shortly before he was due to take the qualifying test for forklift truck driving.*' At age 20 Noel was a first-time offender currently on remand in approved lodgings awaiting a court appearance for fraud against the electricity company, motoring offences, theft and breach of bail. The probation officer writing Noel's SIR anticipated a non-custodial sentence and if supervising would have an overall aim '*to see the client settled in the community with sufficient material*' *and personal resources in order to enable him to avoid further offending'*. The circumstances of Noel's redundancy are those of a young man used to regular employment. Loss of employment came hard on the heels of separation from parents.

In its own way **Harvey's** experience is not too dissimilar to that of Noel because he lost his carpet fitting YTS place due to the firm going out of business. Straight from school at 15 with no qualifications and then the YTS place folded; Harvey *'refused to go on another YTS place because he felt used by the system and so survived by offending and the good will of friends. He is now 18 and on benefit, actively looking for work and at times able to find work of a temporary nature '* Harvey left home in Bath at 15, *'due to poor relationship with father following his mother's abrupt departure from home'*, but had since returned and lived there with his father and brother. His latest offences of criminal damage fitted the stress reaction pattern of Self-expressive offending though as with Noel there was a clear link to a Coping strategy through Harvey's earlier stealing. And again as with Noel the instrumentality of Coping was clouded by the loss of relatives, particularly the ones who might best exercise social controls at a stressful time.

Lee was rather different because he had been offending in Middlesbrough since the age of 14 and by 23 had made eight court appearances. The probation officer supervising him for the current theft wrote: *'He has been involved in petty offences of theft and criminal damage. When he lost his job, Lee also lost his sense of purpose and became seriously involved in thefts and deceptions. Loss of employment has played a significant part in this young man's offending. Poor self esteem, poverty and a sense of uselessness coupled with poor family support has without a doubt led to his offending behaviour.'* Lee left school at 16 with four GCE 'O' levels and worked full-time on a pig farm for three years, until it went bankrupt. He went into voluntary Care at the critical age of 16 due to *'poor relationships within the family — family breakdown'*. Although Lee was separated from his parents at 16, offending pre-dates this. Committed stealing developed after the redundancy at 19 and continued unabated despite three months in a detention centre for theft and violence. Whether there may be any other circumstances is not entirely clear. We know Lee went through a partnership and there is reference to a child with cerebral palsy, though he seems to live on his own at his sister-in-law's house. Lee has debts for poll tax, electricity and gas, a fine payment and a social security benefit overpayment deduction, leaving him with £19 per week. The current circumstances being described by the probation officer would seem adequately explained by Coping, but it was the stress reaction to the redundancy for a young man already used to petty offending which was considered to have made a crucial difference.

Self-harm, self-worth

Reaction to stress can involve offending even when there does not seem to have been the intention 'to commit a crime'. In addition, it is not clear what has been gained from the offence. Even the negative side of strain theory sometimes seems an inadequate explanation. Confidence, self-worth or esteem may be so low that self-harm is beyond either attention seeking or 'a cry for help'.

   Linda is a 23-year-old lone parent with two children living in a London council flat who was herself in care since 13. She has never worked. She is under supervision for arson. However, it was herself whom Linda tried to burn: *'Tried to set herself and flat on fire after leaving her husband who was moving in with his lover. Linda had been sexually abused at 16 by her father who subsequently set himself alight and died as a result.'* The probation officer believes the sex abuse is at the root of Linda's lack of self-worth, *'hence her failure to keep relationships with partners going'.* The issues here are to build self-esteem and worth in order to break a very clear attempt to reproduce past tragedy.

   In circumstances of Self-expressive offending, the self-esteem of the offender under supervision is often destructively low as already reported in the cases of Tom and Lee above. A 20-year-old man who lives alone in a hostel, **Jason** *'has not yet settled into work and found the experience of living alone frightening and confusing. His offences form part of an increasing pattern of petty delinquency and self-neglect. As a result of his experiences he has learned to be negative and mistrustful of others.'* He has been before the courts five times since 18 for a mixture of motoring, theft and assault offences. The SIR writer stated that Jason was *'totally lacking in confidence'.* It is not possible to think of Jason as offending out of resentment or frustration as that would imply a certain confidence — an interpretation of one's situation against which one was reacting. At two and a half Jason's mother placed him in care because she could not cope following a split with his father. Jason was returned home at six, but this failed and he went into care until he was 18. Care appears to have left him totally unprepared for anything at all, which included being unable to work as a kitchen porter. Jason was *'someone who "thinks" failure'.*

   The low self-worth which for Linda turned to harming herself derived from abuse by her father. Fathers do seem to feature in the creation of negative self-images for girls and young women as we shall note below with Pat, but men too are not immune. *Tim* was 20, living on £25 per fortnight reduced Income Support because of 'voluntary' unemployment, alone in his own council tenancy in Coventry. He had left the parental home at 18 through *'disagreements with father because of excessive discipline'*. The current six month probation order was for obtaining a loan by deception and then clumsily attempting the same deception again. *'Tim is a fairly weak person who lacks self-assertion. He appears to have been associating with a more criminally sophisticated peer group and was persuaded by them to offend. His social background appears stable, but he has a very dominant father who appears to have engendered feelings of inadequacy.'* Father had high expectations of Tim who left school at 16 with three CSEs then attended two YTSs, followed by factory labouring from which he was made redundant, although as noted DSS inflicted a different interpretation on his claim for benefit. *'Tim has been unable to fulfil these high expectations of his father which have led to feelings of inadequacy and lack of self-worth. I would like to work with him in the area of self-assertion ideally by introducing Tim to a drop-in group and see how he interacts with other clients, but as no groups are in operation I will pursue individual assertiveness training towards developing increased self-esteem.'* The probation officer's objectives sound rather less offence-focused than might be expected.

In concluding this section on stressful Self-expressive reaction *Pat* links back to the rôle of parents in social control and forward to resentful, frustrated responses which take the form of crimes, though as we have noted not always for gain and sometimes self-harming. Pat threatened to kill someone (we do not know whom) while in possession of an offensive weapon. For this first offence at age 17 she was under supervision. Having left school with seven CSEs at 17 she had already been a temporary civil service clerk, and a chocolate factory operative, and was currently on a YTS typing placement for the usual £35 per week. She had always lived with her parents and the situation seemed entirely to do with the dynamics of that relationship: *'Distressed at not being heard and being treated as an immature girl. Possibly attention seeking behaviour — certainly an over-reaction. Parents very distant; mother over-protective. Her father Pat described as "like a professor" who enjoys explaining things but gets very irritable if interrupted in his own work and hobbies.'* The SIR writer suggested that there had been a failure of bonding between Pat and her mother: *'Pat is a sensitive young woman of above average intelligence who is muddled and unhappy with her feelings, expressing them mostly through piano playing and not to family members. Some work begun to off-set this with herself and mother during enquiries. She has been referred to a psychotherapist.'* A formal referral of that type was highly unusual in our group of offenders. Pat's diabetes is presumably in no way relevant and the home circumstances are materially good and secure.

Resentment and frustration

The sources of resentments and frustrations lie in complex circumstances, which are often seen to be outside the control of the person concerned — illnesses, disabilities, being Black.

Racism

Some aspects of the inability to affect directly the initial circumstances are illustrated by 20-year-old **Craig** serving his sixth custodial sentence, following fifteen previous convictions since the age of 11 as his probation officer claimed: *'Certainly racial prejudice was the major factor in his initial involvement in offending. This young man is a member of one of the first mixed-race families to live in this area. He has experienced racial tensions from a very early age. The family have been "labelled" as offenders and all three brothers have served custodial sentences. Initially he saw no way of changing labels and saw no reason not to offend. Now offends through habit and to take revenge on society.'* The structural disadvantage cannot be denied, but the amplifying effect of that upon the 'labels' which the offender in question obviously views as stigmatising should not be dismissed. The structural disadvantages seem to have their internal counterpart, so in a 'criminogenic' manner those people who are on the receiving end of racism move into situations which make offending more likely.

Racist attacks can be seen as violent expressions of resentment which have a social and political context, although as we noted with Bert's probation officer, who took a psycho-dynamic view, there seems to be a certain reluctance to grasp this. **Keith's** probation officer explained in similar vein the social background to his offending: *'Family dynamics especially rejection by mother and his father influenced Keith's life-style and behaviour.'* Keith, aged 20, is a committed offender who has spent four years in YOI for his *'last two offences* [which] *are the most serious involving an attack on an Iranian cafe owner committed with and under the influence of others when short of cash and accommodation.'*

The cafe owner being Iranian was not an incidental detail: the probation officer aimed to *'stabilise his present life-style by means of a plan directed towards work on his present attitudes to family offending and racial issues'*. The probation officer recognised *'family dynamics especially his relationship with his mother'* as the first major issue, with 'attitudes to ethnic minorities' third after work and finances. Keith had been on two training schemes, one completed; being received into custody terminated the second. Keith viewed his problems as income, work, accommodation and family issues. The Self-expressive resentful offending was still judged to stem from rejection by a parent: he was put in Care at 12 and thrown-out by his mother at 16. And again we still have little purchase on the character of racist offending, for as with Bert, it could have been a Social Activity. It was over racist attacks that we found the least agreement concerning the reasons for offending between the probation officers and the offenders under supervision. Such probationers were most likely to disagree with their probation officer's assessment of the situation.

For people who are on the receiving end of the racism, curiously the explanations are still the same. *Clive* was 20 and living in probation supported lodgings in Nottinghamshire after an unsettled period (he was actually convicted of vagrancy at 19). A first conviction at 17 for burglary led straight to gaol for nine months, though 'offending has reduced in gravity and nature over the years'. The probation officer comments on Clive's leaving home at 17 after 'a strict upbringing and trouble with the police'. Later he became the father of two children who live with their mother. Clive was 'understandably mistrustful of authority' and frustrated with the court processes. The probation officer has 'addressed the accommodation issue by a successful referral to a housing association'. The major objectives were 'to offer an alternative "model" of authority; provide a forum for debate; enable client to look at the impact of racism on his life and future choices; to encourage fulfilment of Clive's undeniable potential'. The last objective was based on Clive's blossoming academic ability at maths and English whilst in YOI. However, when released he went on a painting and decorating YTS during which 'his workmates held him down and painted his face white. Since that time Clive has not wanted to work and has been unemployed. He would like to attend college but accommodation problems and court appearances have prevented him'. Inappropriate over-strict paternal control was assumed to be the source of his leaving home when unprepared and going straight into serious offending, after which Clive was surviving by theft. Although Clive's resentment against authority figures was held to stem from the lack of action over the racist incident, it was presumably not the only one he had encountered.

Disability

The rôle of disability in contributing to resentful Self-expressive offending is hard to judge: 'The school system did not recognise

Lenny's deafness early enough and so he has made limited academic progress and is virtually illiterate.' The deafness and a knee problem were also thought by the probation officer to have affected his employability, basically as a labourer, though peer group influence and the Social Norms of his estate in Bishop Auckland were also important factors: *'Social group of young men on the housing estate, who are unemployable for the type of work available. With a wide knowledge of the scrap business, Lenny always has an eye open for half a chance, but he is more at risk when drunk.'* Lenny was first before the courts at 18 for theft, which developed through drunk and disorderly convictions over his next five appearances, to burglaries. He still lived with his parents whilst his 18-month-old baby lived with its mother somewhere else.

The probation officer had a practical orientation in work with Lenny: *'Establish links with community resources i.e. Disablement Officer, Technical College',* though behind all the peer group activity offending is seen a resentful reaction to unalterable circumstances. *'Stress created for Lenny by family attitudes and growth and development as a twin with more able sister.'* Lenny was partially deaf and although that is a condition known to exclude people from education and employment, if he had been profoundly deaf one might have suggested a different kind of case. Profoundly deaf people may not believe themselves disabled at all, but marginalised, stigmatised and discriminated against for living, perfectly well, in a world of people who just do not recognise hearing as of value: they are not disabled, but have a minority language. Those people with impaired hearing are in the dilemma of being unable to occupy either world with complete ease: there may lie one site for their frustration.

Unfortunately we do not know the physical disability which made 23 year old **Ned** have to leave home at 20 for hospital though it was an *'important physical abnormality which has required surgery from birth to adulthood. Ned was born with incredible physical handicaps which have played a major rôle in his consequent behaviour'.* From the age of 18 each of his three convictions has been for indecent assault. The probation officer supervising Ned's throughcare gave an overview of Ned's offending behaviour in an interesting reversal of the usual offence-led presentation: *'Has drinking problem, personality disorder and both are overlaid by sexual offending.'* The practical objective of throughcare was to arrange appropriate residential accommodation on release from prison, *'because his previous experience is of being unable to cope independently. When alone he is more likely to drink and then offend sexually. Both these areas need confronting in a residential setting'.* It was unusual for a probation officer to be pursuing a residential rehabilitative objective.

Working with resentment and frustration

Though practice objectives with any large group of probationers are
bound to be wide-ranging, those objectives were to be achieved via
relatively limited methods: counselling and skills training with the
client; liaison with other agencies such as social security or housing.
If relationships within the family and adolescent development have
been assessed as of major significance it comes as no surprise that
probation officers should write that they intended to counsel the
client. Re-building, even building for the first time, low self-esteem
into confident assertive, but non aggressive behaviour, is one of the
most significant practice objectives of probation officers because of
the destructive or paralysing force of low self-worth. However,
there is a policy and management issue here regarding 'focusing
on the offence', for often the probation officer would also be
concerned with other family members, beside issues of past life
which did not bear directly upon the actual current offence. **Rob's**
probation officer demonstrates the range. '*Major practical issues
regarding finance and housing have affected Rob's relationship with
his partner* [he has a ten-month-old baby, though his partner also
has access to her two children by a previous marriage]. *I have
been providing debt counselling* [Avon private tenant in rent and
other arrears; disqualified from receiving income support for a
period because he turned-down an Employment Training place
for a real job — the latter failed] *and have given Rob support in
contacting the relevant agencies, e.g. Housing, Environmental Health
etc. . . . By coping successfully with these agencies, Rob has learned
about the network of support available and gained self-confidence from
coping effectively himself.*'

'*Rob is currently being assessed by the Employment Co-ordinator*
[of Avon probation service] *with a view to undertaking a City and
Guilds motor mechanics course* [most of his eleven court appearances
from age 16 to 23 were motoring offences]. *He is awaiting a place
in the Alcohol Education Group and possibly, the Control of Anger and
Temper Group. In addition he is willing to attend the Drivers' Education
Group. Attendance at the above is related to challenging and examining
attitudes to offending and developing appropriate strategies so that the
likelihood of further offending is lessened.*'

'*In addition, Rob welcomes counselling with regard to his early
background and the legacy of insecurity and difficulties he has in
expressing his feelings directly* [left home at 16 for a partnership
after trouble with his step-father and tension over eviction from
the parental council house for rent arrears. They were a statutorily
homeless family living in B & B when Rob's offending began].
Housing remained a problem for Rob: '*At present, housing of an*

extremely poor standard is a major problem and source of anxiety, and Rob will need support in continuing to liaise with the Council and Housing Associations. In addition, both he and his partner wish to work [he had been on three training schemes] *to pay-off arrears accrued whilst he was disqualified from benefit, but child-care is proving too expensive.'* Rob had received good references at the end of one scheme but there were no offers of work. A general objective was: *'To help him build networks of support in the community and develop his Life and Social Skills to lessen his isolation and to enable him to make effective use of available resources.'*

With all that wealth of detail, range of objectives and clarity on how they might be achieved, the categorisation of Self-expressive frustrated or resentful offending rests on the probation officer's concluding paragraphs: *'Also, early background led to poor self-esteem and a tendency to be a loner who bottles-up his feelings. Most recent offences were committed after a domestic argument. Underqualified for level of ability* [rather like Clive] *due to disruption of schooling* [left at 15 with CSE Art] *due to the family's eviction which adds to his frustration leading to offending.'* Rob's probation officer had set ambitious goals.

Counselling is the whole focus of work with 17-year-old **Les** living with his parents in Bristol. *'The major issues in working with this young man are first to attempt to compensate for the damage done during his stay in various children's homes which appear to have had a negative effect on the way in which he perceives adults. My objectives are to work with Les on the way he interacts with others, particularly authority figures with the aim to effect a change in his attitude* [elsewhere: perhaps more understanding from police officers would be of great advantage in this case].' *The Self-expressive resentment was shown in the client's own perception: 'his problems stem from what Les has experienced in his formative years as unfair treatment by those in authority and he is now finding it quite difficult having to take orders'.* The latter is evidenced by his one and a half days on a YTS, two days on another before he left *'due to what he described as being unable to respond to the demands of adults'.* Les, being unable to claim social security, is *'supported by his mother'.* Unlike with Rob, the probation officer supervising Les did not propose to use groups and, given Les's circumstances, welfare advice and liaison with other agencies were not appropriate. So the method is one-to-one casework: *'My objectives in supervision are to counsel this young man on ways to use his negative experiences positively in the future, which can only be achieved by assisting him to get to know himself better. I shall encourage him to think, feel and act positively so as to improve his self-esteem.'* Lastly the probation officer proposed to *'examine why he offends and how to arrest his offending behaviour'.* The offences? Ten convictions for theft since

14 culminating in burglary, assault, going equipped and breach of bail. As with so many of the Self-expressive cases, the main focus of work was something other than offending. That was also true for very violent **Walt**, next.

For those of us not in daily contact with them, it is difficult to imagine just how aggressive young men can be: a major characteristic at which they excel. The aggression is unlike that employed in armed robbery, for example, because it lacks any utilitarian focus and hence is extremely dangerous for those in immediate proximity. The probation officer supervising 20-year-old **Walt** (who also has a MPSO) wants to. '*Avoid being hit*'. Since the age of 18 Walt has made five court appearances for theft, drugs, handling; never left the parental home in London; never had a partnership or children. The probation officer does not see the offending behaviour in itself as particularly important or serious: '*Minor offending behaviour. Client has major problems in self-control; this does not lead to offending as such but does result in aggressive tantrums which prevent people being able or wanting to help Walt. He would see his problem as not having a job, but I regard him as unemployable* [no employment history; left school at 15 without qualifications; never been on a training scheme]. *He has a huge ego. Expresses an interest in working, but because of his total inability to be told what to do, I regard him as unemployable.*' How did he survive? Presumably between 15 and 18 he lived off his parents, though currently he was receiving social security. When the probation officer looks back at the antecedents to Walt's '*Minor, opportunistic thefts plus cannabis*' he or she concludes: '*Total lack of parental involvement has resulted in a lack of ability to control himself*'. One may note that Walt was not described as having been abandoned by his parents or received into care. Beside preventing a breach of the order and avoiding being hit, Walt's probation officer wanted to: '*try to establish a relationship in which Walt feels safe so that he can learn self-control and avoid violent outbursts*'.

The officer supervising 20-year-old **Terry** had a rather more straightforward to define if difficult to achieve task. Terry was the classic Self-expressive offender: '*The client is a graffiti artist and it is unrealistic to expect him to stop as he is fully immersed in graffiti culture. I am looking for commissions for him with an emphasis on legal graffiti work. Terry is currently on a training scheme due to finish in three months and no permanent job to come from this* [left school at 16 with one 'O' level; nine months working steadily in printing, then as a silkscreen printer, and currently on a local charity TS delivering furniture].' At 17 Terry was sent to prison for nine months to rid him of the urge to commit criminal damage by graffiti. After leaving home at 19 in Nottinghamshire he became a private tenant. One judges that the frustration rested in the lack of legitimate avenues for a graffiti artist. In this case, the offending itself does not seem connected to the frustration, much as Walt's probation officer had argued, though in that case there was material gain. Terry would be looking for a driver's mate job until he could afford to take the driving test. The probation officer was concentrating on those issues and trying to maximise Terry's precarious income.

Mental illness

For three decades now the policy context of mental illness has been care in the community. The NHS and Community Care Act 1990 is the latest piece of legislation giving formal expression to the idea of achieving independence for this institutionalised group, though it is still unclear how and whether that can be realised (Stewart and Stewart, 1993b, pp.43–7). With this change in emphasis from institutional containment to community care it has been established that more pressure is now being placed on the criminal justice system by people with mental disorders (Dell et al., 1991).

Not all of those offenders under supervision whom probation officers described as mentally ill had been so diagnosed, nor were some officers entirely convinced when they were. In these cases there is a circumscribed domain of offences characterised by violence and criminal damage, both of which often involved self-harm. Typically, *'Recent offences — public order or similar; hysterical, aggressive and drunken behaviour generally as a response to difficulties in his relationships. Disturbed behaviour since childhood leading to voluntary child care* [first as a 2-year-old, then fostering and finally adoption]. *Described as having a "personality disorder"'*. We have read at length about the tantrums, anger and violence of many offenders and though a feature of this group, there are in addition, beside risks to self and others, an inability to grasp the reality of situations and delusions and projected fantasies. Probation officers often express the belief that institutional care or containment is advisable, perhaps more in desperation than in hope of improvement. For these client-offenders, where serious mental conditions have been identified, there seemed to be little sympathy with the idea that 'care in the community' would actually benefit them.

For 23-year-old **Steve** living in a hostel in London the conclusion was: *'probation at the moment seems somewhat irrelevant to his real needs'*. He was on his second two-year probation order for criminal damage and lesser assault: *'essentially a law-abiding young man. It seems there is a direct link between his mental health problem* *and the offences'*. Steve left home to live with his grandmother in London, from where he got a place in a Richmond Fellowship hostel because he had: *'Long-standing mental health problems, with the involvement of various psychiatric agencies. He is now diagnosed as schizophrenic.'* That diagnosis is clouded somewhat by a comment that whilst at school he was labelled as having 'learning difficulties'. Despite all this, Steve had a go at two YTS: *'worked in a butcher's shop for a while and has helped-out with gardening and odd jobs'*. During the current probation order Steve had said: *'I know I should never have been born. I feel I'm imprisoned in my head. I have an intellect, but I can't get it out. People ask me why I didn't learn to read or write and I can't answer ... '*. The professionals' response was as illuminating: *'The doctor is to some extent throwing up his hands about Steve. I am keeping mine open, but with a growing sense of helplessness, especially in regard to his longer-term future.'* The remarks of Steve's probation officer opening this paragraph are apposite and lead one to conjecture how 'offending behaviour' could possibly be 'addressed' in this case.

One is left with a general feeling that Steve needed supportive residential care, but **Lance** was judged so institutionalised and dangerous that *'he now cannot survive in the community or in bail hostels'*. This 23-year-old Northumbrian was remanded for causing serious injury by driving etc. whilst on licence from a six-year YOI sentence at age 17, previous to which he had already had five convictions from the age of 15 for theft, burglary, criminal damage and motoring offences. The serious offence when Lance was 17 also involved motoring: *'This young man showed no remorse at almost killing school children in a playground, chasing them with a stolen car and his offending persists to date'*, reprised whilst on licence. Lance has moved, when the pressure mounts, between his family and a succession of girlfriends, living a kind of 'nomadic' existence. But the parents are not in a strong position to help as Lance's father has a physical disability and his mother is mentally ill. Lance regards lack of work as his big problem, but he has been either unemployed or in custody since he left school without qualifications at 16, *'despite huge efforts by the PS employment liaison officer'*.

'Lance has a severe personality problem and struggles to cope outside of custody. . . . A tense, volatile and unpredictable young man who can be a risk to himself and others. He continually projects responsibility for himself and his actions onto others. He sees his problems as being lack of employment and family support.' The probation officer's comments regarding employment and Lance's parents have already been mentioned. What are the objectives here? Lance's probation officer, unlike Steve's, is far from despairing. *'I am trying to maintain a steady relationship with Lance despite his tantrums and difficulties,*

which can manifest themselves as deliberate gaps in contact with me. To further assist, monitor and tackle his personality problems I am working towards a future Probation Order being imposed', which is rather unexpected considering his comment on Lance's inability to survive outside custody. A commitment to anti-custodialism. A belief in community care, the power of counselling in a probation setting are evidenced here.

Earlier we drew attention to the possibility of different interpretations of Self-expressive offending based on gender. When focusing on diagnosed psychiatric illness, what differences there are rest on levels of violence and self-harm. **Lei** is a 23-year-old woman who has a Lambeth council bed-sit, but spent much of her time with her sister nearby. She has a poor relationship with her mother. *'The client's anti-social and self-destructive behaviour is the result of deep psychological disturbance manifested in offending from the age of 21.'* She has been convicted of criminal damage and false emergency calls. The current offence also included lesser assault and an SIR was to be prepared whilst Lei was on a hospital order: *'The main issue concerns her mental health rather than offending. She has suffered from schizophrenia and personality disorder resulting in wild behaviour and depression leading to suicide attempts for at least two years.'* Lei's offending behaviour which came to public notice dates from just after *'Incestuous sexual interference at the age of 20.'* Again we are left with a question concerning the pertinence of probation work which is entirely offence-driven. If probation is to offer general social work assessment skills, counselling, advice and welfare there is no reason why it should not benefit Lei, Lance and Steve — within the context of their offending.

A consistent feature of offenders under supervision in whom psychiatric disorder has been identified has been the appropriateness or otherwise of probation itself in the context of deep-seated illness. With **Jenny** *'suicidal depression'* had recently been diagnosed, though the Self-expressive offending was of some standing from the first conviction at 17 for drunk and disorderly and breach of the peace, to the latest at 20 for lesser assault. Parental relations were judged to be at the root of Jenny's problems, not helped by still living with both of them: *'Family background very significant. Jenny has been extremely emotionally damaged by her parents' behaviour and she is following in her father's footsteps regarding drinking* [he suffers from cirrhosis of the liver]. *Offending is mainly drink related. She hates the police and is abusive to them which results in her arrest.'* There is no material gain in the offending, its public seriousness relates to an anti-authority stance when drunk. The supervising officer intended to address the parental relationship as, presumably, the perceived source of the offending, the issue being to restore self-worth: *'Main work has been* *counselling regarding her emotional problems and suicidal depression with the aim of restoring her to emotional health, which hopefully will reduce her need to escape into drink.'* This was to be attempted by looking at Jenny's past history in the family context to identify what seemed to lead to heavy drinking for her, rather than the learned behaviour from her father.

If that was successful and Jenny regained mental health and self-esteem, the probation officer would assist in the job search or training and last but not least in helping her find, *'her own accommodation'*. However, at the moment of the survey Jenny was very low: *'Client's problem is she sees nothing in life to live for, so she wants to be allowed to kill herself and not be stopped by interfering people.'* The probation officer is stepping into a situation which developed into a chronic state over Jenny's adolescence then into an acute crisis in young adulthood, so early and easy results could not be anticipated. It is in these cases where the dual rôle of probation is at its most obvious: all the skills and methods associated with 'social work'; tackling the offending behaviour itself as a community sentence. There remains a policy, if not also a management issue concerning the extent to which the dual rôle is accepted.

The freedom which people have in whether to offend or not involves them in choices. Because there are choices, even if under constraints, probation practice can work towards less or non-offending behaviour. This presupposes that all offenders under supervision have choice and can exercise it. But some of them lack insight and therefore the exercise of choice is that much more problematic. In this respect offenders with mental illnesses present a serious difficulty. The clients of social workers are social subjects constructed by the discourse of social work, but that subjectivity is bounded by the social circumstances in which people find themselves (Philp, 1979). When people are unable to exercise choices they move out of the domain in which social work can be of help. In severe or extreme cases, people with mental illnesses are in the position of being unable to exercise choices.

Concluding with mentally ill clients has helped highlight some of the main features associated with offenders categorised as Self-expressive. We have noted that although the offences associated with Self-expression cover a wide range they tend not to be utilitarian, with anger, violence and self-harm prominent. Explanations and the focus for probation practice tend to be gendered. More so than for our other types, in Self-expression there is somewhat less of an offence focus in work, more of a concentration on counselling and building self-esteem.

4 Social activity

Dull, under-stimulated lad with an obsession for fast cars and joy-riding with his mates. Not guided into socially acceptable teenage male social outlets. Found his own excitement and status on the streets with other like males in stolen cars. Had a reputation for being the best driver in the area. Hated by the local police force (North Shields).

Each person must establish their own adult identity. The social institutions of marriage, the family and work structure aspects of identity, but the socialisation involved in forming an identity for oneself is believed normally to occur during peer-related activities from say 15 onwards. A series of conflicts — with the childhood persona, with parents — needs to be resolved prior to the assumption of an adult identity (Banks et al., 1992, pp.12–13). Crucial to the formation of identity is a passage away from parents, and although this does not have to involve actually leaving the parental home, it often does. We noted in Chapter 3 how early in their lives the young people in our study had left the parental home, the strained nature of that parting, its ambivalence and unsettling character.

It is within such a context of high mobility *and* parental conflict where young people are seeking to establish a positive adult identity that the rôle of the peer group is of special significance. Success in the assumption of a clear adult identity can be evaluated from the self-esteem with which a person regards themselves. In discussing Self-expressive offending we considered how for many if not most of the offenders in our study, the parental home was offering conflict, abuse and rejection. And in any case parental ties have to be cut. Could work, in the sense of regular full-time paid employment, offer identity and security? Work is a social institution in which we as a society have invested massive positive adult values. But in our study, beside those who were currently out of the labour market because they were in custody, only 20 per cent were in waged work (though much of it was part-time), 9 per cent on a Government training scheme, 7 per cent were occupied with caring responsibilities, leaving 64 per cent unemployed. For the general population of young adults regular employment is about 60 per cent (Banks et al., 1992, p.31). Although that still seems alarmingly lower than for the total population, who are so to speak, available for employment at 93 per cent in employment (*Employment Gazette*, March 1991, p.S21, table 2.4), it ought to be remembered that, unlike the people in our study, many young adults take educational courses.

Half of the offenders in our study had been on a training scheme, but these were not well regarded, a view which is confirmed by studies specifically about employment training schemes: '*For young people its* [a training scheme's] *main if not only value lies in the progression to a proper job. . . . If no job materialises then inevitably the evaluation of training will be negative*' (Banks *et al.*, 1992, pp.44, 46). Of those offenders who had been on schemes very few found relevant regular jobs. The resentment of the rest was evident as discussion of Coping offending in Chapter 6 will show. There was a sense of having been used: '*Education for education's sake is a reasonable aim, but YTS is presented to young people as a training scheme and training for training's sake is a contradiction in terms*' (Raffe and Smith, 1987). It is the overall economic climate which is important. Old-style apprenticeships never guaranteed anyone work. In the depression years between the World Wars young men were thrown out of work in droves just before they were due to receive a 'tradesman's wage'.

If work is not providing positive enhancement of self–esteem, because there is none or the young person is just on a training scheme, solidarity with a peer group could shore-up self-esteem and help shape future identity. The peer group may be a useful passage to adult identity because it can provide a social structure which is separate from and challenging to childhood. Young people could gain confidence in their ability to influence the course of events in their own lives. Such involvement with peers is normal; only some peer group activity is (seriously) delinquent. However as youth culture and criminological studies show us, peer groups may also demand from their members what establishment adults call 'delinquent activity' (for example Emler et al., 1987). As proof of the association it has been demonstrated that males with friends who have a criminal record are eight times more likely to commit offences themselves. By young adulthood, so powerful is the influence of a peer group of offenders that the level of parental supervision may make little difference to the level of delinquent behaviour whether or not the parents are operating social controls (Riley and Shaw 1985).

Social Activity was given as an explanation for offending behaviour in 29 per cent of the cases in our study. It became less significant as an explanation as the age of the offenders increased: 45 per cent of the 17-year-old offenders, but only 18 per cent of the 23-year-olds. Social Activity also varied by probation area (the age profiles were the same). Social Activity was very significant in the three north eastern areas, less so in Avon and not particularly significant at all in Nottinghamshire, West Midlands and Inner London. Social Activity was a significant explanation for males, but insignificant for females. There was no difference between Black and White people on this type.

There already exists an extensive literature on peer groups, youth gangs and delinquency which has over this century identified a huge range of activities, proffered explanations and justifications, *and* been highly significant in the development of criminological theorising. There is little point in reviewing these contributions, more than adequately discussed elsewhere (for example Downes and Rock, 1988, ch.6 and 7; Braithwaite, 1989, ch.2). Put briefly, adolescent boys join or form groups of their peers in which status is achieved and maintained by acts which, to say the least test the boundaries of adult tolerance, through to behaviour which directly challenges and opposes law-abiding society. Such adolescent gangs, which may live on into young adulthood are said to be *subcultural groups*, taking (in the classic accounts) aspects of the dominant culture(s) and exaggerating or perverting them. For instance, a significant component of our culture, male-domination, is further perverted into an obsession with power through violence expressed in alcohol-laced anti-social acts often against 'weaker' people: women, old women, Black people and so on.

It has been suggested that in using the term 'gang' we may be enhancing the identity, importance and coherence of the peer groups with which the offenders under supervision in our study associated. Perhaps 'near group' would be a more accurate term as they were likely to be just loose associations of only three or four acquaintances who were probably not particularly friendly and joining them may not entail the ritual which the word 'gang' implies (Yablonsky, 1967). However 'near group' is so ugly and clumsy that even social scientists should feel ashamed to use it. Caveats ringing in our ears, let us stay with 'gang'.

But gangs also imply leaders and followers, solidarity of intention, clarity of purpose. Those characteristics may be seen as positive, valuable assets in the adult world, even features necessary for achieving adult identity and self-esteem, not unrelated to the responsibility we expect of adults. However, by their delinquent behaviour, by offending, members collide with the police and the whole criminal justice system. In our study many offenders under supervision were 'members', even leaders, of such gangs, but they represented a plethora of recruitment to all kinds of Social Activities — theft, violence, graffiti and so on. We shall examine how far the declared aims of probation officers differed depending on the type of offending, for although in this chapter we note that most of the probation officers' aims were closely related to peer issues, some were not. The key identifying phrase for our type Social Activity turned-out to be 'peer group pressure'.

All kinds of gangs

Back in the late 1950s when US criminologists were refining sub-cultural deviancy theory, 'specialisation' was added to the inventory of gang activity: criminal gangs stealing for gain; conflict fighting gangs; retreatist drug gangs (Cloward and Ohlin, 1960). We found several different kinds of gangs to be prevalent around the country which are not easily placed in the Cloward and Ohlin classification (as did Braithwaite, 1989, ch.2). The most frequently mentioned types of gang were those heavily into cars, most of whose members were certainly interested in making money out of auto theft, but also did it for excitement especially if that involved being chased by the police (Light et al., 1993). We also found drinking and drug abuse gangs. There were gangs stealing for gain who were often characterised as part of the criminal fraternity of the neighbourhood which was tolerated and even condoned (Foster, 1990). Obviously such gangs categorised under Social Activity would also overlap with our type Professional. On the fringe of such criminal gangs we found 'style' gangs pursuing fashionable dressing and expensive leisure interests, except that for our offenders under supervision, to obtain these things, theft was necessary — the clothes, entrance fees to clubs and the like being out of the reach of unemployed young men (Hall and Jefferson, 1976). Racial divisions and racism were significant elements in gangs. Gangs of Afro-Caribbean and Asian young men afforded solidarity and mutual protection, whilst some White gangs specialised in beating-up Blacks. Apart from that racist twist, gangs doing little else but street fighting were rarely reported in our study, which is not to say that the rest followed the way of non-violence, far from it.

Super twocers

XJ is 17, lived with his mother and father in Gateshead in the north east of England and was a high speed car thief of the sort much vilified in the mass media. Four court appearances had been achieved since he began taking cars without the owners' consent two years previously. All his sentences so far were in the community, although at the time of the survey he was in custody on remand. He had no income because he refused to accept a YTS place, he had no qualifications from school and had never worked. This supervising probation officer wrote: *'The major issues with XJ are his identity as a twocer; the buzz of stealing high powered cars and relishing in chases with police vehicles and helicopter. All his offending is related to stealing and driving motor cars, undertaken with peer.'* He lives off his parents and his father had *'a high profile as a serious criminal in a home area where a high proportion of young offenders are stealing cars'*. The probation officer sees the practice objectives as *'creating an awareness of and change in behaviour* [through] *discussing employment/training; peer influence; negative consequences of recidivism'*.

Because of his age (20), the unemployed **Gaz** from North Shields, also living with his parents, was able to claim Income Support. His only work since leaving school at 16 without any qualifications appears to have been one welding YTS. He started twoc'ing at 15, and by 20 had eight court appearances and one custodial sentence of fifteen months in a YOI. In the overview, the probation officer wrote: *'Offending occurs in groups and involves cars, i.e. TWOC or going equipped.'* To explain this offending behaviour the probation officer uses control theory: *'Parents divorced, therefore, lack of guidance and support at a critical age. Not given much attention, but given a lot of financial assistance.'* The probation officer wishes to address Gaz's *'obsessive interest in cars. This is an issue for me in terms of the risks involved for others and himself. However for the client, his main issue is to keep out of custody and to offend in a way which means he is less vulnerable to being apprehended.'* Hence the objectives in supervision are to examine: *'the negative consequences of his offending behaviour which are: being a potential danger to the public; and his own loss of liberty. Also to explore his ability to be led by others and to encourage him to seek work and develop constructive interests.'*

In Middlesbrough *'**TC** (aged 17) has been heavily involved with taking high-powered motor cars and bating police to encourage high-speed chases* [this despite a hand injury leaving him without the use of his fingers]. *The housing area has a high level of juvenile delinquency and adult crime. Peer group pressure tends to influence him and his need for street credibility with his friends runs high.'* All of his twelve court appearances since 14, when incidentally he left school without any qualifications, had been motor-related, with one custodial sentence at age 15 for six months. Like XJ he had never worked and would not accept a place on a YTS. So for the probation officer the major issues to address were *'diverting him from custody;*

employment — help him to seek remuneration for work in a "proper" job; improve his self-esteem, to enable him to succeed'. Overall the probation officer thought that TC *'needed help in developing a more realistic approach to life'.*

By the age of 20 **Mark** *'Has grown out of Twocing and is into dishonesty offences, often linked with cars. Now he takes cars and takes parts from the stolen cars for his own use. Initially Mark was involved in offending with a peer group.'* He still lived with his parents, had never left the parental home, had no children nor been through a marriage-like relationship: just like XJ, Gaz and TC. Although currently on basic Income Support through unemployment he had done several jobs of an unskilled, temporary nature: *'However, in the main, since leaving school* [at 16 without qualifications] *he has been unemployed. Epilepsy creates a difficulty in gaining work in his key interest area of mechanics. Often Mark does not declare his disability.'* His first court appearance at 17 led to fifteen weeks in a Detention Centre, followed by three more court appearances leading to two probation orders and one compensation order. *'The Twoc offences were linked with his need to gain peer group acceptance and raise his self-esteem. Mark admits that he knows and is known by the local criminal fraternity where dishonesty is very acceptable.'* The main thrust of the probation supervision was to *'reinforce the work covered by the Schedule 11 4(b) Day Centre which is mainly addressing offending behaviour, challenging this behaviour, developing ways to avoid re-offending and addressing Mark's values and beliefs.'* The latter had yet to be achieved as Mark stated his problems to be just money, work and the law.

In north Bristol, the probation officer supervising **Chas** wrote that his three motoring offences between the first at 15 years old and the current supervision order for Twoc at 17 were *'part of peer group activity — joyriding when homeless which led to stealing cars for re-sale. Chas has grown up with other disadvantaged children who have encouraged each other to commit offences'.* If Chas had not been breached for not reporting, the probation officer would have helped with employment and accommodation, because his mother wanted him out and he would not take a YTS although unemployed for six months after jobs as a tyre-fitter and then panel-beater.

Chas's probation officer also supervised **Dave**, who was from the same gang but in custody on remand and with nowhere to live on release as his parents threw him out because of his offending and unemployment. His last job was seven weeks at Unigate Dairies. He burgled the place after being sacked for bad time-keeping. He had five court appearances since his first at age 15. All the sentences have been in the community and all the offences are motor related. The probation officer wrote that: *'Most of Dave's peer group are* *unemployed and not entitled to Income Support so they try to make a living by selling cars for parts. This began with joyriding and progressed. I suspect he has played-up to the peer group to fit in after being away in a Community Home with Education* [residential child care]. *One sure way to gain respect is to have a criminal record.'* The probation officer was preparing an SIR for (now pre-sentence report) Dave which would recommend another non-custodial sentence, but with a condition of residence outside Bristol as both agreed that local connections make re-offending very likely. His probation officer believed Dave needed to learn about independent living *'without recourse to re-offending'.*

Ron was 20-years-old, started motor related offences when he was 17, and had served three custodial sentences out of a total of nine convictions. Since leaving school at 16 without qualifications he had only worked for the odd day and was currently on Income Support due to unemployment. *'Primarily offences relating to cars and dishonesty. All the offences have occurred with friends and have tended not to have been premeditated but rather opportune joyriding. The client came to England from Northern Ireland at 15. He found it difficult to settle into school and managed to integrate himself by mixing with people who were already entrenched offenders. This led to disagreements at home and eventually he left at 16 and was even more reliant on his friends who were negative influences on him.'* He was living with his girl friend and her daughter. The probation officer mentions under the objects of supervision: *'As the client tends to offend with peers he needs to develop assertiveness skills to resist these pressures. To look closely at the effects (positive and negative) of peer pressure and encourage client to acknowledge the negative side and resist it whilst developing alternative support networks.'*

Stealing cars and driving fast and provocatively to initiate a police chase involves skills which are admired by the offender's peer group. The main motivations are undoubtedly the attractions of excitement, status and self-esteem. In deterring young adults from car crime an alternative to those very powerful forces has to be found which does not provide a 'reward' for the offending behaviour. Motor projects which are open to all young people who are interested can be a more useful contribution to curbing car crime than, say, custodial sentences (McGillivray, 1993).

Neighbourhood thieving gangs

*'***Stan** *is involved in a neighbourhood group of young male offenders. It's his whole life. Also his older brothers are offenders. He's often a target of police 'interest' which causes family bitterness'.* The significance of the social background was believed to be the: *'Shared negative*

experiences in a neighbourhood group of offenders.' What did Stan and his mates do? First before the courts at 13 with eight appearances by 17, he had been convicted of dishonesty offences — burglary, theft and handling, with two custodial disposals. He had no income, job or YTS, and lived with both parents in the north east. After leaving school at 16 with no qualifications he had been on two schemes for a short while, then his father had started him on some building work were they lived in Sunderland. It did not last long. Stan regarded as problematic, besides the lack of money, *'Relationships with the police.'* The probation officer saw the issue to be: *'Persuading Stan he can stay out of trouble and therefore custody.'* That would be aided by further *'Persuading him to take a scheme and look to other forms of income than thieving.'*

Moving down country to the easier economic climate of Avon, **Pete** was *'heavily involved in local delinquent behaviour'*. He was a member of a *'large delinquent group'*. This seems to have been a big gang into all kinds of dishonesty and violence if Pete's record is indicative. Seven court appearances since 15, with one custodial disposal, had brought him to the current probation order for violence, committing theft and motoring offences at age 20. The approach in Avon is to *'Engage Pete in all forms of activity within the Offending Behaviour Group . . .* [because] *He doesn't work in one to one'*. And to *'Enable him to take on responsibility for work.'* The latter is a reasonable objective in an area of relatively low unemployment, for *'This man has been unemployed for most of the time since leaving school* [at 15].*'*

Black and White gangs

Dale had been on the receiving end of racial harassment. He was 17-years-old, living in Bristol with his parents, unattached, never having left home. He described himself as 'mixed' race. The first court appearance was just a year previous to our survey: three more appearances followed rapidly. The offences undertaken as a member of a Black gang were a mixture of robberies, thefts, motor offences, criminal damage and assault. Home life was reasonable, for the probation officer concluded that: *'I believe his social background has had only a limited effect on his current behaviour, but more to do with environment and racial harassment. Because of his lack of confidence and social skills he needs to feel wanted by his peer group. Dale has become resentful of authority due to his own negative experiences with people in authority.'* Since leaving school without qualifications he has had about two weeks employment and 'resigned' from a YTS. At the time of the survey he had no legitimate income of his own. Dale was himself a victim of crime. The number of racially motivated attacks has been increasing steadily, reaching 140,000 in 1992 according to the British Crime Survey. However, there is no specific offence of racial violence and it appears the government has no intention of creating one (*Guardian* 24 January 1994, p.5).

From the same area of Bristol the 20-year-old **Jed**: '*Has grown up in a very delinquent subculture and become totally involved. As he is Black he has been disadvantaged by this and probably feels that he has never had a real chance to succeed.*' The particular part that being Black had played in Jed's disadvantage is obscured by the link with the '*very delinquent sub-culture*'. He had never worked or been on a scheme at all since 16 when he left school without qualifications. He lived with his parents up to his current custodial sentence. '*He is a very delinquent young man who had problems with the use of cocaine and also offending resulting from this and association with equally delinquent friends. He would see being Black and treated in a racist way by police as significant.*'

The case of **Tone** helps us recognise that police attitudes are themselves a problem, but so too is the behaviour of the gang — a vicious circle: '*This young man has been in custody serving a five-year sentence for robbery and assault. His offending is related to his unemployment and the influences of others in similar circumstances. The way Black people are viewed and dealt with by the police and the courts is also a factor. Tone has been brought up in an area with large numbers of young men in similar circumstances and cultural background. The area has acquired a bad reputation with local police.*' The objectives in throughcare were: '*To help him prepare for release; to help him become aware of the difficulties and dangers in prison and to offer consistent support to both prisoner and family.*' Leaving school at 16 without qualifications, he had been on two training schemes, but never in regular work. When not in prison he lived with his parents and siblings in Nottingham. Black youths were being further alienated and antagonised because of police attitudes. Further, similar, offending was likely.

One of the most specialised and bizarre gangs around London must be that of which **Ace** was a member. Again, he was a newcomer to the courts, with his first appearance at 16 for shop-lifting, followed by three counts of criminal damage, to the current theft at 17. '*Ace wants to be recognised and so joined a graffiti gang.*' All his offending was '*Peer group activity*' against a social background of '*Racism*'. He was living with his parents and siblings, and attending sixth form college taking BTEC. The supervising probation officer wanted to address: '*Family relationships; peer group pressure; education — by liaison with the parents and counselling the client; plan his education; examine peer group involvement.*' In Self-expression we discussed another graffiti artist, Terry (p.48), but there was no indication that he was part of a gang. A graffiti gang is one avenue of specialisation that a subculture may take. Terry and Ace indicate the respective places of social control and subcultural theories in explaining offending behaviour. The gang works for Ace whilst Terry just did Self-expressively the thing in which Ace's gang sought specialisation.

Now we turn to the White racist gang of Ryhope, Northumbria. **Kurt** was 17-years-old, left school at 16 without qualifications, and at the time of the survey had no income whatsoever because his bridging allowance had expired and he was not on a scheme. Kurt was on YOI licence having been sentenced for affray. He was a mate of Bert's (see Self-expression, p.31), however in that case the explanation had revolved around family relationships whereas Kurt was presented in classic subcultural terms: *'Caught-up in a mutually supportive peer group in Ryhope which is hostile to Blacks and the police. The last affray involved a racist attack. The current affray involves a riot type situation when police tried to arrest his brother. Kurt's disrupted family, social and educational background intensified his need for this peer group.'* The explanation is highly supportive of Braithwaite's thesis: subcultures await those whose lack of controls leads them into minor offending.

Drink and drug gangs

The classic theory of subcultural deviancy supposes that if young people who seek peer group support cannot find acceptance in the kind of achievement orientated gangs mentioned above they are marginalised into a drug subculture (Cloward and Ohlin, 1960). In our chapter on Lifestyle offending behaviour we deal fully with drink and drugs. Here we examine the gang aspects of excessive drinking and drug abuse. The latter is of course an offence in itself whereas heavy drinking is invested with nearly as many positive male images as work! We conclude from the evidence upon which this study is based that drink and drug abuse is commonplace amongst those under supervision. The two are bracketed together because often the overlap between abuse of different substances makes drawing any distinctions difficult, and because the origins or motivations are similar. Probation officers only seem to mention abuse specifically when it is excessive, the primary motivation for offending, a compelling obsession, or there is a risk to health. However a *gang* of drinkers and drug-takers is a different social entity from individual activity. Here we are concerned with the peer-group pressure and sense of status, the achievement and relief from a supposed boredom, which are involved in a group approach to drink and drug abuse.

Generalisations from relatively small-scale surveys may be tenuous, but it is still worth noting that we found the only drug *gangs* to be in London, whereas the drinkers tended to be in the north east and Nottinghamshire. Indeed one probation officer went so far as to suggest it was a sort of community spirit: even with the destruction of the British coal mining industry after 1992, what former miners and sons of miners did was drink in gangs and fight.

In the case of **Brian**, *'Local culture of youngsters attending local public houses'* is the significance of the social background where *'there is a macho image of young men that they should be able to drink to an unlimited level'*. Brian's court appearances go back five years when he was 15. Convictions were for theft, deception, assault and drunk and disorderly. The first three disposals were conditional discharges, but the latest was custodial and he was currently on a YOI licence. Apart from the YOI spell he has been continuously employed at the same firm, gaining further qualifications — and promotion — to those achieved at school, which he did not leave until he was 18. He was earning £102 per week take-home pay at the time of the survey. Again apart from prison, he has always lived with his parents in Nottinghamshire; he has no children or partnership. The probation officer is certain about the effect of drink in Brian's offending behaviour: *'Originally drink was a feature of our joint work, for all offences are drink-related. Time was taken to look together at his level of drinking and the part played by his co-defendants in the pattern of drinking and then offending.'* The supervision objects, amongst others, were to: *'Offer counselling regarding drink and peers; offer support to client and his family; reinforce the need to control level of drinking; encourage client in continuing in his studies.'*

Ken is *'Always* [when offending] *in the company of others and tends to be easily led. Alcohol plays a major part in his offending. He lives in an area of high unemployment and mixes with a group who have no outside interest other than 'hanging around' and then going drinking.'* Since the age of 15 Ken has been before the courts five times for a mix of worsening offences including burglary, motor offences and harassment: no custodial sentences. He left school at 16 with two CSE passes and subsequently did three YTS over three years. He was still on the last one at the time of the survey being paid £38.80 per week. Ken has lived continuously with his, now, lone parent. 'Real' work was one of the issues, as when schemes ended, *'he was not taken on, did not immediately qualify for another scheme and there is no 'proper' work available'*. The probation officer's objectives in supervising Ken were to address his alcohol intake, peer group pressure, use of leisure and personal responsibility in order to reduce further offending.

Sid was an accepted member of a London drug gang in Kennington, but as a child he was: *'painfully shy and experienced difficulties settling into school. Being self-conscious and defensive he developed a pattern of increasing truancy, becoming associated with and influenced by an unsavoury group of associates with whom he developed serious drug addiction. Offending pattern is now well established as burglary, usually of dwelling houses, to provide funds for heroin addiction.'* The probation officer has described a classic Cloward and Ohlin retreatist. Sid had made nine court appearances since the age of 14; has had two custodial sentences; and was currently on remand aged 23 in a drug rehabilitation hostel, awaiting the preparation of an SIR. Like many another in similar circumstances Sid *'owes substantial monies to various drug dealers'*, never mind his unpaid poll tax. He had left and returned to the parental home several times and was able to live with a friend sometimes, or, put another way, he was homeless. *'Drug addiction has dominated his life since 17 and he would probably be dead by now save for periods of custody. He has now developed respiratory problems.'* He started out from school at 16 as a fruit and veg. market trader, though had not worked since becoming addicted to heroin: *'life since then has been dominated by a desire to obtain drugs illegally'*.

We have read the description of a serious case of heroin addiction which leaves one with an impression of a life ruled by the need to obtain the drug, which can never be achieved without further dishonesty offences. No one is going to argue seriously against the addictive properties of heroin, but cannabis is a different matter. Illegal in itself, obtaining it may often involve offending, so the issue is not so much one of the addictiveness or otherwise of cannabis, rather the different levels of crime involved between hard and soft drugs. **Nick** has a curious mixture of convictions since his first indecent assault at 15: many for possession of drugs and motor offences. His eighth conviction led to prison for the first time where at 20 he was on throughcare. *'A regular smoker of cannabis, he was caught on several occasions. Later involved with others in theft related to their drug abuse.'* When released he will be homeless. His three-year-old child lives with his girlfriend with whom he had a partnership at 17. Whilst in prison, the probation officer's work with Nick was to find settled accommodation on release and, *'generally encouraging him to work and develop a lifestyle independent from his former peers'*.

Mike brings together several aspects of peer group pressure. He is a 20-year-old council tenant living in the north east with his partner and baby. His five offences involve burglary and assault. *'Mike began drinking at 13 and easily adopted the criminal ethic subculture* [at a CHE]. *The* [current] *offence originated from the*

*practice of heavy drinking in a male group at weekends. Mike says
he offends because he is bored and wants to be excited. My objective
is to challenge his attitude to drinking and help him to assess the risks
which he is taking. I shall work on the responsibilities involved with
girlfriend and their new daughter.'* We shall examine next the place of
excitement and boredom in more detail. Interestingly, the probation
work was to focus on adult responsibilites. Stable partnerships and
child rearing have long been held as a significant route out of crime
as we shall discuss in the chapter on Professional offending.

The social activities of the gang

Probation officers supervise individual offenders on a one-to-one
basis, but we have noted that offending behaviour started, led
or dominated via peer groups is a social activity occurring in
an economic and environmental context. Through intensive case
histories we have noted the diversity of peer groups and the diversity
of personal and family circumstances which members bring to these
groups. We should not be too surprised by such variety. Peer groups
are common amongst all adolescents and young adults: only some
of them sometimes involve offending. It is the subcultural theorists
who have fastened our thinking onto the peer group as the milieu for
delinquency. Apart of course from committing offences, which is a
given for the purposes of our study, the unifying threads are: lack
of school qualifications, absence of regular work and the resulting
poverty. Next we shall examine what happens in delinquent peer
groups which seem to give the gangs' activities such attractive
strength for young men. The purpose is to consider how probation
may capitalise on positive aspects of peer gangs, to divert and reduce
offending behaviour. Objectives of this type can probably best be
achieved in groups, projects or schemes.

The gang offers young males relief from the boredom they
find elsewhere and the excitement is to be found, for many, in
offending behaviour itself. As gangs are social organisations there
are competitive issues of leadership and status to be settled. Other
people can be manipulated, 'easily led'. The classic formulation of
peer group gangs is about young males and might run like this.
Bored with school, home life and the church youth club, youngsters
drift around the streets then meet up with others searching for
excitement (Corrigan, 1978). The gang forms around some shared
purpose which gives the youngsters that particular buzz. Because
these youths came together in rejection of the boredom of adult life
and what is on offer to youngsters, excitement often takes the
form of challenging the values of adult society, hence they engage in

anti-social acts most of which will be offences. Leaders emerge from amongst those boys who can provide the excitement. They will often maintain their position through violence, threats and challenges. The 'easily led' must constantly prove their worthiness to live in the presence of such leaders by, naturally, further delinquent acts (classic account in Matza, 1964). In order to be able to commit a stream of delinquent acts, gang members neutralise any feelings of guilt which might trouble them, usually by blaming their victims (Sykes and Matza, 1957). But because the members are ambivalent about the adult world (they want to join it), they do not totally reject law-abiding values, so finding it easy to slip into responsibilities when the time comes. Classically, the time came with regular paid employment, stable-partner relationships (we used to call this marriage), starting a home of one's own and having children (note the chronological order). Now, there is no certainty that the time will ever come.

Drift, excitement and boredom

Stating that the offending behaviour of the peer group is an exciting antidote to the boredom of growing-up makes it sound as though there is something wrong with adolescents who omit this route to adulthood. There has been serious questioning of how rational are the choices involved in 'joining' a delinquent activity peer group (Cornish and Clarke, 1986). It sounds too purposeful, too systematic, and it also ignores the role of excitement, status and fun to be achieved in non-delinquent groups of young people; never mind the occurrence of delinquent acts within legitimate groups. The concept of 'drift' is useful in this respect: youngsters looking around for something they are not sure about. Although of *'a good solid family background'*, a youngster from Middlesbrough *'drifted into offending; peer group pressure — not disciplined living away from home'*. Another 17-year-old, *'drifted into offending behaviour with other youngsters through lack of parental supervision/control/influence. Father in prison'*.

Consider a 17-year-old boy, **Ian**, in Bath with the usual list of offences, *'in general committed with others when he gets carried along by the excitement of the moment. He had been drinking but could not comprehend why people took them* [robbery, burglary, shop-lifting and resisting arrest] *so seriously.'* Ian was imprisoned. *'He under-achieved at school and looked to friends for acceptance and values on which to base his behaviour. Ian is from a loving and caring family but the home policy was not to impose boundaries to behaviour.'* In supervising the throughcare the probation officer views addressing Ian's attitude to his peer group as crucial: *'Main issue influence of peer group and his* *role as the one who will try anything. Ian's first experience of custody has shocked him, he therefore regards this as a problem and does not wish to repeat the experience'.* Group-work is thought to be most appropriate.

Let us pick-up on further mentions of 'excitement' as the motivating factor. In north Bristol 17-year-old **Phil** for whom *'living in Southmead has led to a decision to join the delinquent subculture of those in trouble in the area. The temptation* [to offend] *is too strong and it brings goodies, fun and excitement'.* To address this the probation officer's objectives are *'encouraging client's efforts to find work (he has done so now — builders' labourer £100 per week); help with driving documents when ban is up; ensure he goes to the Life Management Group'.* **Adam** brings out another aspect of excitement. How was all that free time afforded by unemployment to be filled? *'Better use of free time in order to provide excitement and, therefore, avoid offending, as his life-style includes hanging-around and being on the fringe of offending if not actually getting involved. His main problems are the poor use of free-time, though he lives in an area* [of Bristol] *where there are very poor facilities particularly for young people.'* Adam's crimes of theft, burglary and motoring offences were all *'opportunistic and committed with other young men of similar circumstances and style'.*

The other side of excitement was the boredom which prompted offending behaviour, so 20-year-old **Alec** in the north east *'offends because he is bored, is subject to peer group pressure and lives in an area of poor quality housing. . . . Offended within weeks of release from YOI. His parents continue to provide him with a home and whilst they do not condone his behaviour believe themselves powerless to divert him.'* Of **Kelvin**, another 17-year-old this time homeless in central Birmingham the probation officer wrote: *'Member of a group of youngsters who offend for kicks and status.'* **Jim** on the other hand was *'a young man with excellent family support'* despite having been into child care at 16 for a while. The big issues were work and his *'low tolerance of boredom, Jim is apparently an able but lethargic man who mixes with dodgy company which abounds in his area* (in south London). *His mother is hardworking and supportive and does not think much of Jim's excuse of "asthma" for avoiding work.'*

Status

It is often said that peer group social activity offending is something out of which adolescents will grow. **Jerry** (aged 20 at the time of the survey) concentrated all his convictions into his 18th year: three thefts and motoring offences with non-custodial disposals. *'Within a period of eighteen months the client's behaviour deteriorated. He wanted to impress his friends, but he has since settled down after the last court case'.* In confirmation of two usual reasons for quitting crime: *'He* *is now working* [as a roofer for £75 per week] *and has girlfriend so not feeling the need to impress his peer group. Jerry has lost contact with his former associates.'* We should note that finding a non-offending group of friends is a key to involvement in conventional social activities (now coming to be called social insertion). If this kind of offending is something most young men with few educational achievements or job prospects are going to do, probation work must focus on limitation and diversion. As the probation officer concluded: *'Social background was not a problem. It was more about youth and excess energy, growing up and associating for a period with peers who were getting into trouble.'* We should not be too surprised at Jerry's rapid rehabilitation. He left school at 16 with five CSEs and had worked for most of time since then. Stability was also afforded by living with his parents and brother. Jerry responded well to the supervising probation officer's approach: *'Focus was then on his own self-esteem. Helping him to consider employment. Problematic areas were the need for impressing friends. Comes from a good family. He has responded well to supervision, has attended weekly "Offending Behaviour Group" which has enabled him to view his behaviour more rationally. He has been in work for nearly a year and has not re-offended, has a positive attitude. He is someone who has been through an adolescence crisis.'* Jerry was promising material: he had a supportive family; he was not an entrenched juvenile offender; he had qualifications and a work record; and in his own words he wanted *'a good job, a family and nice holidays.'*

Most of these explanations imply that peer groups are just waiting to be joined, like a deviant WRVS rather than being an interactive and spontaneous affair fulfilling immediate youth needs and lacking formal organisation. Though lacking formal organisation, peer group gangs are nevertheless still constantly recruiting and replacing offenders.

Continuing the theme of the peer group as a site of status for young people without close supportive ties at home, and showing that it is not only young males who find this alternative. **Tracy**, aged 20, was an entrenched offender with nine convictions from the age of 16 for theft, assault and motoring offences, but without a custodial sentence. The onset of offending behaviour *'followed the break-up of her parents' marriage. I feel that this young lady received no parental guidance and was allowed to 'run with the pack'. Initially this client became involved in offending as a means of gaining status with her peer group. . . . Almost all her offending has been in the company of other people.'* After her parents' relationship breakdown when Tracy was 14, she was taken into voluntary child care by social services. At the time of the survey she was a private tenant and lone parent in North Shields.

Tracy's probation officer indicates the value of 'rehabilitation' in the sense of helping the client become a citizen rather than 'correct' their offending behaviour (on this aspect of rehabilitation see McWilliam and Pease, 1990). In addition to the parental relationship breakdown and reception into care, a year later at 15, Tracy left school without qualifications and had just two temporary jobs, obtained through her mother, as a process worker *'for a matter of weeks on each occasion'*. But at the time of our survey, the situation for Tracy was changing. *'Recently, following the birth of her son Tracy's offending has lessened and she appears to be taking the responsibility of child care very seriously.'* The probation officer and other professionals have been helping Tracy to secure settled housing and supporting her in caring for her child, *'and encouraging her growing maturity'*. Tracy's attitude had changed to one of, as she put it herself, *'standing on my own two feet'*. It would appear that she had emerged from *'an aimless life-style over the past four years with numerous changes of accommodation'* and through the baby found self-esteem and responsibility.

Status seems excessively important to some young men. **Bill** aged 20 in Middlesbrough was not alone amongst our study in believing small stature was important: *'offends with lads several years his junior, with whom he can act "the hard man". Bit of a "Peter Pan" quality about him, likes to look big in the eyes of his friends, via motor offending. He was the youngest of three brothers whose parents separated when he was 9. He grew up without boundaries that a father might have set. Small in stature at school and prone to being bullied, he coped with this by aspiring to be "streetwise". Now that he is "streetwise"* [part of which was having been in prison — another common trait amongst status-seekers] *he has nothing further he wishes to achieve in his life.'* The supervising probation officer addressed Bill's dead-end self-image also his violence and chronic unemployment (never worked, only done two YTS, both of which he 'bunked-off'). He was on YOI supervision having served a term for assault and motoring offences. There was very little about which the probation officer could have been positive, and so to *'ensure compliance with the legal requirements of the YOI supervision'* seemed reasonable.

It is the status-creating aspect of peer groups which is of significance so that small Bill and *'a youth whose physical maturity has outweighed his emotional maturity'* can use gangs to *'play the "tough guy/leader"'*. For that 20-year-old man living in Coventry, with a string of drunkenness, assault and burglary convictions, there have been *'no learned skills to live independently or external influences to contrast offending behaviour against his community "norm". Lack of self-worth as a youngster promoted his reliance on physical prowess. Now resorts to physical response rather than handle situations in any other way.'* A 17-year-old in the north east *'offends for monetary gain and kudos. There is a high level of delinquency in the locality; peer group pressure has played a large part in his offending. Likes to see himself as "leader of the gang" and probably is. He has moved on from petty shop-lifting to burglaries in the last two years.'* The probation officer explains the situation by the absence of social controls: *'His parents both do shift work and he has long been self-reliant domestically and reliant on friends rather the family.'* Curiously being able to look after oneself domestically is no bad thing and one wonders if this comment would have been made of a 17-year-old female. The point is about, presumably, the absence of social controls at vulnerable times.

If the peer group is a powerful vehicle for establishing and reinforcing young adult male status, probation officers have an exceedingly difficult task in trying to reduce the offending it entails. So when a *'client offends for gain to improve his standing among peers'* the probation officer seeks *'to use that relationship to help him to discover the negativity of his own actions and to help him construct a more positive alternative — to achieve his needs* [for his own flat] *and be valued by his peers';* for even if his peers did not actually value his securing a flat, the client would have something positive which could also be a way into a non–offending network of peers. In that case the probation officer also mentioned that the 17-year-old offender under supervision had to learn, *'owning responsibility for offending'.* There is an implication that he, in classic subcultural tradition, was 'neutralising' his sense of doing something wrong.

Neutralisation of guilt

In arguing for control theory influencing subcultural theory, Sykes and Matza (1957) have claimed that deviants express honourable motives for dishonourable acts, appealing to the higher loyalties owed their peer group in justification of offending. The next case marries guilt neutralisation with status achievement by a violent gang leader. **Beesty** (discussed in Self-expression p.36) a 23-year-old man from Nottinghamshire: *'has a lengthy police record and a very short fuse. Past disposals by the courts prior to the current probation order have failed, that is — fines unpaid, attendance centre order ignored, breaches of a CSO, conditional discharge and probation order. Youth custody also had no impact. This young man was admired by other inmates. He always took the view that people whom he had hit, deserved it or were threatening him first.'* The probation officer is going to, *'Take on a parental role which appears to be lacking in this case* [left parental home at 16, stepfather trouble] *and help this young man through adolescence. Support his attempts to cope alone in* *the outside world, which is a new experience for him.'* One wonders how appropriate that would be for a 23-year-old council tenant living with his girl friend and their six-month-old baby — or any other 23-year-old. This case exhibits some psychodynamic assumptions which are rather out of keeping with the general run of probation officers' accounts of offending behaviour, but there were such accounts and they deserve inclusion.

Aims for practice

Nigel's peer group offending was thought to stem from *'living in close proximity with other offenders who taught him how to steal for financial gain'.* His four court appearances started at 15 and were for criminal damage and motoring offences. As Nigel was serving a YOI sentence the central issue in the probation officer's throughcare was to focus on something important for Nigel himself: *'His offending minimises the chances of him realising his ambition of being a mechanic.'* Hence *'addressing offending behaviour'* in this case became in practice *'to replace his offending with legal diversionary activities and encourage employment'*. Nigel had been on two YTS for a short while and did have one GCSE in maths. Hence there is something, however slim, on which to build.

No one supposes that those thoroughly acceptable and straight-forward objectives are in fact easily achieved. The peer group itself has sufficient power to overturn the most carefully planned practice objectives as **Dick's** case shows. He was a 23-year-old council tenant living with his partner and two children in Sunderland. The same partnership had lasted since he left home at 18. At this point the signs of traditional stability stop. He had never worked since leaving school at 16 without qualifications. He was in prison for drug offences, the last of twelve court appearances of which the first was when he was 12: theft, burglary, motoring offences. *'The client is well-integrated into the local offending culture. His philosophy regarding soft drugs is at odds with the law and is difficult to challenge given the reinforcement which he receives within his peer group'*. The probation officer would be lucky if the *'offer of voluntary support and assistance'* were accepted.

Eight court appearances since age 17 for a string of drink-related offending (criminal damage, theft, deception, motoring offences) did not augur well. **Bret** *'was brought up by supportive but elderly grandparents since his parents divorced when he was 3. He has spent much time with a male peer group because of this'*, although for the rest of the time since 16 he had been working as a builder's labourer (at the time of the survey earning £150 per week). At 23 he was on probation for burglary of a dwelling whilst living with his partner as a private tenant in Avon. The probation officer had clear if complex objectives, somewhat unusually in the case of an 'older' young offender. '*He has attended and participated in an alcohol education group, looking at the role of alcohol involved in his offending; peer group; effects on victims; own family. I am encouraging Bret to examine and challenge his own attitudes especially regarding sexual roles, sexism and racism*'. Further objectives will be analysed elsewhere, but it is important here to draw attention to the effort in this case to address those offence-related prejudices, such as racism, which are likely to be potentiated by peer group pressure. There were several positive elements on which to pin rehabilitation: regular work and a stable partner.

Is 'growing out of it' just wishful thinking? Bret was certainly taking his time and his probation officer was obviously not just sitting about waiting for it to happen. ***Nev's*** probation officer clearly does think he will 'grow out of it'. He was 17, living with his mother and step-relatives in Bath and had '*a short-lived offending pattern. The client offends with friends and he needs to look at this and develop ways of resisting the group consensus*'. The probation officer wrote: '*Client has a very supportive family and stable home. I am not aware of a social situation leading to offending. I feel confident that this is a client who will "grow out of" offending*'. But 'growing out of it' may be more difficult than supposed because we are also told, '*Nev has little insight into his offending and so work initially needs to be done on this*'. Despite his comments to the contrary, judging from what the probation officer has written, negative social background indicators did seem to be present. There was a condition attached to Nev's probation order to attend group sessions. Much group work focuses on using the group to help offenders deal with that other group, a source of their offending behaviour — their peers (Priestley and McGuire, 1985; Brown and Caddick, 1993). Our own study supports the view that younger offenders under supervision, 17-to-19 years-old, seem to respond more readily to project-style groups than to individual counselling or therapeutic-style groups; hence the value of initiatives such as the motor projects.

5 Social norm

Influence of locality — crime the 'norm'; client feels not reaching potential; trapped in cycle of poverty (Council estate in Sunderland, Northumbria).

Response to living environment, lack of funds, unrealistic aims, peer group and family (brothers) pressure to offend, employment problems. Has ambitions encouraged by media in a consumer society. Lives in delinquent area (Sutton Coldfield, West Midlands).

Area of high delinquency where status is hard to achieve. Client comes from a 'hard' family and from a 'hard' area where men are men and women are housewives. Heavy use of socially acceptable alcohol followed by solvent misuse (six convictions include: riding a pedal cycle without lights, culminating in violent disorder; Hartlepool, Cleveland).

The neighbourhood explanation of crime

Besides being one of the oldest explanations for entrenched offending, identifying an area, locality or community of crime also signals neighbourly complicity and the family transmission of criminal values. We learn from social scientists ('Huge areas degenerated from meadow to slum in a generation'), evangelicals ('A citadel of outcasts'), police officers ('The bowels of the earth') and bar-room philosophers ('You had a great influx of discontented people that didn't want to be living here') down long ages that some neighbourhoods, council estates, tenement blocks or 'rookeries' are the homes of every class of villain (Foster, 1990).

This common-sense notion finds the roots of crime to be in certain geographically concentrated areas. The 'Chicago School' of sociology advanced early attempts at a coherent and objective explanation for deviance based upon certain areas of inner cities, the so-called called 'zones of transition'. High crime rates can be associated with 'disorganisation', characterised as split or fragmented 'communities', or alternatively with a high level of subcultural crime. 'Disorganisation' may reside in the paradox of there either being too little or too much 'sense of community' in these urban crime areas. There is too little community in the sense that older residents do not like the way they understand things to have changed in the membership of the neighbourhood: ethnically, economically, in child rearing around the issue of single or dual parenthood, and even in the use of public space. Each change is viewed negatively and constructed into the absence of a coherent community. And yet we can identify coherent and consistent criminal subcultures enforcing territorial rights of occupation over all the residents on certain estates (Bottoms, et al., 1986; Foster, 1990; Evans, et al., 1992; Foster and Hope, 1993, ch.2). The latter is a case of rather too much sense of community residing within a criminal hegemony, though in either case the absence of a common, shared identity in a stable social and economic base, which no longer exists, makes the outcome the same: disorganisation and fragmentation.

Zones of transition

Traditional area explanations rest on the notion of a 'zone of transition' in which the resident population is unstable: families and single people are moving in and out. This threatens the cohesiveness and stability of the area as groups of dependable citizens shrink in number. There is a negotiated order, but it is fraught, fragile and problematic (see the classic exposition in Rainwater, 1971). The areas were described as subject to periods of rapid change and uneven development leading to strain, even breakdown in local order. The zones of urban areas in which different classes lived failed to articulate socially — sometimes expressed as a 'geological fault' between the zones, nicely complemented by descriptions of the dwellings as 'tenement canyons' (in the case of, for example, Glasgow). Pre-figuring strain theory, resorting to crime in these areas was a solution to exclusion and impotence.

Criminology's point of departure from the Chicago School area theory came with the realisation that it was neither philosophically necessary nor empirically possible to identify a geographical place in order to sustain explanatory theories of more general application: subcultural, control, interactionist, situational. However the issue of differential prevalence remains. There are areas within which more recorded crime occurs and there are neighbourhoods or estates within which more convicted offenders live and these patterns tend to persist over time. The theory supposes that the high-risk criminal areas are essentially public places with many social activities, especially by juveniles, going on in the streets, where 'near-groups' may become gangs. Under the surveillance of peers and adults, reputations are earned and respect conferred, thus giving rise to 'community identity'. In this milieu, 'traditions of delinquency are preserved and transmitted through the medium of social contact with the unsupervised playgroups and the more highly organised delinquent and criminal gangs' (Shaw and McKay, 1971, p.260). One of the environmental school's many flaws is highlighted here. If the areas are 'disorganised' how does something as organised as a gang emerge?

Crime and British residential housing

Trying to import into Britain a theory derived from what happens on the Lower East Side or Bay Area proved problematic. Researchers concentrated first on 'housing class' (Rex and Moore, 1967), then housing problems or the growth of communal reputations in study-ing council estates on which there had been the planned allocation of tenancies to 'problem families'. The residents encountered distrust and hostility which restricted opportunity. In this way people in an area became identified as deviants — stigmatised — engendering a self-fulfilling prophecy which perpetuated the deviance of people in the area (for examples of the genre see: Gill, 1977; Reynolds, 1986; Damer, 1989). In the mid 1980s, Foster studied attitudes to law and order on a council estate in south east London: 'Their experience and manipulation of the social world of south London was strongly influenced by the area itself, perennially associated with crime and offending' (Foster, 1990, p.2). Despite substantial post-war rebuilding, the area retained its nineteenth century epithets: 'a bad place, a sink of shadow and sorrow, vice and filth, ignorance and degradation . . . poverty stricken and overcrowded, inhabited by thieves and unfortunates' (ibid. 1990, p.6). The portentous language of social explorers and evangelists may have given way to something more politically correct, but today's message is similar. Foster claims slum clearance policies were instrumental in creating an unstable population of new comers living in badly designed and built council flats on estates with excessive population densities. These features are said to have aided the continuance of crime traditional to the area and endemic on 'sink estates'. Crime 'both of a petty and organised nature was a way of life for many in the area which . . . was generally condoned' (Foster, 1990, p.20). However, the loss and change of slum clearance is hard to match with Foster's concept of the generational transmission of crime. If the culture is disappearing, crime as a Social Norm ought to decline. As we have argued earlier, because the basis for the fragmentation which lets in either an over-weaning sense of community or a vacuum is social and economic breakdown, crime as a Social Norm is a phenomenon capable of reproducing itself (in support of which from the same hand see Foster and Hope, 1993).

It would seem facile to claim that modernist high-rise architecture, the antiquity of sanitary conveniences, penetrating dampness, dog poo on the streets or absence of ring-main electrical wiring had something to do with making areas prone to crime or be the haunts of the offending classes (though Coleman, 1985 comes close). Unfortunately we have a serious problem in explaining the aggregated data. Poor building design and worn-out amenities tend to go together with areas of high unemployment, reliance on social security and high crime or numbers of known offenders. Researchers and commentators have highlighted institutions, such as housing departments, social policies, such as mass re–housing and particularly the industrial re-structuring of the 1980s to 90s (abolition of manufacturing and extraction industries employing plenty of un- and semi-skilled men) as determinants in the contemporary creation and reproduction of neighbourhoods of crime. Of course the built environment has its spatial location determined by ourselves, but there is a particular inertia about ship-building, coal mining and the communities which served them. The 'new' communities where crime tends to be the Social Norm are to be found on the estates and in the towns where once flourished the nation's staple industries.

In September 1991 Britain's first drive-in 'riots' were held on the Meadowell Farm estate in North Shields, Tyneside. Some of the Twocers discussed in Social Activity took part, for example the innominate hero opening Chapter 4. In trying to explain the gestation of Meadowell's notoriety, a recent study considers the usual list: gross neglect of repairs, allocation of tenancies mainly to statutorily homeless people (overlap with lone parenting because of the relationship breakdown connection), very high unemployment, high crime, known offenders (Barke and Turnbull, 1992, ch.5). However, they also stress the strength of social networks and the fortitude of people living in the new-found poverty of 1980s' economic re-structuring. The 'decline' into a stigmatised area was long in the making, the local housing authority playing a sterling rôle, but the turning-point came with the marginalisation of young adult males: no real work nor prospect of it, reduced benefit income (even when over 18), abundant leisure time: 'these young people are growing up at the margins, not only of society in general, but also at the margins of the community within which they live' (Barke and Turnbull, 1992, p.131; see also from a more accessible perspective the wide-ranging study of such estate 'riots' and deprivation in Campbell, 1993).

Within each of the probation areas in our study there were several localities, usually council estates, where crime was high. Some of these estates have been the subjects of extensive investigation (such as Coates and Silburn, 1973: part 2, on St Ann's in Nottingham) and we have drawn upon parts of that work above.

Looking at the issue from another angle, difficult-to-let council estates have been intensively studied, not least in terms of safety and offending. It may be useful to review some of that evidence now. Study after study concludes that people on estates fear both crime and aggressive policing (for example Bonnerjea and Lawton, 1987, ch.4). Many of the cases cited in this study have involved racism and there is strong evidence to support an area-specific interpretation. However, both Black tenant and women's groups have experienced trouble in being acknowledged by the forces of law and order (Ware, 1988, p.5; Limehouse, 1987). It has been suggested that social workers, including probation officers, would be able to mediate between the factions in racially motivated attacks (House of Commons Home Affairs Committee, 1986), a line strongly resisted by activists. Racial conflict was a recurrent feature of the 'riots' of the 1980s, together with high profile policing, from the St Paul's neighbourhood of Bristol (included in our study) to Broadwater Farm estate in Haringey (Gifford, 1986). Public housing estates have been identified as places for anti-crime initiatives because they are seen as 'very close to becoming the new rookeries. They combine stigmatisation, demoralisation and anomie with unusually high rates of offending and victimisation' (Rock, 1988, p.112). Various initiatives involving housing and social services departments, the police and voluntary organisations seem to be able to reverse that decline and restore the ordinary social controls of the neighbourhood, but it is unclear how the projects actually achieve such improvements. That housing deprivation has to be cast in the language of crime can be understood, as one of us has argued, as the criminalisation of the discourses of social policy (Blagg et al., 1988, ch.12).

The meaning of social norms

In our analysis of Social Norm there are two major determinants: the reproduction of communities within which offending, or 'crime', is acceptable and condoned; and socialisation into a criminal way of life within the family. The latter seems to imply that social controls exercised by parents (as discussed in Chapter 3) were absent. Criminologists have often noted the paradox of offenders who espouse the norms of law-abiding people. Are some youngsters learning two sets of norms at the same time? Hitherto we have assumed that social controls must transmit values and behaviour which curb deviance. But parents are quite capable of teaching criminality. One of the strongest predictors of serious delinquency in young adulthood is to have a parent who is an offender (Farrington, 1990).

A measure of the difficulty must rest in the immense diversity of crimes where some are very serious but there is also a great raft which do not have much of a 'criminal feel' to them, say refusing to buy a TV licence and continuing to watch *Coronation Street*; or refusing to pay the poll tax. Practical common sense distinguishes between real crimes and lesser misdemeanours: parents and friends, teachers and probation officers, convey this sense of proportion. If social controls are all about establishing the boundaries of acceptable values and behaviour it follows that in some neighbourhoods a strictly law-abiding set of controls could be vitiated by local norms which approve some illegal activities. Hence we return to the original problem in which socialisation and learned behaviour can allow, even promote, deviance, and appear to do so in a way which could be said to correspond to the boundaries of a neighbourhood, locality or estate. One can readily understand individual families within which offending is approved — the parents do it themselves (analogous to doctoring in a family of medics), but for neighbourhoods and estates a more complex explanation is required. Just by following the law and implementing the 'special needs housing' aspects of care in the community the allocation policies of housing departments can produce concentrations of tenants who are bad risks for offending and bad risks for being victimised. Along with housing families in which parents are themselves offending and hence whose children would be a high risk on Farrington's predictive indicator, a housing department may be offering tenancies to equally high risk groups such as young adults leaving care and men recently discharged from prison. Such concentrations may be located alongside people with learning difficulties discharged from long-stay hospitals and female lone parents re-housed under homelessness procedures, each of which are high risk victims of offending (Foster and Hope, 1993, especially chs.6 and 8). On difficult-to-let estates one third of the turnover of new lettings are to families with the cluster of characteristics described (Foster and Hope, 1993, especially ch.3). All of the probation areas in our study had estates meeting these criteria in some respects and

all of them had inner city areas of mixed housing with criminal
concentrations.

The family supports crime

Larry lived, when not in custody, with his parents and brothers in
Selly Oak, Birmingham. He first appeared before the courts when
he was 13, amassing eight convictions culminating in a run of
burglaries, with affray and fraud. The probation officer supervising
Larry's throughcare believed, *'He doesn't take his behaviour too
seriously* [because] *I feel offending has not been viewed too seriously
by his family. Larry's dad has been in trouble and the older brother is
currently in custody. The family is very close and supportive to Larry.
The affray charge involved Larry and his brother in a fight* [gun in
brother's possession] *at a holiday camp'*.

The family supportive of offending behaviour helps to justify crime
to young adults. In others, the expectation is so high that not offending
would be non-conformity: *'The cumulative effect of communicated
expectations is that **Eddy** will "follow in the footsteps" of his family
i.e. will not achieve status-wise or financially and will follow family
norms regarding attitude to law and offending.'* Eddy was deeply
involved in crime, having twelve court appearances between age
15 and 20 with four custodial disposals, all for burglary. Eddy
lived with his mother, older brother and young sister in West
Bromwich, having been in residential child care from 11 to 16
due to offending. The supervising probation officer located the
guiding inspiration of Eddy's offending: *'Past offending has been
in the company and under the leadership of his older brother'* hence
the practice objective was *'to get him to make decisions for himself,
independently of his brother'*. The PO believed that objective had
been achieved (though if it were only because the brother was in
prison it would be short-lived), along with: *'Raising his awareness
of the inevitable consequences for himself of continual offending — hence
break the pattern and challenge his assumption that he will continue
to offend.'* Apart from the profound comfort Eddy found in his
family (*'his fear of change leads him again and again to decide to
put up with life as it is'*), the PO offered explanations and objectives
similar to those discussed in Self-expression: *'Exceptional lack of
self-confidence and low self-image; built-in expectation of failure with
a resulting apathy about attempting anything new or challenging.'* The
objectives were to help Eddy re-interpret his own past constructively
rather than fall back on his negative *'it's not my fault, look at my
traumatic childhood'* attitude, so work focused on building a positive
self-image and satisfying life-style. The PO's key into all this was

Eddy's growing awareness that 'he now *regards as problematic for him,
his frequent offending and its consequences*'.

Living up to the offending expectations of one's family and
inheriting a position within such a clan of professionals does not,
of course, guarantee success. '*Frank says that he had accepted
offending as a way of life and had seen it as a chance to gain status
with friends. Apparently it is a family trait that the male members
of his family have become involved in offending during their young
adulthood to varying degrees, but that once this has passed they have
settled down to lead responsible and industrious lives. In this sense
Frank sees himself as conforming to the family norm.*' If so, the
period starts at 17 climaxing at 20 with burglary and homelessness.
He had a child by a previous liaison and his current partner
was pregnant. All of which seems to suggest that norms can be
transmitted although the offending family is not too close-knit in
conventional terms.

Violence and drunkenness may also be sanctioned within a
family where that behaviour has been well-learned: '*Parents divorced;
father violent alcoholic with whom later contact led to* **Richard's**
drinking bouts.' Richard's father is a clear influence, though we
are also told: '*Family home of past 17 years situated in an area of
very high delinquency* [east Coventry].' Richard has had eleven court
appearances since he was 15, six of which resulted in prison: '*Alcohol
related offending with motor vehicles appears to be the continuing cause
and effect; status seeking among peers; boredom through unemployment
is a basic factor to all the above.*' The unemployment comment is
interesting as Richard had been on three YTS for two, three and
five weeks respectively (leaving because they were '*unrewarding*'),
but was eight months into employment as a motor panel press
operator at £180 per week.

We will be focusing on substance abuse in the chapter on
Life-style, though here it is important to note the relationship
between learning about drugs within a family and current offending
behaviour related to drug abuse. **Strobe** was a 23-year-old addict
with an addicted partner and 18-month-old baby living in a council
house in Nottinghamshire. '*The over-riding issue with this client is his
dependency on drugs — his numerous problems spring from that.*' Social
background was '*Totally significant — both parents were drug abusers.
No stable upbringing.*'

Contrary to cynical expectation that the criminal Social Norm
of his family would reinforce offending, **Derek** wanted to change,
despite '*his own family being crime orientated; care background reinforced criminal outlook*'. Residential child care raises again the issue
of closeness to one's own family which we noted with Frank, but
also such substitute care can be another site for criminalisation in its

own right. He was a 23-year-old married man with one child and a pregnant wife living in a council house in Nottinghamshire. Put in local authority child care at 10, the year of his first court appearance, Derek had spent years in various homes. Fifteen court appearances and five prison terms later for burglary, robbery and theft, the probation officer supervising Derek's throughcare concluded that his offending was: *'Based on resentment toward society from the way he had been treated as a child and then reinforced with custodial sentences: addictive cycle.'* But one to be broken: *'On the positive side Derek is showing encouraging signs of maturing and giving much thought to his future. He is very willing to work with Probation and seems genuinely determined to avoid offending in the future. Work is focused on how this can best be done. Requires a good deal of time and support but this is not difficult with someone who has had such an apparent change in outlook and is willing to work.'* Part of Derek's *'well-thought-out plans'* was a desire to gain 'O' level and City and Guilds qualifications whilst in prison. His only work so far had been a little double glazing sales and roofing.

Twelve court appearances since the age of 14 for theft with four custodial sentences tend to confirm the probation officer's conclusion that **Martin's** *'Lack of employment opportunities in a large family that was deviant made a law abiding life-style difficult and against the norm.'* Lack of closeness to parents seems to be a recurrent theme in association with offending Social Norms of the family as Martin too was taken into child care at 10 when both his parents were in prison. Against that background Martin *'seems to be moving away from past criminal life-style (no new offence for over twelve months)'*. Martin had done six months YT terminated by custody. It is interesting to ponder on why Martin should be changing: he has no job; he lives with the deviant parents; he is separated from his partner and two children of 3 and 5. Unlike Derek, nothing much had changed in Martin's life. Was he just becoming more successful at avoiding detection? At one point on the questionnaire the probation officer wrote ambiguously in the light of the above remarks and Martin's £38.50 Income Support, *'Although no income he is probably supplemented from other sources!'*

Attachment to crime as a way of life

Stephan had grown up in a part of north Bristol *'where motoring offences are not regarded as criminal'*. The probation officer's objectives were to: *'Achieve a change in attitude towards motoring offences and enable Stephan to make a fresh start — employment being the starting point to achieve independence from the local area.'* He was living in a very overcrowded council house with his mother, two sisters, brother, and various ex-girlfriends. His own two-year-old daughter was living somewhere else with her mother. All his seven convictions from 15- to 20-years-old were for motoring offences: *'Driving opened-up privacy away from home'* — very decidedly an escape from strain.

To free oneself from a subculture of drugs and theft is a fight against social norms. *'Camilla is struggling against her social background and the subculture in which she lives* [in Gateshead, Northumbria with her mother]. *Client is the product of a disturbed background* [at eleven she had a *"nervous breakdown"* and went into residential child care]. *Her father has served several prison sentences and introduced his daughter to drugs and shop-lifting* [six appearances since age 15]. *Camilla's boyfriend was also a regular thief* [leaving her with an 18-month-old baby]. The probation officer knew Camilla was making progress as she *'was a high-risk offender in terms of the life-style she was leading i.e. shop-lifting and drug taking'*, but had managed to complete two-thirds of her order without re-offending, *'which for her is considerable progress'*.

In Chapter 3 certain social circumstances were viewed by some young offenders as outweighing any chance of changing. *Craig's* family (p.43) had been labelled as offenders and he saw no way or reason to change that. The support for his own offending was well established amongst his brothers. His probation officer saw potential for changing Craig by drawing on his sense of community, principally because Craig viewed his crime as 'social action'. *'To use his anger to generate a response which proves his community cannot put him down. He is intelligent and responds to challenges. Hopefully one day he will be a community representative, for both the Whites and Blacks.'* The way out of crime is seem as transcending the 'criminal' label by way of political commitment.

The condoning community of crime fosters a pleasant life-style for some men who can avoid prison and make money with fraudulent social security claims and various 'earners'. In Seaham, Durham **Angus** was a council tenant with his wife and two children. He had tried most of the local 'scams': *'Involved in traditional scavenging, cottage industry type activity supplementing state benefits. Collects scrap metal, beach coal, raises pigs, races greyhounds to supplement his dole. It's a style of life which provides many sources of self-esteem and social approval. Angus avoids custody: he is a successful man!'* After the equally traditional peer group initiation into north eastern offending, Angus *'sailed close to the wind'* as he followed the *'dominant cultural norms'* and was *'not interested in changing his life-style'*. Between his first conviction at 14 and the latest of 15 (progressively criminal damage, theft and burglary), at age 23 he had experienced just one custodial sentence. Probation work is extremely difficult when the social control of 'belief' in the non-offending way of life is just not available.

Socialised in care

We have already noted a lack of closeness with parents even when the probation officer has identified those parents as an influence, because of their own offending, on the delinquent career of the offender under supervision. Experience of residential child care in part defined for us 'lack of closeness' in those circumstances shared by Frank, Derek and Martin. Through the case of **Jane** we shall investigate residential child care as a socialising milieu. In the supervision of 20-year-old Jane living with her partner and 13-month-old baby in a council tenancy in Smethwick, the probation officer was addressing her entrenched racism, financial problems, (rent, poll tax, gas and catalogue debts from £77.30 Income Support), seeking housing in better condition and examining counter-productive attitudes. As Jane was *'distrustful of the system'* the probation officer was: *'Assisting and advising her on how to cope with bureaucracies so that future contacts are more productive'.* Reasonable objectives, as Jane's offending was rarely gainful property theft, but mainly assault of the police on a regular basis since 14: *'Quite marked anti-authority attitudes . . . coupled with strong, delinquent peer group influences and anti-social family have led her into unacceptable behaviour.'* Jane went into residential child care at 5 and again at 14, emerging finally at 18 to live independently, after which experience: *'The general absence of positive, constructive family support and the influence of a delinquent subculture for most of her life has meant that anti-social behaviour and a lack of respect for authority of any sort have adversely conditioned her behaviour and attitudes.'* We can probably read-off 'authority problems' as the probation officer's psycho-analytic version of control theory.

Jane's probation officer points to the powerful influence of peers in negating positive social controls. Much of the peer influence in Jane's past will have been within residential child care. The cultural milieu of care is a 'neighbourhood' or perhaps community within which crime may be condoned. Peer group influence which makes offending a Social Activity is here shown to be the bed-fellow of a community which condones that offending. Of course the staff running child care have not condoned the offending, but the system which they run allows the development of a strong anti-authority community within which offending may well come to be the norm.

It is becoming clear that residential child care is a recurrent theme in offending behaviour and it is neither a coincidence nor insignificant to find residential child care so closely associated with socialisation into a 'community' condoning offending. The chance of achieving any change for **Gordon** was thought by his supervising probation officer to be very low because of *'the whole environment'* within which he had grown-up. *'A very damaged young man who had a severe upbringing due to a drunken, wife-beating father. Gordon was thoroughly institutionalised by "care" and can't cope with a cohabitation and responsibility of a child. He is repeating, behaviourwise, what his father did* [lives with his girlfriend and two-year-old child in her house in Hartlepool, Cleveland].' Gordon was in residential child care from 11 to 17. Court appearances started at 14 with theft and had continued to 20 as: *'A strong mix of violence, theft and involvement with Twoc. Some of it is for excitement, but a lot of it is just to gain money which the state can't provide* [Gordon was in debt for fines, poll tax, catalogue, a commercial loan and Social Fund crisis loan after a year's unemployment following a NACRO YTS and Buxted chicken packing].' The probation officer concludes: *'Inadequate parenting. Lack of work. Peer group situation. Lack of insight and opportunity to do anything else.'* Again, the explanation launches out from the absence of parental bonding as the source of social control, but residential child care became, as for others, the ready-made community within which crime was condoned by the subculture of delinquent peers on hand day and night to reinforce Social Norms.

'Citadels of crime'

In several of the cases we have used elsewhere reference was made to the significant influence of the area, district, neighbourhood or estate where the offender lived. It is useful to review those cases here to explore further aspects of offending behaviour. As noted, there was a particular association of Social Norm with Social Activity, hence our examples here are drawn from cases already used in that chapter.

After the 're-discovery of poverty' in the 1960s, the St Ann's district of Nottingham was an early candidate for an area-based deprivation study, actually conducted by extra-mural students (Coates and Silburn, 1973). Time passes, but only the racism has worsened, the poverty is the same. **Tone**, who lived there with his mother, father and adult siblings, when not in prison, was introduced as a member of a Black gang in Social Activity (p.61). The whole explanation for Tone's Twoc, robbery, thefts and assaults was that he had been: *'Brought-up in an area with large numbers of other young men in similar circumstances and cultural*

background. The area acquired a bad reputation with the local police.'
And so Tone's offending was *'generally a response to unemployment,
racial discrimination, boredom and poor local facilities'.*

The social norms in **Dick's** (p.71) part of Sunderland were
expressed through his gang and so, *'he displayed an offending pattern*
[theft, burglary and Twoc] *common to the area associated with his
peer group'.* Behind that offending pattern we are told there was
a: *'Record of family break-up and lack of parental control linked with
an offending culture common to the local area. The norms which are
associated with stability such as the work ethic are now difficult to
implant in this area'.* The case of Dick, aged 23 who had never
worked at all, but did have two children and a council tenancy
makes an important point for the future of social control. With
the advent of long-term unemployment affecting young adults in
particular it is hard to see what opportunities there are in run-down
neighbourhoods for social control to play its part in promoting
less offending. To what conventions can young offenders become
committed; with what acceptable behaviour are they to be involved;
and in what established morality are they meant to believe? The
economic and social base has been eroded and it is stretching belief
to suppose that parents who are themselves the subjects of such
changes, whilst also coping with multiple deprivation, will be able
to engage very effectively in the social control of errant children.

From this round-up of cases we gain a sense of the principal
features of an area explanation: a neighbourhood with geographical
dimensions which people can identify; a community, often a council
estate — within which the 'gangs' distinguished in Social Activity
can operate freely — where 'crime' in a general sense seems
to be condoned; high unemployment; boredom; few facilities;
police attention; racism. Returning to our notion of over-developed
community, it may be possible to explain the endemic racism
associated with Social Norms. With the break-up of economic
and social structures which we have discussed, the underpinnings
of traditional community are eroded. As community life disappears
there is a crisis of identity which re-communalises on the basis of
nostalgic images of Englishness and racial superiority entrenched
in neighbourhoods with a siege mentality in their citadels of crime.
Probation officers are having to confront this racism as it expresses
itself in offending behaviour.

Neighbourhood crime in the built environment

Next we shall group the Social Norm cases according to neighbourhood to analyse associations and differences between the places and
offending behaviour. Although there is a concentration of these

cases in the north east, no one area stands out in particular, nor is there any dominant urban type. Over the seven probation areas in the study we have represented inner city areas such as Canonbury in London, old towns such as Bishop Auckland, industrial New Towns such as Peterlee and every type of council estate, for example in Middlesbrough. In other words such neighbourhoods of crime as there might be do not depend on any particular form of residential built environment.

Starting in the north east with Cleveland, there is a concentration of Social Norm cases in Middlesbrough itself and a few in the industrial town to the west, Stockton. The probation officer writing the social inquiry report (now pre sentence report) for 17-year-old **Sam** who has always lived with his parents in Middlesbrough isolated the difficulty in addressing his offending behaviour in these terms: '*Sam needs to be made aware of the seriousness of his actions* [theft of a pedal cycle and breach of a conditional discharge] *but this is hindered by the area in which he lives. The area is a severely problematic one, with poverty and deprivation and a high rate of offending. Sam actually states that he is aware of his problems and the problems that are generated in his area. He is depressed about it and sees no direct or immediate answer.*' Considering the economic situation Sam did fairly well to complete 17 months' employment since leaving school, although it was on three different jobs all of which ran out and a NACRO YTS. The probation officer put some of it down to: '*Living in an area with no provision for recreation and leisure activities*'. Also in Middlesbrough but on her own in a council tenancy, 20-year-old **Tina** who was pregnant lived '*in a locality historically linked to crime*'. Leaving school at 15 did not particularly help **Andy**, nor the eight months on a NACRO decorating YTS as he: '*Has been involved in offending since the age of ten years; petty theft and motoring offences*' for which he had already served three custodial sentences by 17. At the root, concluded the probation officer supervising Andy's throughcare, was: '*The poor estate* [in Middlesbrough] *where there is an acceptance of crime as a way of life; poverty, family on income support; educational needs not being met — now academic*', that is the prospect of achieving this, not the needs! Andy was expected to return to his mother on release, a relationship on which the probation officer would have to work. To address the offending behaviour the probation officer would have to '*examine his employment attitude and break the need to retain his public image due to peer group pressure*'. Though there is a clear 'offence focus' here, even 'offender focused' work could hardly undermine such well-entrenched norms without motivation from Andy and structural changes in the form of a prospect of reasonably well-paid work. We have already discussed this recurring

problem of there being a lack of any basis for there to be effective
bonding. All probation officers in deprived areas have to deal
with this difficulty.

Twelve months in prison was the disposal for **Greg's** first
conviction at 17 for burglary. He had a council tenancy in Stockton,
Cleveland with his girlfriend and dependent children aged 8, 4 and
3. He had left home at 16 to live with her and worked as a builder:
*'The fact that he was brought up in an area that has high levels
of delinquency and criminal behaviour and no financial support was
most significant'*. Greg was socialised into the subcultural norm of
offending on their council estate whereas, 20-year-old *'**Ruby** came
from a background where offending was not the norm. Since living on
her own she has been drawn into this culture* [convictions for deception
and handling] *by virtue of the estate she lives on.'* She left the parental
home at 17, never worked, and was bringing-up two children on her
own in a Stockton council house. Ruby 'drifted' into subcultural
offending, with the labelling it entails.

We move further up the east coast to Gosforth, a town on
the northern outskirts of Newcastle where **Morris'** supervising
probation officer implicitly rejects social control theory as significant
by discounting the absence of the father and highlighting the
criminal character of the area. Morris was 20 and started thieving
when he was 12, but: *'Apart from an offence of burglary in a wine bar,
his offences have not been of a very serious nature. I am not convinced
that the absence of a regular father figure is particularly significant.
More relevant would seem to be the high level of delinquency in the
neighbourhood.'* Although leaving school with no qualifications at
16, by 20, unlike his offending peer group, he had worked most
of the time (not YTS). *'Offence was committed whilst unemployed
and he had relationship worries about his girlfriend. Morris now has
a full-time job* [£100 pw] *and the relationship has ended, so the initial
issues seem to have been resolved.'* The probation officer was seeking
to: *'Consolidate the progress which Morris is making of his own accord
by addressing his attitude to offending.'* Poverty formed a background
and the peer group was the pressure to offend in a neighbourhood
experiencing the social and economic disintegration we have so often
observed.

In beautiful county Durham working coal mines no longer mar
the scenery, but in the New Town of Peterlee **Adrian**: *'Lives in a
area of high delinquency. Adrian lacks social skills and there are few
training or employment opportunities. Total lack of leisure facilities or
resources in the community.'* And of course unemployed males have
plenty of leisure time, although in Adrian's case he: *'Was on an
eighteen months' YT joinery scheme';* he had also done three months
of a bricklaying course and been a coal-man for eight months.

There is a sense of the negative aspects of such areas carrying all before them. But the main issue was: *'Extreme discipline and chastisement from an early age. Adrian's father was and still is, an over-zealous disciplinarian. His mother is totally the opposite. There is a need to encourage the right balance.'* The discipline clearly made no impact on Adrian's offending: five court appearances for burglary since 15.

A visible police presence is a distinctive feature of many inner city crime areas as with St Ann's in Nottingham: *'Inner city area — lots of police activity — high policing'*. At 16 **Douglas** was released from custody on a YOI licence after serving four months for theft, burglary and Twoc (with 72 other offences taken into consideration). The current probation involvement followed a motoring offence and breach of bail, so Douglas was on remand. As he was still under 18 and had left his £75 per week building job, he had no legitimate income. Before remand, he was staying at his girl friend's with her mother and younger brother. When on licence Douglas: *'Returned to the same neighbourhood where he is known to the police, friends and former co-defendants. Getting into trouble is a fact of life in this neighbourhood. There are few constructive alternatives available.'* That stated, the probation officer intended to address the offending, but as with Adrian an alternative or parallel explanation was also offered. Douglas had been taken into residential child care: *'at various points in his upbringing through separation and physical abuse from his father.'* In care, he had experienced: *'Lots of difficulties . . . inconsistent parental care must have had a big effect on his behaviour'*. A very similar kind of account is offered for **Patrick**, also aged 17 and staying with friends who lived in another *'run-down, deprived inner city area'* of Nottingham. He was on supervision with section 4a specified activities for burglary. That followed his sixth court appearance since 13: *'The vast majority are for dishonesty where the need to obtain money informed his behaviour. Because of his unstable situation he is at risk of offending.'* Here, the supervising probation officer is clearly drawing our attention to Patrick's lack of legitimate income (excluded from Income Support by age; from Severe Hardship Allowance by refusal to undertake YTS and he will not claim a Bridging Allowance) and very insecure accommodation, since he left the parental home. Hence the objectives of supervision were to *'secure suitable accommodation and employment. Issues are that the client is not motivated and immature and lacking in educational qualifications. There is also very little employment opportunity available for young people who are not prepared to undertake YTS. Douglas has no faith in YTS and would rather not have any money at all than undertake such a scheme [he had done some "casual/knocking").'* Again economic life in the area is seen as intimately connected with offending behaviour. *'Because he has always lived in a home where there was poverty and financial hardship I believe that he has not faith in the system. He like many other young men has become disaffected, apathetic and pre-disposed to offending. The area in which Douglas lives contains a network where stolen goods can be disposed of easily'* because of the sub-cultural tolerance of crime.

In the post-war boom years Coventry led the country in high levels of employment and relative prosperity. Nowadays, 20-year-old **Viny** prospects were few and unemployment afforded him ample leisure time for his 'spur of the moment' burglaries and public order offences: *'Typical offending history related to the home area. No parental control in the formative years — unemployment creates unlimited time for offences to be committed.'* Vincent left the overcrowded family home at 19 to live temporarily with friends and so more secure accommodation was a practice objective. We should note the local and regional variations in accommodation problems. In the north east obtaining council tenancies did not appear to have been a problem, although living on the estates might have constituted a different kind of challenge. In the Ladywood district of central Birmingham, 17-year-old **Zac** lives with his mother who is *'a single parent with five other children living at home. Perhaps of necessity she is quite strict and has high expectations of Zac, which he can't meet'*. The parental exercise of social controls is in tension with peer group pressure as Zac: *'has difficulty in keeping to "rules" at home like time of coming in, contributing to household tasks. He is equally pulled by his friends who want him to join them at all-night parties'*. It was Zac's first offence and: *'The court appearance and subsequent supervision order caused him much anxiety.'* The supervising probation officer reported that he was making good progress, and he was not expected to become involved in further offending. The home area of Ladywood was held responsible for the Zac's lapse into petty offending: *'At the time of the offence the family had moved to the area with its high crime rate and few community resources. Zac was the child of a large single parent family in which the mother was unable to provide the type of stylish clothing which would enable him to "fit in" with his peers. The temptation for Zac to resort to theft was quite strong at this particular time.'*

The St Paul's district of central Bristol has become well known through national media attention as the scene of riots in the early 1980s and spectacular drug dealing in the 1990s. **Ben** was not seen by his supervising officer as a 'criminal', the term applied to the area and his associates. Ben lived with his lone parent mother and self-identified under 'race' as 'mixed'. At 17 Ben was not eligible for Income Support and had done nothing gainful whatsoever since leaving school at 15. Since age 14, Ben had seven court appearances for theft, burglary and handling with no custodial sentences: *'In spite of what his criminal record indicates, I do not perceive Ben as criminally minded, but [he] is caught-up in the wrong environment and peer group.'* Rather over-determining the predispositions to crime, the probation officer concluded that the character of St Paul's had created the deviant social background in which Ben resided, although the root of his problems was lack of confidence and self-worth. However, the probation officer was attempting to do justice to the complex interaction of 'causal' factors which led to Ben's criminal involvement.

Phil who enjoyed the stimulation of offending as a Social Activity (p. 67) with his group, was also under the influence of the neighbourhood. *'Living in Southmead has led to a decision to join the culture of those in trouble in the area. Temptation is too strong and it brings goodies, fun and excitement.'* Unemployed 20-year-old **Joe** was a council tenant living with his partner and baby on £77.30 per week Income Support with debts to poll tax and catalogues. Joe's parents *'suffered from deprivation themselves (grew-up in care), but could not cope with disabilities* [cystic fibrosis of Joe's two older siblings] *plus the lack of money in a high crime area. Joe responded to adult attention at his last boarding school, but on his return home he fell in with a "local crowd" of teenage delinquents.'* The interaction between the idea of an 'area of crime' and delinquent 'gangs' is here suggested to be mediated by parental inadequacy. We have noted in the case of Zac in Ladywood that attempts at parental control were thought to founder on the 'culture of the area', despite the efforts there of Zac's mother. The failure in these cases should not be generalised because 'parental adequacy', in the form for example of appropriate chaperoning in adolescence, can protect against the delinquent subcultural tolerance of a neighbourhood (Wilson, 1980). And for a more purely sociological explanation compared with that offered in the case of Joe, we turn to **Bruce**: *'Apart from living in an area with high delinquency and the reduction in availability of well-paid labouring jobs there is very little in Bruce's social background which would lead to offending. He has supportive, hard-working parents and an extended family.'* He started his court career at 15 gaining eight court appearances for motoring offences, thefts, and burglaries, building to affray and assault by the age of 20: *'Alcohol related and associated with peer group'.* But Bruce does not follow a settled life, *'moving between girl friends and parents at his own convenience'.* He has done some building site work and been in prison twice. The high level of crime and delinquency in the area had overwhelmed parental efforts at social control.

London

The capital contains some of the most deprived inner city areas in the country, having districts still redolent with the nineteenth century iconography of 'criminal rookeries'. Living with his mother on a council estate in Lewisham, south London — rather like the one studied by Foster (1990) — was *Jim* (also discussed under Social Activity p. 67). The probation officer supervising his YOI licence following fifteen months for theft and breach of a PO, his ninth conviction with one custodial sentence, explained Jim's offending behaviour in terms of the area rather than any failure in the social controls his mother exercised: *'Mother hardworking and supportive. Her son has been brought up in an area where "bad company" exists. In this respect the relevant social background is living on a council estate.'*

On the same side of the river, but in Kennington, lived 20-year-old *Priti*. He had been staying temporarily with friends for a year, after his *'mother moved and would not reveal her new address to him because of trouble with the law'*. He has never worked since leaving school at 16 and all his thefts are to finance his heroin addiction. The 'cause': *'Being brought-up in an area with huge heroin problems with an older brother and sister already using.'* Staying south, in Woolwich: *'**Harry** is a young man who has had, for the greater part of his life, many professionals making decisions for him. He now has been given charge of his own life and seems to find it difficult to cope with this responsibility.'* Harry left home at 14, the time of his first offence for burglary, since when he has been convicted of six more offences, *'all financially motivated'*, involving two prison terms. He was only 17 and still the subject of a care order. His life was unsettled and having lost a council bedsit, he was literally roofless. The probation officer identified: *'Problems in the family stemming from his mother's alcoholic life-style. I hope to address his recidivist offending and to look realistically at Harry's life-style and his plans for the future and accepting responsibility for these.'* It was Harry himself who identified a rather different set of priorities to do with Social Norms: *'The area he lives in — burgled often, therefore he does the same to get his own back.'* Offenders are themselves extremely vulnerable to becoming the victims of crime because they live in areas of high crime [Peelo et al., 1992].

North of the river the probation officer supervising **Gary's** YOI licence aimed to: *'Maintain links with his family in Stoke Newington, Hackney; offer support through visits and correspondence; prepare him for his return into the community.'* However, previous reports indicated that: *'Gary lives in an environment where criminal behaviour is an integral part of life; where boundaries on acceptable behaviour are confused. He is very much part of an offending culture . . . all the* *family have been in trouble.'* 20-year-old Gary has eleven convictions, mainly for burglary and three prison sentences.

Although the London cases may mention unemployment, the casual and labouring job market there is undoubtedly easier than in the north east, or even Nottinghamshire. It is, however, noticeably harder to establish a settled life because of the scarcity of good, cheap accommodation with secure tenure. Plenty of private lettings exist, but many are of a temporary character and at prices the clients of the probation service cannot afford. The quality would be awful, hence we find many 'sharing arrangements': 30 per cent in our study were living in some kind of shared household or extended family arrangement.

6 Coping

Offending linked to having fun with peers and obtaining money to survive when homeless (Gateshead, Northumbria).
Loss of employment has played a significant part in this young man's offending. Poor self-esteem, poverty and a sense of uselessness coupled with poor family support has without a doubt led to his offending behaviour (Middlesbrough, Cleveland).

Meaning and interpretation

Our use of the type Coping is intended to draw a distinction between offending 'purely' for gain and stealing in order to have fairly basic things, the lack of which could be considered deprivation. Food, clothing, fuel and shelter are obvious candidates, the acute lack of which constitutes deprivation beyond poverty. Transport and leisure items are more dubious nominees, though we shall note that some offenders under supervision, supported by their probation officers, do claim that stealing to obtain them are 'survival thefts'.

One thing is certain, of all the types, Coping stands alone by involving just one kind of crime: stealing property (which it should be remembered includes here handling, fraud and deception). There is a fine line between stealing for gain and stealing to survive at a tolerable level of poverty above deprivation. As there exists a national scheme of Income Support which supposedly guarantees payments by right to eligible people it may be contended that no one can justify stealing to survive. There are several problems with that simple notion. Some people are ineligible for benefit, for example everybody under the age of 18 (unless they have dependent children, which is an interesting proposition in itself). Others are disqualified by Department of Social Security (DSS) rules, because for example they have committed a system offence such as 'voluntary' unemployment. And yet others have reduced benefits for a further host of system offences or have specific deductions from their 'applicable amount' of Income Support to pay for an ever increasing list of basic living costs: rent, electricity, gas, water, poll tax, mortgage interest and so on. Paying back loans under the DSS Social Fund became and remains one of the late 1980s' most notorious impositions on the poorest people in Britain. However, it has proved extremely difficult to identify cases, quantify the results and present campaigning lobby material in an objective way. For example, it was hard to identify claimants *not* receiving assistance from the DSS Social Fund, but still in need, just as it had been difficult to find young boarders who had been disqualified from receiving benefit under the old board and lodging time limits (on the Social Fund see Stewart and Stewart, 1993c; on board and lodging see Stewart, et al., 1986). The campaigning organisations turned to qualitative material expressed as 'horror stories' which fuelled the government's claim that researchers had been 'scouring the country for evidence of the fund operating harshly' (Lloyd, 1989). In that atmosphere we are rather conscious of the limitation of using qualitative data at this point. We rest our case on the objective character of the sample, the research instruments, completion of questionnaires by professionals and appropriate analysis.

All of these people live below the level Parliament has set down as the basic minimum amount of money people should have when they do not work, if Income Support is their legitimate source of income (for a scene-setting discussion see Stewart and Stewart, 1986, especially pp.48–50). Further to these administrative technicalities, life on social security over a long time is what we have elsewhere described as 'routine poverty': endless scrimping to get by; no savings for occasional durable items (Stewart and Stewart, 1991, p.23). This may mean that some people living for long periods on their full Income Support entitlement believe themselves justified in stealing, for example clothing, because otherwise they would rarely have new garments without going into debt to such as 'The Provident', a clothing club or catalogue company.

The fact that the Social Norms of their family and neighbourhood condone these actions, as we have discussed in Chapter 5, merely serves to support further offending to 'survive' and perhaps lowers the threshold of acceptability. In explaining how Social Norms gain force it is worth considering the suggestion that social controls might be undermined by increasing unemployment: 'The breakdown of social controls is in effect a precondition for the economic determinants of crime to have full-play. However the breakdown of those social controls may also in its turn be determined partly by economic circumstances' (Field, 1990, p.35; also Downes, 1993). As partial evidence for such a case, the general public are now more prepared to ascribe the main cause of crime to unemployment than they used to be: 72 per cent of people asked in a MORI survey for *Reader's Digest* believed drugs to be a main cause; unemployment 71 per cent (increased from 62 per cent in 1989); lack of parental discipline 69 per cent; lenient sentencing 51 per cent; lack of discipline at school 44 per cent; poverty 44 per cent. In reply to that survey the Employment Secretary, David Hunt claimed: *'It is often said that poverty and unemployment create crime. In my experience the converse is true. ... The bulk of thieving today, of course, has nothing to do with poverty. It is the result of wickedness and greed. Almost nobody today robs to buy food, and they do not mug to buy school clothes for their children. No degree of poverty in Britain today forces people into crime to subsist. We should not confuse rising expectations and demands with 'poverty''* ('Minister blames wickedness for crime rise' *Guardian* 21 March 1994, p.2). Of course, one wants to ask, of which was it Mr Hunt had experience, unemployment or crime? In the 1930s, that Golden Age of British Unemployment when workless men marched to London in their tens of thousands, but you could leave your back door unlocked, a Labour Film League movie depicting an unemployed man in desperation stealing bread for his family was banded. The film censors also required the opening sequence of *Love on the Dole* to appear to be portraying a Salford of long ago.

Admittedly Coping and offending for gain are often difficult to distinguish. We shall consider the link between unemployment and crime later in this chapter; however Field's two-way predisposition is intriguing because we are left with control theory firmly in command. Crime rises because social controls are weakened. Unemployment both undermines social control and provides an opportunity environment for offending. One could say that our type Social Norm encapsulates that situation. Taking the Government stance as suggested by Hunt, the effect of the erosion of social control is read-off as 'wickedness'.

So far we have referred only to people who have no paid legitimate work, for whatever reasons — and some of those will have a caring responsibility; but there are also people in low paid employment for whom similar justifications to steal also make sense. We can therefore distinguish several kinds of circumstance in which people steal in order to survive at what is perceived by the individual to be a tolerable level of poverty, including: being homeless and penniless; being long-term benefit income only; having child-care responsibilities. For our type of Coping to operate independently, the offences under consideration must be property offences; the offender must be under 18, out-of-work and not on a YTS; or be subject to routine poverty and have child-care responsibilities.

Needless to say life is not so simple. One day you shop-lift food because of hunger, the next it's a video sold for drugs, and perhaps this young adult has refused a YTS place on ideological grounds. We know that millions of people live on Income Support and millions more work for their poverty. A minority will be stealing in order to Cope or survive, but the great majority will be just coping in the everyday sense of that word. What irony it is that the poorest people are required to exercise such fine ethical judgement in these matters, and with harder outcomes for themselves, so much more often than the well-heeled. In order to gain some purchase on these circumstances and the judgements involved, an estimate of the level of poverty in which offenders under supervision live, will help.

Poverty and social security

There are several ways of examining poverty amongst offenders under supervision and all are beset with problems. By the very nature of who they are, this group *probably* have money and goods obtained illegally. In making a poverty profile are these stolen items to be counted? Surely it is reasonable to assume that the illegitimate income of a thief will be vastly greater than declared legitimate gains? When a 'criminal' is engaged on a spate of stealing for gain (which we discuss under Professional), that may be the case, but we have every reason to believe from the reports of probation officers that there are many offenders who are stealing in order to Cope and whose declared legitimate income is very small.

It is conventional nowadays to take the level of Income Support as the measure of poverty, below it constituting severe deprivation, even destitution. Unfortunately it would require a social security assessment on each case to construct such a measure and surveys do not reveal sufficient detail to make that possible. Part of the cliché about offenders following a 'chaotic life-style' extends to their knowledge of their own social security position. A further difficulty involves the treatment of housing costs. Most people on Income Support have (most of) their housing costs met by Housing Benefit; however the poorest of the poor, especially young people, do not, for various, often highly complex, reasons. It forms yet another element in why we can claim they are in such extremely straitened circumstances and are Coping by stealing. Those complex circumstances are most easily explained in terms of their homelessness. In developing a poverty profile of offenders one compromises and either uses the stated weekly income where known, or uses 'unemployment' as a proxy. In our studies we have employed the former approach, whilst accepting doubts as to its reliability — and actually for that reason have made no attempt to link stated income to applicable social security benefit.

How poor are offenders under supervision?

As shown in Table 6.1, means-tested Income Support was the principal current, or expected, source of income for more than half of the offenders in our study; wages for only a fifth. Both unemployment and DSS rules hit the youngest people in our survey particularly hard and it should be borne in mind that YT places are neither universally nor readily available. Being disqualified from benefit, over two-thirds of 17-year-olds had no reliable source of income and only 14 individuals actually received the bridging or hardship payments which are supposedly available to those who cannot get a training scheme place. Seven per cent overall were dependent on irregular one-off payments from the probation service Befriending Fund (mainly 17-year-olds) or Social Fund crisis loans (mainly 20- and 23-year-olds). Subsidies in cash or kind, usually from parents, were the principal source of income for more than a quarter of 17-year-olds and one in ten of all ages. The financial pressures on 17-year-old offenders and their families are unequivocally established. The link between youth destitution and crime can be gauged from the national DSS-funded research which found that 30 per cent of the young male applicants for severe hardship payments had previous convictions (MORI, 1991, p.187).

In a similar study to ours by the National Association of Probation Officers (NAPO 1993, p.4) rather higher levels of reliance on means-tested benefits and lower levels of 'no income' were reported (79 per cent and 3 per cent respectively).

Table 6.1: Source of income currently received, or expected on release from custody

% of age groups	17 %	20 %	23 %	all ages N	%
Wages, full- or part-time	18	21	22	276	21
Training Scheme Allowance	20	5	3	105	8
Income Support, Hardship	20	66	67	748	56
Another Benefit	3	7	10	98	7
One-off Payments	14	6	4	96	7
Subsidies from Individuals	27	8	4	151	11
No Income At All	27	3	2	114	9
(multiple responses)	N = 315	614	414	1343	

Multiple response means that individual cases may be included under more than one category (except 'no income') as applicable to their situation.

Among those on means-tested benefits, a fifth had some of their income directly deducted at source to pay off (mainly) previous Social Fund loans, fuel and rent arrears (a relatively high figure considering that only a quarter had independent housing with rent and fuel commitments at the time of the survey). The NAPO survey found a quarter to have deductions from benefits and concluded: *'It seems certain therefore that at least 28 per cent of the probation caseload are living below Income Support level'* (deductions plus 'no income') (NAPO, 1993, p.7). It should be pointed out, however, that claimants with deductions are only in that position because they have incurred a liability by not having paid previous bills or because of an arrangement to pay their current accounts directly. They are not being financially punished by the DSS for a system offence as are claimants on reduced benefits or with disqualifications.

More than half of those with a known regular income actually received under £30 a week for their own needs and those of any dependents. Tables 6.2 and 6.3 indicate that those with the lowest income were unemployed single people, and particularly 17-year-olds disqualified from benefit, who were living either on their own or within extended families which were supporting them. However, nearly half of parents with responsibility for children had a family income of less than £60 a week. Overall 54 per cent of these young people were in debt in addition to any direct deductions, particularly with outstanding fines (37 per cent), poll tax arrears and catalogue debts. The general impression was one of poverty and financial pressure.

Information about weekly income was given for 81 per cent of those who were not in custody. As Table 6.3 shows, just 10 per cent had over £100 a week of legitimate income and all were on wages. At the other end of the scale, two-thirds had less than £40 and

Table 6.2: Weekly income currently received by household composition

% of household	Single, Couple %	Nuclear Family %	Extended Types %	All No.	%
Nothing	8	4	18	110	13
£1 to £19	5	1	6	41	5
£20 to £29	48	10	38	306	37
£30 to £39	17	6	12	99	12
£40 to £59	7	17	4	58	7
£60 to £79	3	19	6	70	8
£80 to £99	6	10	6	56	7
Over £100	7	18	9	86	10
	N = 198	143	485	826	

Table 6.3 Weekly income currently received by age *(does not include Housing Benefit)*

% of age groups	17 %	20 %	23 %	all ages N	%
Nothing	38	5	4	114	13
£1 to £19	12	2	2	41	5
£20 to £29	14	49	39	318	38
£30 to £39	16	11	9	101	12
£40 to £59	4	8	7	59	7
£60 to £79	8	7	11	70	8
£80 to £99	4	7	10	59	7
over £100	4	10	17	86	10
	N = 222	395	231	848	

18 per cent had under £20 a week — which must be regarded as poverty in Britain by any standard. Can we compare these figures with any kinds of standard? There are two fruitful avenues. First, there is the European Union measure of 'poverty', as reported by O'Higgins and Jenkins (1990). The measure of poverty is taken to be having less than 50 per cent of median average equivalent household income for single person households. Although a strict use of that measure is not possible, taking the wages mentioned by the young adults in our study, an average of £106 per week after deductions seems likely for 1991 for single people in circumstances relevant to offenders under supervision when in work. Comparing the two sets of figures we can estimate, on the EU measure, that 72 per cent of the survey sample would be judged to be 'in poverty'. We appreciate this is a comparison of young offenders in work with all young offenders' circumstances outside custody. A comparison with all young adults is likely to produce an even worse result.

A second way of making a comparison is historically, against offenders under supervision in a previous epoch. The value of doing this lies in matching like with like. A study of probationers comparable with ours was conducted from the Home Office in 1965, and the revealing findings on income are presented in Table 6.4 at 1991 prices. The proportion with no income at all is more than four times higher in our study, and the generally higher income levels which were recorded in the mid-1960s can be attributed to 59 per cent of probationers being employed then compared with only 21 per cent in 1991 (Davies, 1969, pp.61, 81). It was this kind of finding which allowed Davies to claim: *'There was every indication, indeed, that the probationers and their families were for the most part well in the mainstream of Britain's economic affluence'* (Davies, 1969, p.31). That finding of worsening poverty

Table 6.4:   Weekly income of probationers in 1964–65, at 1990–91 rates

	%
Nothing	3
Under £36.40p	12
. . . Up to £72.80p	33
. . . Up to £109.20p	32
. . . Up to £145.60p	14
. . . Up to £182	3
Over £182	2
	N = 461

Derived from Davies, 1969, table 5.31 by a multiple of 9.1 from the following base: National Assistance basic scale rate for a single householder 1964–65 = £3.175p (63s 6d); Income Support applicable amount for a single 18–24-year-old 1990–91 = £28.80p.

amongst offenders is reflected in the recent evidence which shows that income inequality over the last 15 years has left the poorest tenth of the general population no better off than in 1967 (Goodman and Webb, 1994).

The next crucial issue is whether the poorest offenders in our study are in the Coping category. Whereas 13 per cent of all offenders in our study were without income, 17.5 per cent of Coping offenders had no income. For those Coping offenders with an income it tended to be just lower than that of all offenders. Even more dramatic was the age distribution of Coping offenders by income: 48 per cent of 17-year-old Coping offenders had no income and they constituted 82 per cent of offenders with no income. This reflects directly the effect of social security regulations and YTS opportunities on younger people in our study. The gender distribution of Coping offenders by income is interesting because it apparently shows that men in this group are worse off than women: only 8 per cent of coping women offenders had no income, compared with 21 per cent of men. And where there was an income, Coping male offenders still tended to be worse off financially than women. The reason for this lies in caring for dependent children: the women were doing it and hence had additional Income Support; the men were not. Overall, 27 per cent of offenders in our survey had dependent children, whereas 32 per cent of Coping offenders had children. We may conclude that Coping offenders were, as a group, somewhat worse off financially, though, 17-year-olds apart, not markedly so. We shall see from discussion of the cases the crucial importance of financial circumstances, commitments and ability to manage in determining Coping offending, rather than simply income level alone.

Unemployment

Leaving out those who were currently in custody, we know that 20 per cent of offenders were in waged work, and 9 per cent on a government training scheme, whilst 7 per cent were occupied with caring responsibilities, leaving 64 per cent of the young offenders in our study unemployed. The unemployment rate ranged from 51 per cent in the West Midlands to 76 per cent in Northumbria. It was not worse in the 'inner cities' than in less urban areas: it was worse in areas of highest general unemployment. To compare those massive rates of unemployment with the national average (which was 6.7 per cent for Great Britain in January 1991 when our data were collected) or even the appropriate regional rates would however be misleading, principally because the unemployment rate for under 25-year-old males was nearly twice that for the over 25s (Office of Population Censuses and Surveys, 1992, table 6.23, p.30). The rates of unemployment in our survey roughly follow the variations in the percentage of the whole work force unemployed in the relevant 'travel to work' areas. Hence in our seven probation areas, the highest rate of unemployment is to be found in the North East's 'travel to work' areas at 10.84 per cent, then Nottinghamshire at 8 per cent, West Midlands 7.96 per cent, London 6 per cent and Avon 5.7 per cent (*Employment Gazette*, March 1991, p.S21, from table 2.4, for January 1991). At its higher level, the distribution in our study directly mirrors the national profile. The NAPO study found exactly the same proportion of unemployed offenders under supervision (NAPO, 1993, p.1). Also in 1993, the Association of Chief Officers of Probation issued an employment status analysis of the 30,000 pre-sentence reports undertaken nationally between January and June of that year. It revealed 70 per cent unemployed; 20 per cent employed; 4 per cent on education or training schemes and 6 per cent 'other' — remarkably similar to our results (ACOP News Release, *Unemployment and Crime*, 17 September 1993).

Using national, published data, Dickinson has attempted to demonstrate a link between crime and unemployment claiming a 'close association between the unemployment and offending rates of young men . . . this indicates that unemployment is a cause of crime'. It should be made clear that Dickinson is referring to property offences only and totally excludes so-called 'personal' offences such as violence and sexual crimes. It is unclear what has happened to drug offences in his analysis, and he also ducks the issue of drug-related property offences (of which more in Chapter

7) — if 'unemployment is a cause of crime' is it also a cause of the increased drug use which occurred during the same period and is intimately linked to property offences?. Dickinson does not claim a simple relationship between unemployment and, specifically, burglary, 'but unemployment must be regarded as a major factor motivating crime'. Unemployment is seen as the catalyst to increased offending for young people deprived of educational and economic opportunities who, because of that, are 'least affected by social restraints' (Dickinson, 1993, pp. 31–2).

We know offenders under supervision have left school at the earliest opportunity, have truanted, do not have qualifications; but is all of that deprivation of opportunity or is it rejection by them of the education from which they could have benefited? Perhaps the mass youth unemployment for which the decades of the 1980s and 1990s will be historically famous has eroded social restraints against offending and engendered a feeling of cynical apathy about the possibility of any kind of legitimate self-improvement because the kind of opportunities on offer appear to be of little value, as evidenced in the strong anti-YTS sentiments we shall discuss. The crucial issue after the age of 18 is whether a job could in principle provide a 'living wage' to raise a family with stable prospects. Young adults have little faith in training schemes either providing those circumstances directly or leading to them. Through their probation officers' comments, many young adults seem to be suggesting they can only put together a 'living wage' out of several ill-paying activities. Coping offending is one strategy in such an environment.

Offenders who are coping by stealing

Coping by stealing was an individualistic business. More so than any other type it was driven by the actual circumstances of each person in their household. Also Coping theft was less opportunistic than that in, say, Self-expression, because the reason was linked directly with needing something which the offender did not have. As an intention to steal for a purpose is implied here, Coping must always sit on the boundary of Professional theft. One may judge from the preceding discussion that Coping theft will be highly structured by economic situation and social circumstances: patterns of offending behaviour are clear for this type. Hence chronic unemployment; the routine poverty of child rearing on social security; survival situations such as leaving home or absconding from detention. Within those general contexts the DSS regulations have their effect causing or potentiating survival thefts by leaving people without sufficient income. When people are in poverty over a long period of time the likelihood of debt increases greatly. Probation officers may be expected to address offending behaviour, and they do, but as we shall note, they are also concerned with the poor budgeting skills of offenders under supervision who cannot cope, precisely because such situations may lead to Coping offending.

Out-of-work

Let us open by considering that boundary between stealing for Professional gain and Coping. **Lawrence** from Northumbria was a 23-year-old family man offending for money because he was unemployed. Despite qualifications (one 'O' level and five CSEs) and YT (one year construction) he had been unemployed for four years until a joinery training scheme with the Apex Trust. Reference to that scheme indicates that Lawrence had been in prison — eighteen months in fact. All his six convictions since he was 15 were for burglary: *'All Lawrence's offences are entering premises both dwelling houses and business to steal property to sell for financial gain.'* How can one decide whether his offending was Professional or Coping? Lawrence was currently on a suspended sentence supervision order for another burglary. He had electricity and consumer credit debts to pay out of his £76.50 employment training pay. Along with his partner, Lawrence also lives with their three children aged 8, 4 and 3. The two YTS were the only legitimate 'employment' which Lawrence had known since he left school at 16. *'The client regards Employment as the most serious problem and the major cause of his offending. Being unemployed means limited finances, increased stress at home, leading to offending purely for financial gain.'* The probation officer accepts that assessment and was working on employment and financial management: *'Encourage the client to make use of community resources such as Job Centres and Job Clubs.'* However, there were other aspects of his offending behaviour to raise with Lawrence: *'To create an awareness in the client just what the consequences are for the victim, himself and his family.'* The probation officer understands the circumstances which pressure Lawrence towards such Coping offending: *'The client has had limited access to opportunities which could improve the quality of his life. He is a product of his social environment which recognises that illegitimate opportunities become an acceptable risk to take.'* He also acknowledges that offending behaviour has to be addressed — *'To help the client recognise the times when he is vulnerable and likely to offend so that he can develop strategies to cope with those situations and be diverted or the risks of re-offending reduced.'*

We have considerably less detail about **Scott** who is also unemployed in Sunderland. Though Scott lived with his parents he had a one-year-old baby who lived with his girlfriend and a problem for Scott was: *'Having to live separately from his girlfriend and child'*. Unemployment was an issue for both his probation officer and Scott who left school at 16 with no qualifications and had only done two months of a YTS. By 20 his sole contact with the world of full-time regular employment was a Re-start interview with DSS. He had Income Support for £26.05 and no deductions or debts. Appearances before the court totalled nine and began when he was 15, following a mixed course of theft, drink related offences, criminal damage, handling, motoring: *'Background of marital difficulties and alcohol related offending, but main problem now is unemployment. In this area if you have a criminal record your chances of succeeding to make a good and honest life for yourself is almost nonexistent.'* The probation officer's doleful conclusion reads like a resigned acceptance of the Social Norms which condone re-offending because there can be no escape at present levels of unemployment.

Employment prospects in the North East were so poor that moving in search of work was often considered, though there were many difficulties for 17-year-olds such as **Kevin** who had already experienced homelessness and destitution after leaving his mother's home following a disagreement. In those circumstances Kevin committed three burglaries for which he was given six months YOI (only one previous conviction). On licence with a Cleveland probation officer and back with his mother, the focus of work was unemployment: *'Client prepared to go to London to find work. To encourage Kevin to take-up an offer of full-time employment offered by his relatives [although] his literacy skills are in need of improvement as lack of them hinders his employment prospects.'* The probation officer hopes that this will lead to a satisfactory income with which he can be independent as at that time he was living off his mother. It might have had the added bonus of providing a circle of non-offending friends.

Often the offending occurred only when the young adult was unemployed as with **Simon** who was 23 and still lived with his parents in Cleveland, although he had been through a partnership and left (no children). Having left school early at 15 without qualifications he had completed two YTSs, a vandal patrol and a NACRO decorating scheme, and various seasonal fairground jobs. At the time of the survey he was employed full-time as a fork lift truck driver at £157.50 per week. His fine of £740 was outstanding as was his poll tax liability. Of his offending career the probation officer wrote: *'Most of the offences are of dishonesty and in the main, stealing from cars. All were committed at times of unemployment.'* He had eleven convictions since he was 16 and one custodial sentence of six months YOI. The probation officer has no doubt about the background: *'As Hartlepool is amongst the worst areas in the country for unemployment, this has been significant. He has only offended when out-of-work. When he has a job, this has never been an issue.'* Straightforwardly enough Simon's probation officer wants to focus on the employment and use it to deflect him from further offending: *'Having quickly obtained work in a permanent capacity shortly after being placed on probation, I want to help him keep it and clear his large amount of outstanding fines, thus giving him a "clean sheet" for the future.'* Perhaps Simon's age was working to his advantage in the exceedingly tough job market of Hartlepool.

Bicky on the other hand was a 17-year-old Hartlepool lad who refused YTS, was unemployed, lived with his mother and stepfather and was hence totally dependent upon them with no legitimate income of his own. The situation was further stressed as he was the father of two babies, 9 and 20 months who lived in *'council accommodation with mother.* At some time whilst he was 17 Bicky had lived with his girlfriend, but separated (*'Lack of money keeps him separated from his girlfriend'*: without more information it is difficult to know what to make of this because if they were living as a couple Bicky, his girlfriend and their children could claim Income Support). Bicky's supervising probation officer was seeking to gain *'the co-operation of the client to enhance his job-search skills and promote employment opportunities via a probation linked employment project'.* This is one of the ways in which the probation service can be of clear, positive value to young people trapped in extremely difficult economic circumstances over which they have no influence whatsoever. However, as the probation officer points out: *'As this area is an unemployment blackspot many young people are lacking in motivation because their situation appears hopeless to them.'* It would be difficult to persuade Bicky to accept the project because of his antagonistic attitude to YTS: *'His offending* [handling, theft, burglary since 15] *is closely linked with "lack of money" made worse by his refusal to accept Youth Training. Were employment available to him he is likely to stop offending.'* The probation officer believes failure of social controls may underlie the unemployment situation: *'Parents' separation/divorce followed by "stepfather difficulties" may have influenced offending behaviour in addition to "failed schooling", but the main reason* [for offending] *seems to stem from unemployment.'* The offending behaviour career would be different, even absent, if the economic situation were different. Probation officers, and all other agents with public responsibilities for deprived young people in these times face a serious problem of credibility when confronting the employment issue in the one-dimensional world of YTS.

According to the probation officer supervising **Victor's** voluntary after-care following imprisonment for assault and three burglaries he was: '*A petty offender who is opportunist — would probably not offend at all, if in employment, but is also easily persuadable by friends to participate*'. 23-years-old, he has had nine court appearances since he was 11 for burglary, theft, violence, possession of offensive weapons and so on, resulting in three custodial sentences: '*Poor family history and fairly low mentality mean this client was born with disadvantages. It's meant job opportunities are limited, so he has turned to petty offending in an effort to make money — so far unsuccessfully, as so much in his life.*' At the time of the survey he was back at his parents' house in Hucknall, a small town north of Nottingham, but had left when he was 18 because of overcrowding and that remained an issue: '*I have known Victor for five years. He has always maintained that accommodation or lack of it, is the main problem. We have not been able to secure permanent accommodation during this time.*' Victor has had a few jobs such as a YTS industrial cleaning and packing, though the spells of unemployment have been long: '*When in employment, there seem few problems, but he reverts to petty offending when he needs money, usually stealing scrap metal to sell for cash.*' Victor has a complaint that payment of Income Support has often been seriously delayed. Accommodation and benefit problems have plagued him to such an extent that his probation officer felt deflected from the primary objective: '*These two problems have clouded the issue of offending behaviour*'. The probation officer was realistic about the future possibilities, limiting the objectives to: '*Maintaining contact (knowing at some time he will re-offend). To encourage him at least to widen the time between committing offences.*'

Poverty and child care

Although the offenders under supervision in our study were all young people many had family responsibilities. Nearly two-thirds of the women had children and overall 27 per cent of the whole sample had children (more than 500 children in all). Most of those children were very young: 86 per cent of the eldest or only children were aged under 5. The father was often absent. Of the men who were fathers, 59 per cent were not living with their off-spring at the time of the survey.

Bringing up children is extremely expensive and trying to do that on benefit income alone constitutes the circumstances we have referred to as routine poverty. The problems may be exacerbated by disability of the client or a family member. Stealing had to be a Coping strategy for **Claudia**, who at 20 was bringing up two children aged two and a half and six months, living with her in a council tenancy in St Paul's, Bristol: '*All shop-lifting of children's clothes. Offences only committed because of poverty and the need to provide*

for her children'. She had been unemployed since leaving school at
16 without qualifications, soon having her first baby at 17. Benefit
income, which included Attendance Allowance toward the 24-hour
care of one of her children, totalled £76 per week. There were
deductions and it was unclear whether they were taken from that
amount or separate: rent direct £5.24; electricity direct £10; poll tax
direct £10. Claudia also had a consumer credit debt to a catalogue.
Known shop-lifting commenced when she was 19. For the first
two Claudia was conditionally discharged. Indeed her probation
officer recommended to the court that she should be conditionally
discharged a third time, but the magistrates handed down a two year
probation order: *'Offending is only committed because of poverty. Little
or no work to do on offending behaviour.'* The probation officer was so
confident about Claudia's ability to comply with the order that at the
half way stage a discharge was to be requested. Claudia's probation
officer had *'no concerns about her parenting'*, although Social Services
had Claudia on their 'At Risk' register, which was, presumably,
some kind of helpful precaution on their part because of Claudia's
difficult circumstances.

In prosperous Bath lived 20-year-old **Dody** looking-after her
3-year-old child in a council flat. When she was 16, Dody's alcoholic
mother could not cope with her and the baby, so Dody was put in
'a council hostel for one-parent families'. Dody had never lived in a
partnership. Considerable debts of poll tax, electricity and catalogue
credit were owed from her £53.15 per week benefit income. She had
never worked since leaving school at 16 without qualifications. *'Her
earning capacity is very limited and long-term reliance on benefits has
led to inappropriate behaviour* [meaning offending?].' There were two
sets of convictions when Dody was 19 for handling large amounts
of stolen goods. Her probation officer certainly implied that Dody
was trying to Cope by dishonesty, but believed peer group pressure
actually motivated her to do the deed: *'The aims of the order are to
encourage the client to develop assertiveness skills so that she can resist the
pressures of friends and to support her in her attempts to put her financial
situation in order.'* To address the first issue the probation officer
proposed attendance at a women's group. Debts and peer pressure
were linked as Dody only gave in to the latter when the debts *'get
out of proportion and can't be avoided'*. The probation officer would
advise on debt management and budgeting.

When attacking qualitative analysis critics often accuse the
writers of scouring the countryside for the worst possible cases.
Rebecca is our *first* contribution! She was 20 and homeless in
Northumbria, though in the week of the survey she was actually in
the family unit of a hospital, *'awaiting a local authority tenancy'*. Only
her 2-month-old baby was with her; the 3 and 2-year-old children

were living with Rebecca's parents. When she was pregnant this last time, Rebecca did not seek any *'medical intervention'*, although apparently there had been: *'Social services involvement because of risk factors to the unborn child'*. At the time she had no income because the DSS had *'not yet sorted it out'*. She had been without benefit income for ten months, living a: *'Homeless, rootless, drifting existence since December 1989'*, which date was the commencement of her drug and alcohol abuse. The probation service had made her a grant from the Befriending Fund. The offences for which Rebecca was currently under supervision were shop-lifting, theft and fraudulently obtaining drugs. That was her fifth appearance before the courts since she began at 14 with burglary. Rebecca had *'Never been employed or on any training scheme'* because of motherhood at 16.

Rebecca's probation officer proposed an inter-disciplinary approach involving social services and health: *'Work towards maintaining some stability in client's life. Addressing drug related problems lack of income and homelessness. Once stabilised, to support her to maintain herself and her child in the community in her present drug and alcohol free position. Increase Rebecca's awareness of "risk" factors in her behaviour. Unpick multitude of 'problems' which led to previous nomadic existence.'* The probation officer believed a certain rigidity in the outlook of Rebecca's parents led to her 'rebellion' at 14 when she got into solvent abuse. That in turn resulted in voluntary local authority care from which she frequently absconded. Living rough and on the run, she stole. From 15 to 18 there was a period of stability and Rebecca did not offend, but *'offending occurred again when a social relationship began to break down. Parental conflict continues to exacerbate problems'*. Rebecca *'is unhappy about all these issues and motivated to keep her baby and establish a permanent home'*. Even though she was surviving whilst homeless and on the run, an aspect of Life-style offending especially because of substance abuse, Rebecca was still Coping.

Coping as an aspect of Life-style also appears with **Jean** because homelessness involves getting by on very little, often employing Coping strategies to survive. Substance abuse is not a necessary precondition of Life-style offending, though of course it is a major factor. *'Lack of money motivated Jean and she was spurred-on by encouragement from others. With inadequate funds, poor housing and an unsettled life-style Jean went tagging around after her partner who has drifted to various parts of the city to live until he gets fed-up and wants to move again.'* They teamed up when she was 17 and not getting on with her parents. Then the convictions began: three for theft and DSS fraud. There were two children, aged 6 months and 2 years who lived with her in a council tenancy on a Selly Oak estate, a southern 'suburb' of Birmingham: *'The partner comes on and off the scene frequently'*. They lived on £59.69 Income Support per week and there were serious debts of fines, rent, poll tax, catalogues and credit cards. *'Jean sees survival on a limited income as problematic and that she gets so little support from her partner.'* The objectives are typical of those with a woman client, as we have noted in Self-expression, focusing on domestic responsibilities and the wife rôle: *'In order to help her organise finances and prevent the need to further offend, work has revolved around budgeting and financial problems — negotiating with agencies such as the housing department.'* The tendency for social workers (including probation officers) to ignore domestic violence may well have declined since the criticisms of Maynard (1985) as this extract suggests: *'Jean has relationship problems with her partner who drinks heavily and has violent tendencies. . . . she fears his drunken outbursts'* (Stewart and Stewart, 1993b, discuss the practice issues pp.55–6; and evidence pp.66–7). However, despite the critical tone readers will have noticed, Jean's probation officer still proposed the traditional social work response where children are involved: reconciliation with the abusing partner: *'Efforts have been made to mediate between the two and increase the partner's awareness of his responsibilities to Jean and their two children.'* The probation officer wanted to improve the domestic situation and was also going to: *'Represent his interests to various agencies such as housing and gas'.* We do not know if Jean's partner was also under supervision, but if he was not there is an issue here of 'offence focus'. The probation officer appears to be providing a general welfare service to a household rather than addressing the offence.

That other major crime, watching the TV without a licence to view half of the output, had brought 20-year-old **Clare** before the court in Durham: her first and only offence. A council tenant, she was the lone parent of an 18-month-old baby, having no contact with the father and living on £53.25 Income Support. Clare also had a one-off Social Fund crisis loan at the time. There were direct payments for rent, electricity and of course the SF loan. The TV fine, water rates, catalogue and coal bill were all in arrears. She was on a money payment supervision order: *'Through mismanagement of income and expenditure got into debt and defaulted on fine payment.'* The probation service assistant was concentrating efforts on helping Clare manage her finances more responsibly and *'liaising with organisations to whom client owes money.'* After leaving school at 16 with four GCSEs (*'cannot remember subjects'*), Clare was on a supermarket check-out for a year, then: *'Mother put client out of family home when she became pregnant, so she has had to fend for herself since as a one-parent family.'* The immediate circumstances surrounding the petty offending, of an unstable partnership and routine poverty, sit within the social background of Jean's early parenting, relationship breakdown with her own parents, and having to leave home at a time of extreme financial and emotional pressure. Sometimes even solicitors show sympathy in such cases: '**Whip-round by lawyers saves mother from jail.** *A pregnant mother of six about to start five days in jail was saved when solicitors held a whip-round in court to pay her £55 fine for TV licence dodging' (Guardian* 26 November 1993, p.3).

Re-capping on the features that have emerged so far in this section, Coping offending in circumstances of child rearing involves fairly petty offending, often fraud, and it often has a late onset, but is always directed to a practical cash result often said to be 'for the children'. There are considerable debts for household necessities. We can also note background issues involving homelessness, or insecurity of accommodation and relationship breakdown. **Sally** was a lone parent with children aged 4 and 2 whose first and only conviction at 22 was conspiracy to defraud the DSS: *'She has had to exist on benefits from an early age with two young children and she considers benefits are very low.'* The probation officer remained neutral throughout: *'The client considers she has too little to live on and paying debts etc. comes low on her list of priorities.'* The practice objectives address both offending and the pressing welfare issues: *'To help the client cope with her difficulties without seeking solutions outside the law.'* Income Support was £65.50, with £9 gas direct a week, rent arrears for her Durham council house and poll tax arrears. Sally had left the parental home at 18 to live with her boyfriend, who later cleared off, and: *'Has never worked due to becoming pregnant young.'* The probation officer regarded the factor which precipitated Sally towards the offence to be: *'Mixing with criminally sophisticated people well-known to the courts.'* The last point suggests that even DSS fraud may require sub-culturally learned skills.

It is useful to compare **Stella** and **Sue**, both living in the North East, because Stella's one and only offence involving use of a stolen credit card leading to a year's probation was prompted by *'her situation as a single parent which produced financial and other pressures in 1990'*, whereas Sue had a very long and criminally relevant background. Sue, 23, had set up with her partner in a private tenancy in Bishop Auckland when she was 19 and pregnant. There were two children aged 3 years and 6 months at the time of the study. She was the *'youngest of a large family — observed matrimonial violence and a drunken father — poverty as her mother struggled to cope'.* Convictions for thefts, twoc, criminal damage and assault began when she was 15. Similarly, Stella left the parental home at 18 for a council tenancy in Middlesbrough to *'live with the father of her children',* aged 1 and 2 at the time of the study. So both women were in nuclear families, with presumably unemployed men-folk as the households received Income Support. What we note is that when the women are the offenders under supervision and the probation officer offers a Coping explanation, it is not couched in terms of unemployment, but of child-rearing. That has been a feature in the previous cases, but one to which we have not referred because the absence of a male partner could be thought to place in importance 'poverty and child-rearing' above 'poverty and seeking a job' in areas of horrendous unemployment. On the evidence of Sue and Sally, we have to suggest that Coping is justifiably understood for women in terms of bringing up children in routine poverty and budgeting problems, whereas men do not appear to have child care responsibilities in quite the same kind of way. Of course, Coping offending explained via 'unemployment' in the case of men could always be a metaphor for child-rearing and the rest.

In confirmation of these points, the issues for the probation officer in working with Stella involved: *'Poverty and child care . . . Practical advice and help required. Vulnerable mother who had recently lost her own mother.'* Because of fine non-payment, Sue attended a money management course — very practical of course and geared to her emerging rôle: *'Advice about alcohol and family dynamics with the cohabitee who is now her husband.'* And it would be wrong to suggest that issues of unemployment for clients who are mothers were always ignored. Sue's probation officer concludes by commenting: *'There are no organised community structures to allow her to have a choice of employment or DSS. Trapped by social structures and lack of training for many types of employment.'* This probation officer was well aware of the issues we have just considered. There was a regional variation here. First, a higher proportion of offenders under supervision in the North East had dependent children than those in the Midlands and southern probation areas and secondly, the rates of unemployment were massively higher in the North East.

To demonstrate the complexity of reasons for theft and investigate further the gender issue just raised, we turn to **Owen** who, on release from prison, would be living with his parents in Walker, a town between Newcastle-upon-Tyne and Wallsend. He left home of, *'his own choice to stay with friends when he was 16'* and then found his own accommodation when he was 19. At the time of the survey he was imprisoned for burglary and theft, the ninth conviction since age 12, and fourth custodial sentence. The explanation of the offending behaviour is an interesting mixture: *'Mainly of a dishonest nature in order to raise cash. Some of it was spent on his children, some on drugs. Because of lack of money at home, this was the only way he felt able to get money to enjoy himself.'* The two children are 3 years and 3 months, each living *'with their* *respective mothers'*. When he returns to his parent's home, Owen will be joining a household with an epileptic brother and asthmatic father. The probation officer's throughcare work was to concentrate on two areas: *'To ensure an unproblematic return to the community and assist Owen re-integrate'* and *'To ensure family contact is maintained during sentence so that a home is available on release'*. Employment is a serious problem for Owen. He left school at 15 and although he had done maths, English, carpet fitting and electrical installation at FE, on two YTS placements he lasted just half-an-hour. Perhaps we have a partial answer to the gender division in child care, poverty and Coping offending. The responsible men are just not there, though sometimes goods are stolen to provide treats for their kids (Campbell, 1993).

Survival and homelessness

So far we have considered Coping offending behaviour within the relatively stable context of households. The youngest offenders who had left their families or had absconded from an institution were often homeless and sometimes starving.

Niall's *'mother decided he was beyond her control when he was 15* [she had him put into "voluntary child care"]. *Since then she has only reluctantly allowed him home and then only for short periods.'* It was at that age Niall began appearing before the courts — five times for thefts, Twocs, handling, burglary, resisting arrest: *'Most offences stealing from cars as a way of survival between employment, particularly when living away from home.'* At the time of the survey, Niall was homeless, staying temporarily with friends living-off £15 DSS Bridging Allowance. Attached to Niall's probation order was a 4a activity requirement to attend a 'life management group' as part of Avon's PACT programme (intensive probation). However he was, *'in breach of PO for failing to co-operate with PACT or keep appointments'* and the probation officer was recommending revocation of the order. PACT may not have been an appropriate probation response to Coping offending: it certainly was not typical. **Danny** was also 17 and living in north Bristol, but he was 'literally roofless' and his probation officer believes his peer group had a hand in the situation: *'Lack of parental concern, local peer group made survival through crime then homelessness acceptable to Danny.'* Since the age of 16, *'theft was as a means of survival'*. YTS was not acceptable to either Niall or Danny, who *'would not co-operate with the careers office'*. Again breach was likely as Danny was reluctant to report.

London has been enticing young people to its racy, indulgent, exciting, temptingly rich life-style despite many campaigns, such as 'Why Not Go To London?', to persuade naïve young provincials that without the prospects of a job or somewhere to live they would be joining a long queue of homeless and penniless hopefuls. It is not really surprising that young people are attracted to a city in which it is possible to survive on a circuit of lodgings because of voluntary agencies, numerous opportunities for food gathering, and being in a large milieu of like people. One should be aware of such stereotypes, for leaving the family home can also be at the time a rational solution and a traditional path. **Nolan** went to London when he was 15 following violent abuse by his step-father in Ireland. He thought he would join *'the rest of the family. Nolan is illiterate. The family do not give the impression of caring much. His elder brother is too controlling.'* He used to work with his brother in a scrapyard for £80 a week of which he gave his brother £30. On leaving he was: *'Caught-out as he had no money, so stole a car'*. Nolan was being supervised by ILPS on a Supervision Order.

Finding suitable accommodation can become the single most important issue in the supervision of some offenders as for example in the kind of situation faced by **Hartley**, a 20-year-old man homeless in London. He was psychiatrically disturbed and had been evicted by four hostels in three months. We are not told when he came to London, just that he appeared to be instrumental in his parents' divorce when he was 10, after which he went into residential child care. *'Offending occurs when he is greatly stressed, and has deteriorated since he came to London where he has been homeless and had no support networks.'* Depression was thought to underlie all Hartley's four convictions since 18: motoring offences, assault, handling and theft. *'The major issue is housing, in that Hartley is currently living in an unsatisfactory bed and breakfast hotel which he hates. Because of his emotional instability and loneliness we are looking for a hostel which provides quite a high level of support* [a "personality disorder" had been diagnosed]. *However, these are few and far between.'* Even that difficult goal was only seen by Hartley's probation officer as a stage *'eventually leading to his having his own flat'*.

For women, pregnancy is a further complication to being roofless and without income. **Emma** was 16 when the grandparents who looked after her died, and her father deserted, leaving her alone in the house. At first she was staying with friends in London, where she was to train as a hairdresser until her pregnancy became noticeable. Then she was homeless, but found a hostel place. From her £28 per week Income Support there was a Social Fund Loan repayment of £4. Also, there was £10 rent direct for the hostel. *'Emma came from an extraordinarily violent family who had all either died or abandoned her by the time she was 16. She is now pregnant, penniless and homeless and if this would not drive someone to occasional* *shop-lifting nothing would.'* The probation officer's sympathy is illuminating, as that kind of comment was quite rare in our study.

Sharon *'has committed offences to make ends meet. Her background — with some time spent in care* [as a baby] *has been instrumental.'* Although she left home at 16 to live independently, convictions did not start till 18 and by age 20 she had four: handling, fraud, theft. She had worked as a care assistant for a year. She was pregnant, homeless, staying temporarily with friends somewhere in Birmingham, and said to be in receipt of £56 per week income support. The probation officer did not judge offending behaviour to be the focus of work: *'This young lady has more welfare problems than offending ones. Her boyfriend has left and Sharon is unsure of whether she wants the baby, however, it is too late for an abortion. She has very little skills with both looking after a child as well as herself. She is also technically homeless — yet does not want to go to an allocated flat. My main work is crisis orientated all the time from DSS payments to trying to find emergency accommodation which she then does not want.'* The probation officer believed Sharon would have real difficulties with child rearing and as all the work was *'crisis intervention at the moment until baby is born'*, tackling Sharon's shop-lifting or getting the fine repayment under control had to wait. The DSS regulations were still proving a trial for Sharon and her probation officer as they had earlier; *'for a while she had no means of income due to not receiving DSS at age 17'.* Affected by DSS regulations in a rather different way was **George**, aged 20, who was living in Oldbury, a district of Dudley in the West Midlands. George had followed a nomadic existence (discussed in Life-style p.123), but at the time of the survey lived with: *'His mother, a one parent family who is already struggling to exist with the three younger children and George's return home has brought its additional problems with it'.* The burglaries and thefts had been: *'Carried out during a time of great insecurity and without any noticeable support from parents or guardians at a young age'.* The trouble with DSS concerned George's size: *'When George moved into our area his benefit was stopped because George failed to show appropriate identification. George's low esteem of himself is confirmed by his small stature, brought home to him by these demands for proof of his age. George and his mother are unable to find his birth certificate.'* Again as with Sharon, George's case had involved the much disparaged 'welfare' work of the probation service before offending behaviour could be addressed.

We have learned from conventional criminology that youths offend for excitement in groups as a Social Activity. Some do; but they may be the fortunate ones. **Rik** was staying with his brother's family at the time of the survey in the eastern 'suburb' of Birmingham, Chelmsley Wood. At 16 he had been deserted by his parents (*'a large, disorganised and fragmented family'*) and the first court appearance at 17 confirms him as something of a folk devil: theft, attempted burglary, Twoc, burglary and 114 offences taken into consideration. But his current probation officer wrote: *'Offends when he is homeless and hungry. Broken family and homelessness as a young teenager. He does not enjoy or want to offend'*. Curiously Rik did work, *'days, occasionally weeks at a time at casual painting and decorating'*. And when he did not work it was due to: *'Malnutrition!'*.

If youngsters left the parental home during relationship break-down between the adults, they were likely to have to Cope with survival somehow. *'**Jonathan's** offending started during the period of his parents' separating* [at 13].' He amassed nine convictions for burglaries, handling, thefts and Twocs, and as might be expected finally received a custodial sentence. At 14 Jonathan was *'beyond the control of his mother'*, but his behaviour in residential child care was increasingly disruptive leading to being placed in a secure unit. 17-year-old Jonathan, who on release from the current custodial sentence was expected to live with his lone parent mother in Redcar, Cleveland, after a three year separation, had *'frequently absconded from care establishments and was offending as a means of surviving'*. Though a rather sceptical sounding probation officer added: *'Latterly he maintains it was also a means of survival as his then girlfriend's father was drinking all the money'*.

We have noted the pattern of offending behaviour potentiated by residential child care (in other chapters — Self-expression: Alan p.32. Social Activity: Tracy p.68. Social Norm: Eddy p.79; Derek p.80; Martin p.81; Camilla p.82; Jane p.83; Gordon p.84; Douglas p.88. Life-style: Spencer p.125; Spider p126; Matt p.126; Max p.139. Professional: Guy p.149; Ernie p.149; Bob p.150; Dean p.151; Ivan p.152; Albert p.154; Neale p.156; Curtly p.161. In this chapter, besides Jonathan: Rebecca p.107; Niall p.112; Hartley p.113; George p.114). We have emphasised the association of residential child care with Coping because the Self-expressive or subcultural reaction of absconding will mean that these young people are without any legitimate way to survive. Also on discharge from care young adults have been thrust into poverty in bleak environments.

Budgeting and debt management

Focus on the offence if you can, but many offenders under super-vision are in the poorest households in the country, so probation officers find themselves having to confront the seemingly intractable debt problems of their clients. There was detailed discussion of the counselling offered to **Rob** by his probation officer under Self-expression (p.46), part of which involved difficulties with money: *'Major practical issues regarding finance and housing have affected Rob's relationship with his partner. I have been providing debt counselling and have given Rob support in contacting the relevant agencies.'* Rob wanted a council tenancy, but he had arrears to his private landlord: *'In addition, both he and his partner wish to work to pay-off rent arrears accrued whilst he was disqualified from benefits'.* If rent is in arrears it is most likely that repayments will be deducted at source by DSS from Income Support. This reduces disposable income and hence capacity to juggle the creditors each week, and cope with other debts. Commercial debt, for example on credit cards, to catalogue companies such as Kays or Great Universal Stores, or to cheque traders such as 'The Provident' have to be distinguished from arrears of rent and fuel because the potential consequences are much more serious, like eviction and disconnection of electricity, and most likely to affect people on social security (Ford, 1991). The gas and electricity distributors often collect 'fuel direct' off the Income Support, but there is an increasing trend now the technology has arrived to install power card meters which can be pre-calibrated to recover arrears and charge for current consumption at the same time. However little fuel is used, if the meter is not fed via the card to reduce arrears, the supply cuts off: new technology has produced the major advance of self-disconnection (Birmingham Settlement, 1993).

Although 'primary' debts of rent, fuel and fines may be more serious in that they can lead to homelessness, disconnection and imprisonment, creditors of commercial loan debts ('secondary' debts) tend to exert more immediate pressure for payment. Offending to Cope with that situation may ensue. At the time of the survey an SIR was being prepared on 23-year-old **Gavin**, on remand for burglaries, theft, arson and motoring offences, with only one previous conviction. Before the remand he was a council tenant in Newark, Nottinghamshire with rent arrears, outstanding fine, poll tax debt, catalogue, credit card and commercial loan debts. Since leaving school at 16 with two CSEs he had completed one YTS, laboured for eight months, done three months YTS road maintenance, then eight weeks at a chicken factory followed by sickness and a year unemployed. It was the commercial loan which unhinged Gavin: *'Got into trouble with loan sharks after becoming unemployed and couldn't pay. Stole property to sell to pay off debts. Loan shark is not licensed and threatening injury.'* Given the seriousness of the offences, the probation officer believed Gavin would receive a custodial sentence. No dependent children were involved. Gavin's attempt to set-up home with his girlfriend fell through. The reason for the loan sharks' tough line lies in the 'secondary' creditors' lower relative formal power to extract the debt and of course the fact that they are not making money when the re-payments cease. Such creditors walk a fine line of indulgence and persuasion as it is in their interest to extend re-payments indefinitely.

The same Coping reaction to serious debt can be seen with **Ray**, aged 20, who was living temporarily with friends on an outer estate to the south of Bristol. He had completed a two-year YTS on painting, decorating and scaffolding, after which he got a job as a scaffolder for 16 months, since which he had been unemployed on £28.80 Income Support. He was in prison serving three years for robbery and the probation officer supervising his throughcare wrote: *'No previous convictions. Drawn into two serious robberies by more experienced criminals as desperate way of solving pressing debts.'* As with Gavin, Ray's debts were commercial loans. The probation officer followed a social control explanation and linked it to Ray's inability to manage his finances: *'Disrupted upbringing after parents separated. He lived with each parent in turn and was denied stable rôle model particularly with regard to handling money.'* The practice objectives were two-pronged: *'Get him thinking about the distress he caused to the victims and awaken his own compassion; analysing the magnitude of his debts . . .* [with a view to] *Persuading him to adopt alternative budgeting strategies to avoid re-offending.'*

Dudley had done eight months in retail sales, some part-time, little else since he left school at 16 without qualifications. When unemployed he started offending and by 20 had four court appearances for theft, burglary and currently assault and criminal damage with one custodial sentence. At the time of the survey he lived in a Sutton Coldfield council tenancy with rent paid direct, but he had left his father's home when 16 and the result was devastating. *'One frightened and inadequate client ill-equipped to achieve independence, but trying hard to do so.'* The probation officer reported that encouraging Dudley to share his difficulties had taken a long time. The aim of practice was to empower Dudley to sort out his own problems, whilst being aware that in the recent past he was not able to do so: *'To help clear the administrative problems concerning heavy rent arrears and at the same time help with the social skills that are necessary for this. I have attempted to encourage maturity that will lead to steady employment and accommodation, but such developments require a good deal of time.'*

Dudley's offending was: *'Largely a re-action to a troubled past, to anxiety, insecurity and an immature response to provocation and comparative poverty.'* We note that Self-expressive reaction to stress, largely accounted for by absence of appropriate social controls, has repercussions in later life. Young adults are not prepared for the independence they have achieved when making the break or escape from a negative home situation. *'Leaving home so young was devastating. Dudley was not able to cope and only now is learning social skills necessary to survive with little money and few prospects.'* Some may carp about a 'welfarist' approach here, but if this is not genuinely offence focussed what is? Offence focus is an issue in Coping offending because, as we have discussed elsewhere, when the offender is trying to survive poverty working on offending tends to be drowned out by demands on the probation officer to relieve desperate situations (Stewart et al., 1989). Other aspects of probation work demonstrate the artificiality of a split between offence-focus and so-called 'welfare work' (for an example in working with the female partners of male prisoners see Peelo et al., 1991; for a discussion of that artificiality see Smith et al., 1993).

7 Life-style

Offending is linked to drug addiction and alcohol abuse. Unemployment and its consequences in the long-term have prevented this man from becoming a member of main-stream society (Sunderland, Northumbria).

Chronic and chaotic multi-drug use associated with huge number of burglaries (Inner London).

Recent offences are public order or similar. Hysterical, aggressive and drunken behaviour generally as a response to difficulties in his relationships (Avon).

Introduction

Life-style offences relate to those ways of living in which committing a range of offences is highly likely, or certain aspects of the way of life are actually offences. That way of life is alienated from, and mostly antipathetic to, accepted ordinary social norms. Subcultural theory explains such behaviour in drug 'gangs' as an adaptation when people fail to achieve in other kinds of deviancy. Although many of these offenders have known homelessness, we shall see that nearly every circumstance in this chapter is drink or drug related.

The Employment Secretary, David Hunt, has spoken of: *'Some of the so-called cultures springing up in our country* [which] *reject all decency and civilised values — the cultures of the housebreaker, the hippy and the hoodlum'* (**'Minister blames wickedness for crime rise'** *The Guardian* 21 March 1994, p.2). And if one wondered whether such 'life-styles' were related to offending, Hunt obligingly makes it clear in the very next sentence: *'The bulk of thieving today, of course, has nothing to do with poverty.'* Drinking alcohol and being homeless are not of themselves offences, although there are several kinds of offences associated with various drugs. There are two sets of points to be made here: first, the way of life which people taking drugs or large amounts of alcohol follow frequently involves dishonesty offending to support consumption. Secondly whilst under the influence of abused substances they may commit violence and public order offences which they would otherwise have avoided.

Having one's life dominated by drink or drugs is seen as a choice, though it could be that other, personal, circumstances have led to the way of life. Similarly, it is sometimes claimed of homelessness that it too is a chosen way of life. Whatever the truth of that in any particular case, homelessness, particularly 'street homelessness', involves survival strategies and as we have noted in Chapter 6, one of those is theft. Others' strategies are perfectly legitimate if time-consuming, such as cadging off market traders and collecting debris. These latter tactics are more successful in the biggest cities where there is just more market trading and rubbish. One of our offenders who lived in a burned-out car on a London council estate said he collected thrown-out hi-fi, even CD players, off skips and tried to repair them or sold them on for repair. As well as public order offences, street homelessness may also involve begging and vagrancy which are themselves offences. Begging has been a traditional, if illegal, way of coping and surviving 'street homelessness', but the Prime Minister's (Mr John Major) remarks on the subject may have paved the way for a more strict enforcement of the law: *'It is not acceptable to be out on the street. There is no justification for it these days. It is a very offensive problem to many people who see it. If people are in desperately straitened circumstances we have a social security safety net in this country which they can use. People should be rigorous in reporting beggars to the police.'* (**'PM attacks 'offensive' beggars'**, The Guardian, 28 May 1994, p.1). In furtherance of this aggressive anti-poor policy the government have recently created a raft of 'life-style offences' related to those people who are homeless: squatting, aggravated trespass, 'new age travelling'.

The link between drug addiction and property offences is now well established (Pearson, 1987; Parker et al., 1988; Hammersley et al., 1989). It has been estimated that £4 billion worth of property stolen each year is sold to finance drug purchases. Police studies have shown that nearly all the country's 25,000 heroin addicts fund their habits through property crime, at about £600 a week each (for current political context see The Guardian 12 February 1994, p.1; for background discussion see Jarvis and Parker, 1989). There have been various attempts to determine drug use amongst offenders. In a study of prisoners it was found that a third self-reported cannabis use before entering prison, a tenth each for opiates and amphetamines and 5 per cent cocaine (multiple response categories). Clinical drug dependence was reported by 11 per cent of the sample. Just over half of the Black prisoners said they used cannabis and a third of White men, although: 'Black inmates were less likely to be dependent on drugs and less likely to inject'. The study also reported that drug dependent men were more likely to have committed burglaries than those who were not dependent and that they had served more custodial sentences (Maden et al., 1992).

There is a possibility that probation officers under-report the incidence of drug use and relatively over-emphasise alcohol problems because they do not recognise or, lacking access to services, they do not wish to know about the former, whilst they have both competence with, and probation-related services for, offenders abusing alcohol. Our study can shed no light on that issue, except to state that we judged the probation officers to be limiting their explanations of Life-style offending to 'serious' substance abuse (for evidence on probation officers' under-stating drug problems and how to help offenders with a drug problem see Fitzwilliam-Pipe, 1992). The probation officers clearly excluded from their explanations, which we can categorise as Life-style offending, social drinking which was controlled, as well as the moderate or occasional use of 'soft' drugs. Black offenders under supervision in our study were under-represented in Life-style and we are led to conjecture whether there was a tolerance on the part of probation officers to dope-smoking. Being homeless was used as a social circumstance or background explanation to the actual offending behaviour. The new Life-style offences had not come into effect and are, therefore, not mentioned.

Homelessness

Survival offences of the kind discussed in the chapter on Coping are an integral part of homelessness. There is a serious problem with the notion of 'choice' in homelessness as a way of life because, besides the implication of intentional control of the situation, choice also suggests that homelessness has positive features which people might seek. The reality is quite the reverse. In none of our cases did anyone in any way suggest that homelessness had been sought after. If that is so, homelessness lacks a major feature of sub-cultural deviancy: something positive, beneficial and enjoyed. Unlike the offending associated with subcultural deviance, homelessness brings no material or emotional rewards.

Hence homelessness cannot be a life-style because it is not a sub-culture, but as with Coping offending, we shall see that homelessness is intimately associated with Life-style offending.

The evidence indicates that probationers are much more likely than clients of other agencies for young adults 'with difficulties' to be without independent housing and therefore dependent on either formally provided services, such as probation-arranged accommodation, or informal support from their relatives (Stewart and Stewart, 1991, p.17–18). That situation itself is in part explained by the very large proportions of probationers who have spent at least part of their childhood in residential child care and cannot therefore rely on the sort of family support most young people leaving home would expect (Stewart et al., 1989, para.5.22) and that is despite the requirements in the Children Act, 1989, which places a duty on social services departments to provide accommodation and 'advice and assistance' up to the age of 21 to those previously in care or accommodated.

As criminal justice policy has moved more towards 'punishment in the community', probation officers will have to exercise ever closer supervision over offenders. Of course it is not a new problem, but probation officers will have to take an increased interest in housing as it would be difficult to maintain surveillance over a homeless person. Although the Home Office initially acknowledged this issue (Home Office, 1988a, para.3.18), later pronouncements envisaged a perverse re-thinking. Anything to do with housing would be contracted-out to the voluntary and private sectors on the grounds of 'housing' involving specialist skills which probation officers supposedly lack, the promotion of the 'independent' sector for its own sake, or to attain 'value for money' which can only be achieved by 'the disciplines of the market' (Home Office, 1990b, paras.9.13, 10.5, 10.9, 10.16; see Smith et al., 1993, on some paradoxes of 'partnership'). The expectation of confronting offending behaviour becomes unrealistic when taken out of the context of the offender's social circumstances as we shall be noting in the practical realities of the cases next (for a full discussion see Raynor et al., 1994).

Probation officers were aware of the breakdown of social bonds which has usually preceded homelessness and the Coping offending which results. For 20-year-old **Marvin,** homeless in London and facing breach proceedings on his current probation order for going equipped, it started with: *'The break-up of his parents — felt abandoned by mother and left* [at 7] *to live with a father in Southampton he didn't get on with. Marvin started to drink in his mid-teens, this disinhibited him and led to further gratuitous offences. Latterly, homelessness* [when he left his father at 18 for London] *has added* *to offence predilection.'* There have been six court appearances since he was 16. The probation officer stated that Marvin was disabled by: *'Drugs, alcohol and mental illness'*, though he had worked whilst in London, as a roof tiler for four months and a night porter for a year until his arrest on the current offence. He lived a: *'Chaotic life-style — no accommodation or regular employment; no ability to plan and follow through plans; alcohol and drug abuse; mental instability — feelings of paranoia and aggression.'* But Marvin was not unaware of the state he was in: *'Client most worried about his mental state specifically related to relationships with women and generally feeling unsettled.'*

George (discussed under Coping p. 114) was 20 and living with his mother and siblings in the West Midlands: *'This client had completed nine months of a two-year order when he was transferred into his own area. The client had previously led a nomadic life-style, until the imposition of the probation order which required him to live in a hostel. He had recently regained contact with his mother which necessitated a move to live with her.'* We have already remarked on George's low self-esteem due to his small stature, confirmed for him by requests for evidence of identity. George's confidence had failed to develop since residential child care, hence the probation officer was to: *'Incorporate an element of confidence – building at all times'*. To make that a practical reality the probation officer intended to: *'Enable George to request and obtain copies of birth certificates to lessen the frustration this causes him'*. The case is also a good example of the amount of liaison required when the Benefit Agency proves unhelpful: *'Negotiate continued payment with local social security until documents are forthcoming'*. The case also illustrates that Life-style can change.

Amanda was 17, not on a YTS, living with friends in Wallsend, Northumbria and shop-lifting, having left the parental home at 16. She had been around: six months a pizza cook, two months in a bottle factory in Scarborough, one month in a restaurant, two weeks on a NACRO YTS in Byker, three months in a bakery in Northern Ireland. *'Amanda's background has little to do with her offending, the main influence has been unemployment and homelessness.'* **Amanda** had ended up back near her parents after following an unsettled way of life for a year, working her way around these islands. When just 17, if one does not or cannot choose the educational road, the alternatives to reasonably paid regular waged employment are highly restricted and mainly involve staying at home. Doing anything else magnifies the chances of homelessness dramatically. But young adults want to leave home. Amanda's offending of motoring, theft and shop-lifting started when she left home. *'Amanda does not have a supportive family and at the age of 17 years has no accommodation of* *her own. Not only is she homeless but she also has no strong ties with any particular area. She has no income because she is not on a scheme and she is 17. She has at least experimented with drugs and I believe there is the possibility of future problems there.'* Without that vital family support the probation officer hoped *'to try to provide one consistent focus in an otherwise chaotic situation and to ensure that options are kept open in relation to accommodation and employment even if at present she doesn't wish to avail herself of what is most realistically possible.'* A hostel place and a YTS place were realistic, but like most actual hostel dwellers Amanda *'would like a flat of her own'*, and like most people on schemes Amanda would like *'full-time, reasonably paid employment. Absence of these is what Amanda regards as problematic about her circumstances and she is of course quite correct'.*

Homelessness, as one might expect of the 17-year-olds in our study, involved the background circumstances of unemployment, lack of 'suitable' YTS and DSS regulations. There were often further issues around relationship breakdown, but can we speak of a sub-culture of homelessness? If the Coping-type offending which we will note in the following cases is a product of a way of life, we would be justified in arguing for this kind of homelessness being sub-cultural in itself. However, we will also note the association with a Life-style of offending around drink and drugs abuse. Homelessness is also episodic and usually of fairly short duration. At any one time very few offenders are actually homeless, but many of them have been or will be. In the mid-1960s Davies found only 4.9 per cent of probationers to be of 'no fixed abode' (Davies, 1969, table 3.1 and p.37). In 1991 we found 6 per cent homeless or in B and B, 5 per cent temporarily with friends and 9 per cent in hostels or supported lodgings (Stewart and Stewart, 1993, from table 11, p.15). Not all of those offenders were homeless, but what we do know from the probation officers' comments is that such circumstances, experienced at some time in their lives by far more than that 20 per cent of offenders, involve insecure and unsettling changes of extremely poor accommodation.

Living from day-to-day is a basic characteristic of chronic homelessness and 20-year-old **Will** was doing that in Blaydon, Northumbria. His accommodation was so unsettled it *'varies from day-to-day'*. He had slept rough on and off since adolescence, but returned to the parental home now and then, *'depending upon relationships at the time'*. Will had done some work though always of short duration. At the time of the survey he had not been claiming Income Support for several weeks because of: *'Unsettled accommodation, failed to sign-on since before Christmas'*, hence in order to survive: *'Will commits offences on an almost daily basis. At his last court appearance he was sentenced for over 100 offences'*

— a motley collection of theft, assault, breach, criminal damage, motoring offences, going equipped (six court appearances since he was 16; two custodial sentences). We will note in Professional offending that not claiming social security benefit is often a sign of relative success, though clearly not for Will.

Another 17-year-old lad in Blaydon was on a supervision order with intermediate treatment (which he completed) for a dwelling burglary which was his first offence. **Vincent** had left the parental home many times since he was 16, often sleeping rough and at the time of the survey he was: *'Living in the central heating system under a block of flats'*. Because of Vincent's unsettled way of living, the probation officer had *'spent about three months chasing him* [to report] *then gave up. He has re-offended and hopefully when he comes to court contact can again be established.'* Like most of the homeless survivors we have discussed, Vincent too: *'Was not motivated to seek help'*. In near-by Hartlepool, **Spencer** was a homeless, mentally ill 23-year-old man who: *'Offended from an early age* [10], *developed a pattern of offending whilst absconding from care establishments to which he was admitted at 10-years old where he "learned the trade". Failed in family/schooling/employment/marital relationship.'* Although said to be 'staying temporarily with friends' the probation officer notes that Spencer is: *'Currently homeless and the main objective is to help him find suitable accommodation. Secondly, to assist with job-search/training via a probation-linked employment project.'* Such welfare work is an essential pre-requisite before other probation practice can be attempted. Neither Vincent's nor Spencer's life revolved around drugs and drink. Their circumstances are adequately explained, as discussed in Chapters 3, 4 and 5 by failure of social control and the criminal subculture of residential child care. On that basis, whereas it is difficult to discern a subculture of homelessness in these two cases, it is possible to view them as offending to survive. However we are not being told that Vincent and Spencer are in fact Coping, and homelessness itself is not coping because it constitutes failure.

Street life: drugs, drink and crime

The point that homelessness is not a subculture and hence only an aspect of Life-style offending, or any other type of offending, is not so clear cut as the cases of Vincent and Spencer might suggest. Homelessness, because it involves trying to survive whilst lacking a basic of life in our country — secure shelter, is strongly associated with Coping as we have shown, but it is also associated with Life-style. Homelessness is not strongly associated with other offending types. Therefore, in this chapter it is particularly important to consider the connection between offending, homelessness and substance abuse.

Dan was on remand for robbery and theft. There was a residence condition attached to Dan's probation order and he had been in supported accommodation, but on release from custody was expected to be NFA. All his theft offences were drug related shop-lifting. The probation officer identified no positive aspects to Dan's life of chronic alcohol abuse and heroin addiction. His three year old child lives with its mother: *'Dan's father died when he was 3, so he was brought up by his mother. At that time Dan's mother had an alcoholic partner who abused her and the children for five years. Mother died when he was 19; has lost contact with sister. Dan feels guilt relating to his behaviour whilst his mother was alive. Now he has no family, friends, home or ties. Had a child, but there is no contact now and chronic drug abuse.'* Staying in London W1, **Spider's** *'fascination with the West End scene'* was likely to prove greater than his probation officer's attempts to: *'Clarify life-style, debts; help him look at self; stabilise and prioritise; to live safely'.* At 23 Spider was 'literally roofless' following child care of various kinds from being abandoned by his father at the age of two until the statutory end of care at 18: *'Spider was bitter at parental abandonment and sexual abuse whilst in foster care'.* He had left school at 15 without qualifications: *'No history of paid employment'*, though there was evidence of ill health related to drug abuse. How did Spider manage? *'Offences related to involvement in street life and prostitution.'* There were about seventeen court appearances for offences related to soliciting and 'several' spells in prison for non-payment of fines. Most of his income was from prostitution.

A chaotic life punctuated by crises is characterised by homelessness, drug and alcohol abuse for 20-year-old **Matt** who 'drifts' around the west country. At the time of the survey he was in St Paul's, Bristol, though he returned quickly to Barnstaple, Devon. The probation officer's objective had been: *'Initially to break the cycle of crisis to crisis which stopped any other work being effective.'* Matt had injured himself whilst in care for being 'out of control', following violence from his step-father: *'History of self-abuse; spent time in hospital as a teenager before going to Richmond Fellowship hostel'* [specialist residential therapeutic communities for drug addicts — access difficult]. The explanation concentrates on the absence of social controls: *'No consistent parenting or secure boundaries. Now either homeless, squatting or in B and B. No stability or security, lacking confidence and community ties, employment or relationships. Hence drifting into crime.'* Most of offenders who were homeless do not seem to have been motivated to change, but **Denis** was keen to change: *'Difficulties at home and poor relationship with parents led to homeless,* *rootless and lonely life. Lack of stable accommodation, or decent work or enough money make it very difficult for him to get life together even now that he wants to.'* As with Matt, lack of social controls was the reason for those later developments. Trying to achieve re-settlement would involve *'looking-out for vacancies in suitable accommodation projects'*, rather than a flat on the open market.

Curiously when set against their chronic homelessness, in most of these cases, the offenders had a work record. Denis for instance had done a DIY course while on Avon Probation PACT and a fork lift truck training course using charitable money raised by probation. There had been five months on Avon Motor Project (many Twoc convictions) and several casual jobs a few months at a time: *'Since doing the fork lift truck driving course, had two very short-lived jobs; sacked from both. One for swearing at the boss, one for poor time-keeping.'* This work record was punctuated with long spells of unemployment, often attributed by Denis to accidents which were the by-products of drinking. **Leo** had worked for a year as a labourer in north Bristol after leaving school at 15 with three CSEs, but a row ended the job and he had not worked since. Still only 17, he had no income at all at the time of the survey. Offending coincided with leaving school and after five court appearances for theft, criminal damage and motoring offences Leo's probation officer saw him as: *'Persistent. Maybe due to drugs or alcohol — possibly parents' divorce and poor relationships with both parents'*, whom he left at age 17 to sleep rough. He was, at the time of the survey, staying temporarily with friends, but the probation officer viewed his condition as homeless.

If the Department of the Environment's suggested changes to Part III of the Housing Act, 1985 go through, 17-year-old **Griff**, his partner and 4-month-old baby, all living temporarily with friends on a difficult-to-let council estate outside Newcastle, could no longer be defined as priority statutorily homeless. Not that anyone was actually doing that, but Griff left his mother's home at 16 because of: *'Breakdown in relationship'*. The government believes such people will have to come to a reconciliation and not expect prioritised re-housing before applicants waiting patiently in the queue. Griff's circumstances are certainly an example of those the government has targeted, although Griff himself would probably not recognise this and his probation officer does not refer to statutory homelessness, preferring with consummate realism to pursue probation sponsored supported accommodation. Griff is on a supervision order for serious assault and has two previous motoring convictions: *'Offending is solvent abuse related'*.

Griff has no income at all because after exhausting his Bridging Allowance he failed to keep appointments to claim Severe Hardship

Allowance. These and other practical issues distract Griff's probation officer from any other work and yet another aspect of that distraction was that: '*Lack of stability has led him to live very much in the here-and-now with little regard for consequences of action to self or others. I feel that his lack of self-regard and unstable life-style and consequent offending relate directly to social background.*' Hence the probation officer's considerable efforts at counselling were deflected by the need to engage constantly with welfare issues and liaison with other agencies: '*I worked jointly with the Juvenile Justice Centre in examining and helping the client to understand the patterns and influences on his offending. He is now living at an unstable address and has no income, so tackling these issues is the primary focus of current work: referrals to accommodation projects, careers interview, referral to DSS. Griff has also undertaken individual work in respect of solvent abuse and has been referred to the Intensive Probation Unit for a course on drug problems.*' Solvent abuse is a serious health risk, but: '*At present securing legitimate income and suitable supported accommodation are the primary objectives of supervision. Until these issues are tackled, I feel it is very difficult to move forward on further work re: solvent abuse and associated offending.*' Trying to engage with the local authority homeless persons unit to secure housing for single probationers is usually pointless. There might have been more chance with Griff because of his partner and baby. Trying to take a statutory route into re-housing is time-consuming and complex. From cases we have examined the motivation of the probationer (who should also be a parent), besides the negotiating skills of the probation officers, were important in securing public housing although the available council stock was also a clear factor. In our study, there were more council-housed offenders in the north east than in Avon or London.

Learning to be a heavy drinker

For males, social drinking is part of growing-up: both part of becoming accepted into the adult world and a way of testing its boundaries or rebelling against its norms. **Warren** was thought to have joined in with Byker's drinkers too soon: '*I think the fact that Warren was brought up by his grandparents who failed to pick up the fact his involvement in drinking at a young age has been significant in both his lack of achievement at school and subsequent offending* [five court appearances for public order and theft from 17].' By 20 he was on probation for assault, burglary, handling, criminal damage and public order offences. His probation officer was: '*Working with him to minimize his use of alcohol. Objectives: to make Warren aware of the* *situations which are risk provoking for him and how to minimize the risks. He sees that his offending is alcohol related, but likes the effect it gives him.'* Warren was on medication for epilepsy. The offences were all, *'committed on the spur of the moment with the peer group, usually on the way home from the pub.'* Warren had been socialised into a drinking peer group and was beginning to worry about crossing that boundary between increasing use and drinking out of control, where a Social Activity becomes a Life-style.

Karl was in approved lodgings with a pregnant partner so his probation officer was looking for suitable accommodation and trying to: *'Break into the cycle of offending with proposed intensive supervision via an 4a specified activity.'* A social control explanation also links with the social norms of St Paul's Bristol: *'Family situation is very difficult as his mother has been depressed following the disintegration of her marriage and there was no discipline* [Karl was in voluntary child care twice]. *He is part of a strong criminal culture of heavy drinking and out-breaks of violence.'* It should be clear that in a drinking Life-style we are not necessarily identifying 'alcoholism', but excessive consumption which involves offending as part of the weekly routine.

Use of leisure was regarded as a serious issue because bored young men with plenty of time can, like **Richard**, aged 20, look for excitement in drinking with their mates because they are easily bored. He had learned about drunkenness and violence with his father in drinking bouts (see Social Norm p. 80). *'Individual counselling on alcohol abuse. Richard was a weekend drinker under peer group pressure.'* His eleven court appearances since age 15 were mainly for motor and alcohol related offences: *'Richard's response was to sell his car so that he would not be tempted, but the problem is that he now feels this has freed him to drink during the week also.'* The probation officer believed Richard was not acknowledging what was happening to himself and thus putting at risk his full-time regular job at £180 per week as a press operator in Coventry. *'He feels there is no problem and does not feel that his attitude puts him at risk of committing other offences, despite a previous record of alcohol related offending.'* It was important for **Mike's** probation officer to: *'Challenge his drinking attitudes'*, as he was at the time of the survey a security guard on £80 per week in Northumbria. Mike said he offended for excitement through boredom (see also Social Activity p.64): *'The offence originated from the practice of heavy drinking in a male group at weekends when he was unemployed.'* At the age of 16, Mike was put into voluntary child care at the request of his mother. He had been, *'educated at a special school and began drinking at 13, easily adopting the criminal ethic and subculture'*. At the time of the survey he was a council tenant living with his partner and one year old child.

Alyn has two convictions for driving with excess alcohol: '*Working hard all week, earning, in his view, the weekend out with his mates drinking. He consumes too much alcohol at each session, thereby leading to the offences.*' This could be seen as: '*A traditional, cultural view of how one spends the weekends*' in Beeston, Nottinghamshire. Alyn had never been unemployed from the building trade, never claimed social security and lived on his own in a private tenancy. The probation officer pursued a rigorous programme after which Alyn took '*the view that whilst not an alcoholic in the true sense of the word, he needed to change his pattern if he was not to become addicted*'. The cultural expectation of heavy drinking was there for **Jake** as well, a 23-year-old Middlesbrough steelworker, son of a steelworker. He was serving three years at the time of the survey for conspiracy to supply drugs, the seventh conviction since he was 14, mainly drunk and disorderly. The probation officer supervising Jake's throughcare was preparing him for parole, return to his council tenancy, 9-month-old twins and massive debts of electricity, gas and catalogue. Jake's attitude to '*easy money*' would be addressed as '*high spirits when drinking resulted in incidents occurring*'. Things tended to get out of hand.

Drug culture

In discussing the 'drug gangs' distinguished under Social Activity we have already identified the general characteristics of those addicted, noticeable amongst which was homelessness (see Sid, p.64). Serious addiction meant that the offender was unable to work for health reasons. The whole of the drug offender's time seemed to be spent stealing and buying drugs, within a network of users and suppliers (Pearson, 1987). **Priti** (see also Social Norm p.91) aged 20 was homeless, living temporarily with friends in south London: '*Heroin addiction; stealing to finance habit and maintain himself; unsettled — in and out of custody or on the run*'. The prospect of achieving the objectives of re-settlement seemed remote though '*Priti does see heroin addiction as the problem*'. The probation officer's concluding remarks were chilling: '*Waste of intelligence and ability, feeling of hopelessness*'. Four prison sentences and his current remand had not dissuaded Priti from his habit. **Dick** too was in prison, for possession of drugs, and was '*well-integrated into the local offending culture of this area* [Sunderland].' That culture (see Social Norm, p.85) was totally supportive of Dick's activities regarding drug use or abuse and is worth bearing in mind when considering the discussion in the next paragraphs: '*His philosophy regarding soft drugs is at odds with the law and is difficult to challenge* *given the reinforcement which he receives within his peer group.'* In a sense the attitude of drug users who steal to finance their habit in a manner which seems to be under control is similar to Professional offending for gain, but for those in the drug culture, both stealing and the object of desire are illegal. Whatever, probation practice was not thought to be getting anywhere with Dick, who *'sees crime as a natural means of easily supplementing his income. Given his view of the probation service work with Dick is difficult'* (undermining of probation plans discussed in Social Activity, p.71).

'Race' and drug use

In the chapter about Social Norm offending we considered theories which linked crime with certain parts of the city and we have just discussed an example in Dick above. Probation officers have tended to set their Social Norm explanations in the context of a geographically identifiable sub-culture of deviance, and one major deviant feature was drug abuse. We actually meet *Jed* in Social Activity because we were using his case to investigate the group dimensions of drug offending. Jed lived in St Paul's, Bristol, an inner city area mentioned extensively in Social Norm, who regarded himself as a victim by *'being Black and treated in a racist way by police'*. The probation officer viewed Jed as a *'very delinquent young man who had problems with the use of cocaine and also offending resulting from this and associations with equally delinquent friends'*. When place, 'community' and single interest shared illegal experience come together as with Jed in St Paul's doing drugs with his mates, probation officers tend to write of a subculture in a manner redolent of traditional criminological theory (for example Cloward and Ohlin, 1960). Or, paralleling the 'female explanation' problem in Self-expression, are we witnessing the 'Black explanation' of drug abuse? It will be recalled that Black people did not feature prominently at all in the social division profiling of Life-style, but Jed, Priti and Nick were all Black. Are the probation officers trying to give us a different explanation of the way young Black men become involved with and use illegal drugs? Let us consider *Courtney* as a test case on this issue.

Courtney was 23 at the time of the survey, having made his first of thirteen appearances before the courts of Nottinghamshire when 15, building from burglary, theft, handling stolen goods and fine non-payment to criminal damage, demanding services with menaces, possession of an offensive weapon; and cultivation and possession of cannabis. Since he left home at 20, Courtney had lived on Income Support with his partner in a council tenancy, where there were arrears of fine payment, rent, poll tax and water rates, though at the time of the survey he was in prison. Courtney had never worked since leaving school. The significant social background was judged by the probation officer supervising Courtney's throughcare to be: '*Cannabis — relates in part to his Rastafarianism and general social life (he runs the local blues parties).*' Subcultural deviance seems to rest on rock n' roll and his religious beliefs. Almost as an after-thought the probation officer offers the familiar social control explanation which illuminates a little more of a complex life: '*Took a lot of responsibility as the eldest male child following his father's death when Courtney was 13*'. Courtney stopped going to school at 13.

In almost total contrast consider a White 23-year-old, whose parents were middle class. A '*very criminally sophisticated subgroup*' in Coventry had led '*intelligent although naïve*' **Wayne** astray. He was in prison for supply of drugs. His first and only other offence was for possession of drugs. The probation officer supervising Wayne's throughcare regarded social background as unimportant: '*Comes from a fairly well-established, hard-working home where parents . . . owned their own hotel. Wayne was possibly overindulged by his parents who didn't lay down boundaries at an earlier stage. There has been no background of poverty or social deprivation, but in attitude he admits to having pursued a hedonistic life-style without regard for others.*' The probation officer had divided objectives into those to be achieved should Wayne be given parole and more long-term and diffuse ones should that fail and he become a voluntary after-care case: '*The major issues have revolved around preparation of a home circumstances report (statutory). His previous drug abuse and rather cavalier attitude to drug supply is another area of concern. He has passed a very unstable, insecure life-style in the past two years which he recognises he must change if he is to survive within society.*' Of primary importance were his relationships with parents, with whom a '*satisfactory and stable home life*' might develop, and then with his girlfriend. Wayne may have been swept along by the excitement of the illicit drug culture, but he was not presented as part of it: he sought the drug culture and it used him, destabilising his life. Unlike the other Life-style cases so far the probation officer's practice objectives are reminiscent of those in Self-expressive offending behaviour, a feature we will note in the next case too.

Don initially overcame his problematic teenage background which involved Self-expressive attention-seeking offences of violence and school burglary, only to relapse, after losing his job at 20, into drink and drug related offences: public order, possession, theft, fraud. High wages for three years as a pipe fitter in Stockton enabled Don at 19 to buy a flat on a mortgage, but he threw in his job following poor timekeeping and needed money: '*it would* *seem that the way of life and peer pressure enabled him to accept drink and drugs'*. Although for the probation officer supervising Don's throughcare, *'looking at the drug problem* [was] *one area of work'*, there was as much concern about his return on parole or release to his mother's house with her three other children because: *'Lack of parental control following mother's change of partner* [had led to Don being put in various] — *schools for disruptive pupils* — *spent some three years in care from age 13 to 16'*. As Don's only chance of accommodation on parole would be with his mother, the probation officer would focus on *'ensuring that he can accept rules that his mother will lay down. Relationship with girlfriend* — *they can fire each other up* — *work on expectations'*. The objectives in this and the previous case do not have the hopeless defeatism that has characterised practice with Life-style offenders so far. With Wayne and Don the 'culture' may be overcome by potentiating the already formed social controls. Taking a more materialist stance, homelessness had not been a destabilising feature and some kind of work record had been established.

The probation officer supervising **Roger's** throughcare was preparing a home circumstances report on him at the time of the survey and was very clear what ought to happen: *'The plans are that he should go to a drug rehabilitation unit in Sheffield. He needs to kick his drug habit and to achieve this he needs to stay away from Coventry'*. All of Roger's offences were drug related , a problem which seems to have started when he was 17. He was placed in residential child care at 7: *'Felt rejected. Moved from place to place whilst in care, rebelled, turned to drugs'* — the classic Cloward and Ohlin (1960) explanation. In Gosforth on the northern outskirts of Newcastle, **Oscar's** *'pattern of offending is worsening as he is getting older'*, though it was not a case of all his offending being drug related in the usual sense, for: *'When under the influence of LSD, he commits unpredictable offences* — *and alone'* (handling, criminal damage, burglary, assault, breach). The offending was explained both as a Self-expressive reaction to stress and a coping strategy whilst unemployed: *'a scapegoated young man who is virtually illiterate. He has been the butt of cruel jokes over the years* — *beginning whilst he was at school and in remedial classes. He is inarticulate and given his low intelligence, almost unemployable at the moment. When jobs are scarce for capable people this young man with very little going for him stands no chance at all of finding work. Bored, unemployed without income he has offended.'* The probation officer suspects that Oscar is mentally ill, *'possibly drug related psychosis due to prolonged heavy usage of LSD'*, but the condition remained undiagnosed as Oscar was not prepared to seek medical help. At the time of the survey Oscar was on the run: *'He faces very serious charges* — *arson with intent to endanger life; criminal damage totally* *destroying at least one car valued at over £10,000. Custody seems almost inevitable; prepare him for VPAC* [voluntary probation after-care].'

In this unpromising group where the usual run of problems for probationers was made worse by addictions, it was possible to find a more hopeful story. For 23-year-old **Marianne** the negative experiences of her early life were to be completely reversed in a very traditional manner: *'Initially everything in her life seemed problematic to her. Had a mental breakdown, probably drug induced — committed further offences — fresh probation order. Gave birth to a baby — complete change in behaviour.'* Marianne had a violent alcoholic father and an ailing mother from whose house she wished to escape at 18 into a partnership and a council tenancy in Avon. She had received little support and guidance from her parents. Quickly abandoning her job as a machinist she became involved with her cohabitee in a, *'long list of convictions and a history of minor drug abuse — resulting in armed robbery'.* The current probation order related to the armed robbery offence, and *'involved group work to address offending behaviour and . . . placements to involve her in community work with disadvantaged groups'.* Those objectives were successfully achieved as Marianne, *'has completely changed her life-style following the birth of her child.'* It would be difficult (but not impossible see Keir, p.137) to find a male Life-style offender in our study for whom that was true. Because social controls seem to work better for females it may be marginally easier for probation officers to achieve their goals with female offenders.

Black and White differences

If we compare the last five offenders who were White with the previous three who were Black, the clearest distinction concerns 'drug culture'. The 'Black explanation' invariably refers to living a drug culture life-style in which using appears to have been unproblematically accepted by Jed, Priti, and Courtney. By contrast the White offenders Wayne, Don, Roger, Oscar, and Marianne are explained Self-expressively, in reaction to a stressful situation, or related to other illnesses. They are not presented as part of a laid-back accepting drug scene, but more like victims. For these ten cases we have controlled for other key issues in Life-style such as homelessness, probation areas and age, hence this difference is not likely to be coincidence. Probation officers seemed to be more clear about their objectives, more positive about the outcome and more understanding of the overall circumstances when their client was located in a household, rather than homeless, and had the trappings of the institution of the family about them, rather than being enmeshed in the 'drug culture'.

Clear differences have emerged between Black and White offenders. Probation officers have a sophisticated interpretation of the way in which soft drug use may be a part of a coherent Afro-Caribbean subculture whose members engage in activities defined as criminal without an imputation of pathology by the probation officers concerned. White Life-style offenders do not seem to have a subculture which supports and polices itself, hence they are more likely to be characterised as having a 'chaotic way of living'. We will carry forward discussion of some of these points in the next section on Life-style offending and family life.

Drink, drugs and family problems

We have discussed the relationship of drink and drugs to home-lessness; learned social drinking which is out of control; drugs as part of a culture. We next turn to difficulties in personal relationships and consider the rôle drink and drugs have played. Violence within the family will be a feature here. As with much of Self-expressive offending we have considered, the probation officers' practice in these Life-style cases tends to be focused less on the offence than the dynamics of relationships and welfare issues, even though that bucks the trend of the new orthodoxy.

Frederick is a case in point where violence in his relationships involves alcohol misuse. *'Initial offending at the age of 15, for dishonesty, purely for kicks and secondarily for gain, by his account . . . recent offence* [assault, criminal damage] *a result of intra-family disputes'*. Having set up home when 17, by the time of the survey he was 23 and living in a Durham probation hostel, estranged from his wife and children. Frederick had been unsettled by his parents' move to the north east when he was 12: *'Has had a problem with drink, less so now, which was a factor in some of his offending, records suggest and a response to boredom, and break-up with his wife. The current offences result from him living with his sister and husband, now he and his wife no longer together, and the strain in the household: tension between him and brother-in-law.'* In preparing Frederick's SIR (now pre-sentence report) the probation officer identified *'alcohol, violence, need for structure in life — i.e. accommodation and employment, plus support in the event of reconciliation with his wife'*. Frederick was not unaware of these issues and before the current incidents he had been making progress: *'Response to previous supervision very good'*, but without his being too clear or decisive about how accommodation and employment could be achieved (*'virtually illiterate'*). He saw returning to his wife as the key. *'Estrangement from his wife appears to be a major factor for him*

— think he sees this as central to rehabilitation, but is he realistic about it happening? *If not, access to his children would be a major goal and he needs accommodation and a regular income to provide for this to happen on an organised basis, he says.'* The probation officer had a realistic programme of supervision in mind comprising welfare work on accommodation and employment; addressing the alcohol misuse; *'seek the underlying causes'* of his violent behaviour and *'find alternatives and make him aware of its unacceptability';* support and mediation over the marital relationship.

Drunkenness within the family, relationship breakdown and child neglect were amongst the key concerns for the probation officer preparing an SIR (shop-lifting, criminal damage) on 20-year-old **Rosemary** who lived in a mother and baby unit in Coventry (that is, she was homeless). The 13-month-old baby was with her, the 2- and 3-year-olds were in foster care. Rosemary had herself been in care, on and off, from 10 until 16, when first her own mother and then her grandmother could not cope with her: *'Very chaotic, unstable home background characterised by her father's alcoholism and her mother's nervous breakdown.'* Rosemary was constantly absconding from residential child care. Offending started at 17 with drunk and disorderly, deception, fraud of DSS: four court appearances in all. *'Rosemary began to drink heavily and offend following the breakdown of relationship with her cohabitee. Alcohol abuse led to some offences. She comes from a well-known family where most members have offended . . . She has absorbed anti-social norms of behaviour which include the abuse of alcohol and offending as appropriate remedies to problems.'* Social services were taking the major initiatives through Rosemary's allocated social worker as *'she has very low standards of child care which are now being addressed'.* The probation officer's objective was *'to secure a low tariff disposal in order to enable social services to continue working with her'.* Perhaps also thinking of the outcome for the future: *'At all costs I wish to avoid a custodial sentence which would lead to her children being received into care and the loss of her place at a mother and baby unit.'*

Ralph did not have a problem of unemployment as he received £150 per week at a labouring job. Since leaving school at 16 without qualifications he had worked his way through five labouring jobs and two months in prison. Spells of unemployment were directly related to his drinking as were the offences: *'Wild behaviour characterised by early interest in cars and theft later exacerbated by incipient alcoholism . . . Parents divorced when 8. Mother alcoholic. Family existed entirely on benefit. Poverty and lack of control from an early age plus encouragement to drink heavily have greatly influenced his behaviour.'* The probation officer was hoping to establish Ralph away from his current environment in Lambeth as his alcoholic mother was tending to undermine efforts to control Ralph's own heavy drinking. Ralph saw his problems as alcoholism, living with his mother and *'emotional stress and sadness following separation from his partner and their child'*.

The social background of **Keir**, aged 23 living with his mother and brother in Bristol and earning £100 per week in a shoe factory, could best be understood in terms of the absence of social controls, which we outlined in Self-expression. Keir's offending from the age of 15 resulted in eight court appearances for theft, abuse, drunk and disorderly, assault, criminal damage and burglary, all characterised by: *'Excessive consumption of alcohol . . . Also involved was a tendency to lash out as he lacked the verbal skills to deal with difficult situations in other more constructive ways.'* Heavy drinking allied to offending had been learned within the family: *'also older sibling with drink problem and more serious criminal record'*. Keir attended a special school because of his behavioural difficulties from 10 to 16. He left home after a row about his offending only to return a few months later when his mother had her leg amputated. His mother's condition was a shock to Keir and seemed to have changed his attitude to the drinking and offending aspects of his life. *'He continued to work full-time, but returned home to care for his mother and to help with housework. He has found supervision invaluable in supporting him during very difficult periods during which his mother nearly died. He followed advice given and was able to facilitate family discussions and engage help from social services and occupational therapists, gaining confidence in his own abilities and useful knowledge for the future. He also sought help when his relationship with his girlfriend foundered. Again, he responded to and practised, strategies suggested, and has successfully re-negotiated the basis of their relationship rather than allowing set-backs to give him an excuse for lapsing into heavy drinking. He has developed a wider circle of friends and social support and is now assertive and takes responsibility for his own actions and feelings. Although he realises that, at present, his mother's poor health is problematic, he has been able to discuss his fears and face the worst.'* There seems little doubt that it was the event of his mother's ill health in Keir's life which led to the change in him upon which his probation officer could work: building his confidence; empowerment to deal with agencies himself to improve well-being and the home care of his mother; identifying for himself situations which triggered drinking rather than solving problems; a wider network of friends, probably non-offending, who would not continually reinforce Social Norms condoning crime or defeatism concerning personal improvement. The case is an example of attachment to other people or 'embeddedness' leading to reduced criminality.

Living in a flat in Hackney with her parents and her four year old child was 23-year-old **Sarah**. Her first and only offence of possession and intent to supply heroin might have only occurred the year before, but: *'Drug history in the family led to her own addiction'* and she was unable to work because of that and *'associated abscesses'*. She had left home at 13 to live with a man and although not leaving school until 15 was actually: *'Working in a factory at 13'*. Most of the probation work was liaison: *'with social services re: child protection; working with the drug dependency unit; housing association applications'*. Presumably the drug addiction developed when she was living away from her parents. Sarah herself had trouble understanding and using 'helping' agencies because a major objective besides offering a safe, confidential environment for addiction counselling was for the probation officer to: *'Make better sense of all agencies involved and their rôles for the client'*.

Personal problems

We shall conclude this chapter with a brief examination of Life-style offending as a 'personal problem'. We have concentrated a lot on the settings within which substance abuse occurs. The Life-style aspects of homelessness were socially rather than individually explained. Here we are concerned with just the individual person's reaction and how it may be understood. As an example: *'**Gloria** changes from a shy demure young lady to a foul-mouthed aggressive "monster" when drunk and she has a major alcohol dependency problem which she largely denies. Primarily over-strict parenting has produced her low self-esteem and inhibited personality when sober.'* The thrust of probation work was: *'Getting Gloria to accept that she has a major alcohol dependency problem and then encouraging her to persist with any therapy to which she will agree.'* **Dawn's** worsening alcohol problem also stemmed from family experiences: *'Mother's frequent changes of partner and mental ill-health have given Dawn little stability in her life, and poor rôle models. She married before she was ready for it, to try to find security, and the relationship soon broke up. She had few adults to turn to and could not organise herself or her life for a while. She began turning to alcohol to cope with her feelings.'*

Let us try to present in detail the part played by alcohol in **Stefan's** low self esteem. He was 23 with only three court appearances since he was 21, for criminal damage and twice for driving with excess alcohol: *'Always following heavy drinking sessions. This apart, not motivated by crime'*. Before he left the parental home when he was 19 because of *'poor relationship with parents'* Stefan obtained seven school qualifications and then worked as an electrician. A leg injury in a car accident and his alcohol problems affected his ability to work. He had been through a partnership with no children. He ended up in a hostel in Cleveland: *'Although Stefan's family background was supportive, he was in his own eyes a failure to his parents. Failed a medical for the armed forces and a failed personal relationship left him with very low self-esteem. He turned to alcohol which for a period took over his life.'* Stefan's probation officer believes he can *'raise his self-esteem and help him fulfil his tremendous potential'.* An objective which, from the probation officer's assessment, is set against very difficult background circumstances: *'Supervision has attempted to "pick him up" by finding him suitable hostel accommodation with constructive support, re-establishing contact with his parents via a sister and getting him back into the work-place through his participation in hospital voluntary work. Stefan's only problem in his eyes was lack of finance, but he now is beginning to see what he needs to do to change this.'* For Stefan alcohol abuse was less a criminal career progression from anti-social activities as a juvenile than a Self-expressive reaction to personal problems. However we were clearly told that alcohol dominated his life and involved offending.

The story of **Max** in contrast with Stefan's, where Self-expressive drinking led to Life-style offending, illustrates progression in what is thought to be the traditional manner from peer group Social Activity to entrenched Life-style substance abuse. As so often personal factors also played a part in the case of Max, who was 23-years-old lived in his mother's council tenancy in Bristol. He was on probation for a lesser sexual offence, making his twelfth court appearance since he was 13 for theft from a meter, criminal damage, malicious wounding, harassment, and fine default. When he was 8, after being physically abused by his father, Max went *'to a school for emotionally maladjusted'* children, returning home briefly before again going into residential child care until he was 16. His *'very poor level of literacy and numeracy'* did not help him in the work-place. Besides a bricklaying YTS at an assessment centre Max had only found casual labouring work for brief periods. Max was a: *'Glue sniffer. Very poor self-presentation including speech. Very limited academically. Extremely withdrawn. Poorly clothed.'* If Max was handicapped by his *'drink and solvent abuse — emotionally disturbed and mild learning difficulty'* his mother was *'anaemic, drinks heavily at times'.*

The family situation was dire as Max's mother's, *'benefits have been severely reduced when she lost her job having taken time-off for sickness and to help her daughter in emergency during pregnancy. Mother collapsed with severe anaemia during summer and eats an inadequate diet due to reduced benefit. She had recently claimed Income Support after being on sickness benefit. Amount of reduction not known.'* There was a Social Fund loan for a new bed of £105 to be repaid at £5.50 a week. Max's mother had considerable debts of rent, electricity (£15 per week repayment), hire purchase, a commercial loan and water rates (£5.10 per week). *'Both Max and his mother are desperately short of clothing and often go hungry.'* The probation officer charts this sad history: *'Of limited intelligence, immaturity, basic insecurity, low self-esteem and few constructive leisure activities, Max began offending with the more delinquent peers he met whilst in care and also began sniffing glue. Later he began to drink heavily. Once he reached school-leaving age no support was offered and a lack of structure rapidly led to more offending. Very poor life skills despite being in care. Once YTS ended, nothing else was offered and few facilities exist for the like of Max, unable to cope with residential settings or group work. Changes in social security have proved disastrous for Max's mother. Max has made efforts following individual counselling to stop his addictions, but he cannot afford clothing to replace his old stuff (covered in glue). Family too poor for a Social Fund loan. His present appearance makes integration into the community impossible. Most offences are impulsive and committed whilst drunk or under the influence of solvents. He has never had a girlfriend and has shown signs of greater awareness of this lack.'*

Needless to say the probation officer's objects are many and varied: *'Help to keep a roof over his head by liaising with the housing department re: the suspended possession order* [Notice to Quit]; *debt counselling — reschedule the family debts. Continue to work on Max's relationship with his mother; maximise income by challenging benefit decisions.'* And turning to the offence focus: *'Minimise chances of re-offending by improving basic communication skills, life and social skills and networks by encouraging leisure interests and voluntary work to raise his self-esteem. Develop a range of interests including literacy and numeracy. Develop problem-solving abilities so that he does not resort to alcohol or solvent abuse at times of stress. Find him training or work by referral to the probation service employment co-ordinator. Develop skills for independent living and help Max seek suitable accommodation. Sex education and advice about relationships.'* Everything really.

Conclusion

Max was a complicated and grim climax to this chapter. Though homelessness, drug culture, and learned behaviour condoned by family and friends are easily shown to be aspects of Life-style offending, it is of course individual people who are affected by substance abuse and who in turn affect the lives of those around them. The section on drink, drugs and family problems demonstrated the individual accommodation people reached, or failed to reach, with those substances in such circumstances. On the positive side, Keir's reaction to his mother's serious illness brought about an ability to control his own life, with, so his probation officer indicated, considerable help. A crisis can make things worse or better. Like Stefan's car accident it can be associated with the loosening of social controls or as with Keir and his mother's leg amputation, or the birth of Marianne's baby, a crisis can activate attachment and commitment. This is an anti-deterministic point, for even in the most unpromising situations people can make personal choices which lead to various outcomes associated with more or less offending.

8 Professional

Opportunistic, mainly theft from cars, motivated by need to obtain money. Not persuaded to remit by several custodial sentences or current probation order (Middlesbrough, Cleveland).

Well known to Probation Service and adult criminals in the area. No stability to life. Accepts custody as part of life-style. Unwilling to change (Peterlee, Durham).

Introduction

The image of the professional offender is of a hard man, calculatedly committing property offences for gain. Our study serves to confirm what is known about the routes into crime. Many young men who become committed offenders began with parental encouragement or the active support of their other relatives, often brothers. Subcultural deviancy plays a rôle in loosening social controls, teaching the trade and fostering acquaintance with a criminal network; so what begins as joy-riding can quickly progress to ringing cars (Light et al., 1993). In residential child care, young people find the support of a subcultural peer group and learn skills marketable in the criminal world (Dimmock, 1993). Care was decidedly a relevant background. Overall 26 per cent of offenders in our study were known to have been in care, but of the Professional offenders 31 per cent had been in care. There was every reason to suppose that all the traditional routes into an entrenched life of crime, and perhaps new ones, were readily available to young people (Foster, 1990; Hagell and Newburn, 1994).

However, a popular view is that things ain't what they used to be: 'A lot of younger guys come up today who didn't come up the way the older criminal did by being a thief or fence or whatever'. Thus did Derek Maughan the drug smuggler bemoan the passing of the Golden Age of British Crime: 'Now all of a sudden, they're buying three or four thousand Ecstasy pills in Holland and getting £15 or £20 a time for them. They're making bundles of money. They're millionaires at 23' (article by Duncan Campbell, 'Strong-arm men' *Guardian 2*, 23 March 1994, p.12].

The reality is more mundane. The offenders under supervision in our study are no Krays, Richardsons or Maughans. Our use of the term 'professional' for this type is not meant to imply real professionalism in committing offences, simply that the person was judged to be offending for gain in an instrumental manner, in a way which mimicked legitimate employment. Most of our Professional offenders might have identified with crime and been *committed*, but they were not very *successful* in the sense of Shover's useful dual typology for analysing ageing amongst professional property criminals (Shover, 1985, p.24). With the implementation of the Criminal Justice Act, 1991 the percentage of offenders on probation service caseloads who fall into the Professional category is bound to increase. The Act increases the scope of people who will, without choice, be supervised on release from prison, through supervision being an automatic condition for certain sentences.

We have regarded offending as professional when it was specialist and *sufficiently* successful to provide a fairly regular income. But in other respects what at one stage can be labelled Professional may just be a more skilled and longer-term version of Coping, and Professional is certainly resonant of conforming to the criminal Social Norm. In a sense Social Norm is a justifying or explanatory background to Professional offending. In Chapter 6 on Coping we have already illustrated the difficulty of identifying the boundary between Coping offences to survive and Professional offending for gain. Prostitution is a different kind of Professional crime to the usual run of property offences and will receive separate discussion. Certain offences of a Professional nature are open to women and the opportunities for crime by women are increasing in the field of fraud and deception for example, rather than just shop-lifting. We will note that offenders who make a living from what they do are less likely than others to co-operate with their probation officers, less likely to have their probation officer's 'sympathy', and less likely to ask for or be offered welfare help and advice.

Offending careers

'Professional offenders' will usually have committed many serious, mostly property, offences for which, if caught, they will in all likelihood have served several prison sentences. Young men seeking to become Professional offenders will identify with crime as a means of livelihood. As they improve at their craft they will become more successful at committing offences, which means sustaining themselves financially by their thefts without going to prison. But after a while, in their thirties, nearly all of these committed offenders will remit, settle down, whilst just a few will go on to become the 'background' operators whose shady dealing is hard to detect, such as Angus discussed in Social Norm (p.82).

As the oldest people in our study were only 23 it is difficult to relate our data and findings to the standard literature on professional offending, concerned as it is with older men, the remission of offending behaviour, or entrenched, relatively successful, serious crime. In the main we would not expect to find Professional offenders on probation, in the English and Welsh criminal justice system that is, but, if they so elected, we may expect to find them on voluntary throughcare and after care. Prisoners on parole or other licences would be under supervision whether they liked it or not.

Probation practice and professional offending

If a young man or woman finds the criminal life glamorous, appealing and apparently attainable he or she will identify with it, accepting its standards in an attempt to be a successful criminal. Rational calculations may be made about the risks involved. Prison is a risk or a cost of this chosen way of living which in most cases will mean an interuption of one's Professional activity. Probation on the other hand may be an annoyance, but gainful theft can continue. Hence in interviewing for pre-sentence reports probation officers seek *inter alia* to establish whether the accused has a Professional stance, for if he or she has, probation would probably be irrelevant. If the offence is low in the tariff and a non-custodial sentence is possible, probation officers should, on grounds of avoiding custody, consider seeking a community service order rather than supervision.

Knowing about Professional criminals may help probation officers to identify early signs of a dangerous progression. Probation officers can counter the allure for young adults who: '*In their youth . . . came into contact with older skilled, and successful thieves . . . and they are attracted to the criminal life. The tutelage they receive from their older rôle models is extremely important in the development of their criminal skills. Eventually they approach crime as a vocational calling*' (Shover, 1985, p.26). As we have pointed out, professional criminals will be on caseloads anyway because of probation officers' responsibilities for ex-prisoners and officers have, therefore, to consider what appropriate objectives they could pursue with committed offenders. Finally, there is a parade of relatively un-successful Professional offenders for whom probation officers will be made responsible because the actual current offences are insufficiently serious to attract a custodial sentence. When a Pro-fessional offender is being supervised on licence as motivation is likely to be low the probation officer has a problem of what to do with the client.

Differential expectations

When addressing such offending, probation officers are often trying to alter the expectations that the probationer has of the outcome because, following Glaser's differential expectation theory, *'a person refrains from or commits crime because of his or her expectations as to its consequences'* (Glaser, 1980, pp.138–9; and for discussion of the 'rational choice perspective' see Cornish and Clarke, 1986). That means in terms of practice that the probation officer has to convince the offender that further crime is not a rewarding activity by pointing to the choices available of other, more rewarding activities which do not carry the possibility of prison. As we have noted time and again, however, offenders under supervision point to lack of money caused by unemployment as the reason for stealing or whatever, so they may interpret their situation as lacking any rewarding avenues. Those probationers were like younger versions of Shover's ageing criminals who: *'Had they seen an alternative path to the kinds of goals we generally interpret as signs of modest success, they would have taken it'* (Shover, 1985, pp.125–9). There is a convergence of offenders with non-offenders in their perspectives on life as they age. The practice point is to make that convergence happen sooner in the offending career.

It is unclear why social controls, internal or external, cannot feature in the influences which lead to the law-abiding choice of rewarding activities in the theory of differential expectations. People can choose to offend or not. If that were not true, probation would not be possible, so probation officers have to be concerned with the causes of crime in order to pursue activities which reduce the likelihood of offending. Choices may be constrained, but they remain choices — a truth which applies generally; for although we are being very clear about choices here with Professional offenders, other offenders under supervision were also capable of choices.

Giving up crime

Shover identifies several reasons for the remission of offending, but they all relate to men older than our age group. However, two are relevant to our study: personal changes because of experience; interpersonal contingencies (Shover, 1985, pp.80–91).

Experiential changes amounted to watersheds in the mature criminals' lives: 'They decide that their earlier identity and behaviour are of limited value for constructing the future' (*ibid.*, p.83) and the cause was a derogatory comparison with their peers. They despised the club they had joined of failed ageing thieves, of jail-birds without a real family life. As we have discussed in Social Activity it is of prime importance for probation officers to break into the 'subculture' of gangs by dissuading vulnerable youngsters from gaining their esteem and purpose for living from such peer groups which engage mainly in opportunistic offending. Admittedly it is a difficult and time-consuming matter to help these young men find confidence in themselves to achieve what they want without reference to the approbation of the offending peer group. One of the difficulties seems to have been that the probationers failed to achieve in the legitimate worlds of home, school and work. As an alternative they have sought a sense of identity and worth in the offending peer group. Or, as another alternative, their negative reaction to the strain of situations with which they could not cope expressed itself through Self-expressive offending. Where are probationers to find their sense of achievement and purpose away from crime? Of course once that source has been located, other positive features begin to flow such as a non-offending circle of friends who begin to alter the meaning of 'social norms' for the entrenched offender.

Traditional criminology has appeared to suggest that all we need to do is await nature's course: job, partner, babies equals non-offending (for a witty riposte to 'maturity' explaining remission of offending see Wootton, 1959, p.164). We have noted time and again that the young adults in our study certainly had partners, and a fair number had children, but very few, of course, had legitimate work (see Ivan and Neale as a partial example of this; below pp.152, 156). Shover's older men told of how they had squandered legitimate jobs and of how relationships with women in their youth were exploitative. Some of our cases illustrate the possibility of such regret, for example 20-year-old **Brent** living in Bristol and on probation for burglary: '*He had two good jobs since leaving school, one in the accounts department of the* Bristol Journal, *commenting, "you don't realise how good a job is until you leave it". He has realised how difficult it will be to get a job like that again*'.

With Shover's ageing male criminals, a change in attitude came in their early thirties when they met someone with whom they wished to live a family life and, significantly, her relatives could form the non-offending group which would give the support necessary to confirm the change: 'Successful participation in a personal relationship, a job, or some other conventional line of activity provides personal rewards and reinforces non-criminal identity' (Shover, 1985, p.96). There is no particular order in time to these life-events (interpersonal contingencies) which lead into a law-abiding life, just as there was none which led to youthful involvment in crime. Hence if the change is 'a social and interactional one' the probation officer's counselling can be valuable in bringing about the changed way of interpreting past events and current experiences.

Entrenched criminals

We can begin with committed offenders who were, within the limitations we have mentioned, successful. A consistent theme will be the difficulty of bringing about change in these offenders through probation supervision. The probation officers working with them had a struggle to meet basic National Standards of compliance. Breach of the probation order was always in mind. **Ryan** was a 23-year-old south Londoner who was employed as a *'chauffeur, security person and bodyguard'* at £500 per week. Six months in youth custody was his one custodial sentence out of six court appearances since he was 17, for motoring offences, theft and burglary: *'Began to offend when he left school in order to obtain money to enhance his life-style. Ryan has since chosen to follow a criminal life-style.'* He still lived with his mother, without family commitments of his own, although he had been in residential child care from the age of 2, when his mother had a nervous breakdown, until he was 16. Ryan was not interested in changing: *'Not a probation recommendation — no obvious work focus. The previous response to supervision was not satisfactory therefore I doubt about his willingness to comply with obligations on this occasion.'* As with nearly all cases where the offender under supervision took a more committed professional approach to crime: *'The main and only objective has been to establish an adequate pattern of contact . . . He failed to do that and has now been breached.'* It was similar with 23-year-old **Howard** who *'drifts between his mother and girlfriend'* and their 6-year-old child in Hendon, Sunderland: *'Reporting only. The client seems to make quite a good "living" from his offending* [burglary, shoplifting, handling] *and nothing I say is going to deter him. He sees lack of money as his problem.'* Whereas Ryan worked earning serious money, Howard had only completed two 12 months YTS (one Apex) and two weeks as a packer. Howard too had spent time in prison, three spells from his 12 court appearances since he was a 14-year-old. His petty thieving and twocing had developed: *'Tends now to get involved with more sophisticated successful offenders'*. The probation officer offered a social control explanation: *'Earlier,* *no father figure, after a messy divorce and no apparent rules or guidelines to operate within'*, so Howard fell in with *'a social group of offenders, needs approval, has to be at the centre of things, quite immature'*.

Burglary was all **Spike** knew, 23-years-old at the time of the study and in prison for burglary of dwellings. Since leaving school at 16 he had worked for three weeks whereas in six court appearances he had been sentenced to imprisonment three times totalling nearly seven years: *'All serious dwelling house burglaries in order to obtain and sell high value items. Has no idea of the consequences for his victims'*. If probation officers were able to encourage offenders to relate to their victims, there was likely to be some chance of actually addressing offending. The importance of a probation officer's influence in encouraging concern for the victims of crimes points us towards the kind of offending focused work which is relevant with this group. Alternatively a welfare issue may be the key. On discharge from prison the probation officer believed Spike would be homeless, so that was to be a focus of the throughcare: *'To get him to accept that decent accommodation will be a good basis for the future and that offending is not the only way to gain attention. He needs to rely less on the 'system' he knows so well in courts, prisons etc. and begin to make relationships of mutual trust'*, but the social background was unpromising. *'He feels cheated because the woman he thought was his sister is actually his mother so his "parents" turned out to be his grandparents. This needs attention.'* Hence Spike discounted the family support he might have been able to use in order to resettle and remained with the 'comforting' institutionalisation which the criminal justice system had afforded so far. He saw the problem as being, *'too well known'* in his small town in Nottinghamshire *'as a burglar and so needs to move away'*. The probation officer concluded: *'Realism is the aim'*. The probation officer's 'personalist' dynamic explanation of Spike's offending behaviour is rather naïve in the context of the lack of fit between probation assumptions and Professional offenders. There has to be some correspondence between the perspective of the probation officer and the man who has made the calculated decision to continue Professional offending.

Experienced probation officers know which offenders are likely to respond, but that does not prevent the courts from ignoring the considered recommendations of probation officers in their pre-sentence reports. *'**Erol** was placed on probation despite comments made in the SER that he would not co-operate in any meaningful way and had a history of paying rather scornful lip-service to the requirements of statutory supervision. He has a history of extreme violence and is involved in professional crime. Supervision tried to focus on the issues of re-housing* [Erol lived with his mother in Gosforth on the northern outskirts of Newcastle], *offending* [current offence burglary and possession of offensive weapon; previously five court appearances for burglary, wounding, theft, assault and a 'not guilty' verdict for murder; two prison sentences of one year each], *and counselling on the illness he is currently suffering* [said to have a severe liver complaint]. *There is no longer any contact with Erol as he has made threats, totally avoided any meaningful communication and is currently facing serious charges relating to the administering of a noxious substance, i.e. ammonia.'* Erol had never worked at all, indeed he, *'completed his education in Youth Custody'*. Erol's offending is judged to be a reaction to the very common background circumstances of probationers in our study of: *'Single-parent upbringing in an area of delinquency. Poverty. The origins of offending behaviour probably lie in the fact that the mother (a single parent) was excessively over-indulgent and could not impose control. Thereafter via special schools and YC he has graduated to professional criminal circles and became involved in offences of excessive violence.'* So Erol, like Ryan, had experienced some form of residential child care. The probation officer tried *'to gain some credibility in order to motivate Erol to communicate some of the problems he was worried about. Unfortunately Erol, who should never have been placed on probation, regards any discussion of personal problems as unwarranted curiosity, against which he is totally defended'.*

So strong was the influence of the neighbourhood that *'Guy felt he needed to leave the area to change his behaviour'*, a council estate in Stockton where he lived with his partner and their 2-year-old child. He too was totally unco-operative with his probation officer who would: *'Continue to pressure to get Guy established in some legal employment and to alter his attitude to RTA offences'*. Unsurprisingly Guy had never had 'legal employment' and had only managed two months of a YTS at Cleveland Wheelbase four years previously. Guy *'opposes Employment Training for ethical reasons'*, though not apparently burglary, theft, and non-payment of fines, for which he was imprisoned; but the big problem was *'calculated disregard of RTA regulations!'*. We noted how **Angus** had fitted snugly into the dominant Social Norms of economically depressed Durham county (p.82). He was a *'successful man'*, avoiding prison as a small time crook working the 'black' economy and fraudulently claiming Income Support. Angus would not change: *'Client sees getting caught as problematic. Not interested in changing his life-style.'* As there was no point in 'addressing offending behaviour' with Angus, *'latter part of Order remains for minimum enforcement of conditions'*. Not far away in Bishop Auckland lived 20-year-old **Ernie**, on remand for burglary, theft, motoring offences and criminal damage. Since the age of 12 Ernie had made eleven court appearances for the same type of offences and served three custodial sentences:

'*This man offends in order to get the things he wants. Punishment and prison are like water off a duck's back.*' He was a: '*Deeply engrained delinquent in habits and attitudes*'. However Ernie had a: '*Terrible start to life. Institutionalised from an early age. Reluctant to listen to views other than his own*'. When Ernie was six his parents separated and he was neglected. It is not known how long he was in residential child care. He had never worked or been on a scheme. There are limits to person-centred understanding.

In Life-style we explained how people addicted to various substances offended in order to support their habit. After a while there comes for many a stage where Professional offending for gain and Life-style offending for drugs are indistinguishable, making the point of supervison obscure. **Bob** was supposed to be on probation for burglary. From the age of 12 had had made twenty-three court appearances and been imprisoned four times: '*Bob was initiated into offending whilst in care* [from the age of eleven at the request of his parents for unruly behaviour] *and has continued ever since. At one time he had a serious drug problem which brought him to homelessness and further offending. Now, he just doesn't know how to go about living a "straight" life. Parents could not cope with either of their two sons and put both into care at about 11 years. They have been very inconsistent in their care and concern since. Bob was moved around a great deal whilst in care and did not get any sense of self-esteem, confidence, skills etc . . . Survived as best he could in what he felt to be an alien adult world.*' Bob had done unskilled casual building labouring work on the side for years. He was Coping in the past when homeless, combined with Life-style offending for drugs. At the time of the study this now committed offender had abandoned his 3-year-old child. Bob might have acquired the relationships which we are told lead to the remission of offending, but he clearly had not formed an attachment to them. He had been 'on the run' for over a year. It may be that in that respect our group of Professional offenders are atypical as other evidence does point to the significance of close personal relationships in avoiding offending. In particular, people released from prison are less likely to re-offend if they return to a network of close relationships (Haines, 1990).

No remorse

Probation officers often judged young offenders to have been 'easily led' by more sophisticated criminals, by whom, presumably, were meant those who avoided detection and made enough money out of stealing to live well. A major objective was to avoid the allure of such criminals by encouraging young offenders to take command of their own lives, decide what they wanted and how to get it legally, free from the behest of peer pressure. Much of the confidence-building and encouragement of self-esteem was directed to that end. In the case of the more committed or entrenched offenders we can note a definite move towards whole-hearted acceptance of criminal values. For instance, when addressing offending behaviour probation officers often encourage the offender under supervision to realise the effect of the crime upon the victim: see it from the victim's point of view. On the other hand, the Professional offender has to block all such understanding and empathy in order to carry through the crime efficiently, surrounded as it often is with the possibility of violence. A sign that the probationer has gone beyond some threshold of feeling for the victim and entered the Professional realm is the absence of remorse.

Iggy was a late starter with his first court apperance at 17, although it was for burglary, assault on the police, theft and TDA for which he was sentenced to six months YOI. A second six months followed when he was 19, for similar offences. At the time of the study Iggy was serving his third term for burglary of a dwelling, handling and breach. The probation officer supervising Iggy's throughcare noted: *'This client has proved quite unco-operative for the last two years. Not prepared to co-operate with non-custodial alternative. Refuses to accept any help or even report as required. Does not regard his criminal activities as problematic. Thoroughly irresponsible; no conern for others and no remorse. Offends almost immediately he is released.'* When Iggy was 18 his parents *'asked him to leave'* so he went to stay with his sister in Bath: *'His parents have done their best to help him'*. In contrast, *Eric* had started, or been found out, much earlier with his first of nine convictions when aged 11, running up even more custodial sentences than Iggy — five. At the time of the survey he was on probation with a day centre attendance requirement for burglary of commercial premises. All his offences were theft and burglary. *'This man is devoid of the usual feelings of restraint that govern most people. He seems to feel no remorse or regret for offending. Punishment accepted without demur, but ineffectual.'* Eric left home at 17 *'to live with a girl'*. He had no children and had never worked. Although: *'Family discipline nil. Parents were divided on handling. Client played one off against the other'*, Eric was back living with them in Bishop Auckland. Two possible explanations should be considered: either Eric was a 'psychopath' or he had access to a subculture which supported property offences (Cleckley, 1964).

Most of the offences in this chapter involve stealing property, but sometimes the targeting of certain victims makes the offending much worse, or so the tone of *Dean's* probation officer suggests. Dean was only 17, on remand in prison and also on a supervision order, his sixth conviction since he was 15, with one custodial sentence. '*Offending has escalated to serious dwelling house burglaries against elderly people while they are in their homes.*' When Dean left prison he would be homeless in Northumbria and he would have no income as he refused YTS and would not claim DSS Severe Hardship Allowance: all fairly reasonable indicators that he was a committed offender. It would seem Dean too learned the trade in residential child care: '*Disrupted family life. Parents separated. Parents requested he be taken into care at age 12 because of aggressive and disruptive behaviour at home and school. Began offending when in residential care.*' With that background Dean left care at 16 to burgle and 'stay temporarily with friends'. The probation officer was addressing five issues: '*establishing reporting contact; accommodation; employment or at least claiming severe hardship allowance; pattern of offending; type of offences committed (vulnerable victims i.e. elderly).*'

No change

Ivan was probably beyond probation help, drifting between custody and homelessness. At the time of the survey he was 23, on throughcare whilst serving a sentence for handling and motoring offences: his nineteenth conviction since the age of 13 when he burned down a hut. His offences were: '*Mainly driving — obsessed with cars. Occasional drink and threatening behaviour and assault*'. On release he will return to debts of fine, poll tax, electricity, catalogue, credit card and commercial loan. He has some children, somewhere. He went into residential child care from 12 to 18. Curiously he has held a: '*Variety of manual jobs; mainly been in employment. Last job held as road sweeper*', until custody during 1989 after which Ivan '*seemed mentally disturbed and unable to hold down a job*'. Obviously, for all his thefts he has been demonstrably unsuccessful, but he is Professional in the sense that it is the only life he knows and all he does. The probation officer believed Ivan's social background to be of the utmost significance. '*Total disruption throughout childhood seems to have left Ivan unable to cope with life at all. Prison has compounded this and he seems destined to drift between custody and NFA for the rest of his life — quite beyond any probation help.*' Despite that doleful conclusion the probation officer had objectives which mingled nobility with sarcasm in '*trying to get Ivan to face up to responsibility, accommodation, relationships, unreasonableness; trying to get client to take some responsibility while providing some help; helping sort-out endless financial problems. What the client regards as problematic: Unfair that he is not allowed to drive whatever and whenever he feels like it even whilst disqualified. All other means of transport are "not on" for him, e.g. walking, bus. That I don't help him* *enough and drop everything else when he arrives to see me at a different time from his appointment.'* Ivan counts as Professional, but he is far removed from the stereotype of a cool, rational calculator.

'Wickedness and greed'

We have already quoted (Coping p.95) at length from the Employment Secretary, David Hunt, who believes: 'The bulk of thieving today, of course, has nothing to do with poverty. It is the result of wickedness and greed'. While probation officers are inevitably and properly concerned with less metaphysical explanations of crime, they were realistic about the immediate motives of professional offenders and the possibilities of change. It did not escape their notice that offenders under supervision stole to enhance their lives: just wanted more money; were not prepared to work for wages when they could have done so. They might, as we have seen, condemn at times, but moral judgements did not prevent them from trying also to understand.

Aiden was 23. He had lived with his partner since he was 19 in their Nottingham council tenancy. They had two children, aged 1 and 3. The probation officer was preparing Aiden's SIR: *'Over the last year the client stole regularly from his employers. He now faces a prison sentence as the most likely outcome'*. This was Aiden's first offence. He received £112.50 wages per week out of which there were debts of rent, poll tax, electricity, catalogue, credit card and commercial loan. *'Both me and the client see the court appearance as the most stressful current problem . . . In the longer term financial problems are great. A large number of unpayable debts exist.'* Aiden's income was limited but he wanted expensive things which, initially, credit could provide: *'Living in our "consumer society", perhaps a "middle class" or "keeping up with the Jones's" approach to possessions (flash car, hi fi etc.) led to debts which were then only payable by finding an extra income, which eventually was through theft.'* Aiden had eight school qualifications, had always worked full-time since he was 16 — building trade, assistant manager in retailing (presumably when the thefts occurred); at the time of the survey he was a packer. A 'consumer culture' is seen as encouraging crime, rather like the drug culture in Life-style. The probation officer supervising 20-year-old **Callum** in Newcastle took a similar view: *'Callum feels himself an outsider in society. Offending is an alternative to the "consumer" society when he has no cash. Wants possessions which are portrayed as hallmarks of success by society.'* This is an apparently straightforward explanation in terms of Merton's anomie; but one can also say that massive and conspicuous inequalities in consumption are liable to weaken the bonds which tie the more fortunate to conventional lines of behaviour: 'When you ain't got nothing you got nothing to lose' ('*Like a Rolling Stone*', from Bob Dylan, 1965, *Highway 61 Revisited*). A person will be especially likely to consider criminal options when they see no prospect of a change in this state of affairs.

With 23-year-old **Albert** the probation officer supervising his throughcare (robbery, burglary, motoring) can understand the long term poverty of Albert's life, but still believes that financial gain was the motivation to offend: '*The main pattern of offending is entrenched, and are offences of dishonesty for financial gain. There are also a number of motoring offences committed while in the company of older peers when he was much younger* [first two when aged 12]. *All his offences have been committed against a background of long-term unemployment. This as well as being a low-achiever and labelled disruptive at school has had a significant impact on Albert.*' Through '*domestic difficulties*' Albert left home on a number of occasions from the age of 8 and so, as could be anticipated, went into residential child care. Albert had never done legitimate work of any kind since leaving school at 15, but had served seven previous prison sentences. When released from the current term, Albert would return to his wife and two children of 7 and 6 in their council house on an estate outside Sunderland. In the circumstances the probation officer had a daunting programme: '*The major issues are offending behaviour, family relationships and employment on release. The main focus is to create an awareness in the client of the consequences of offending on the client, his victim and his family. To stimulate and promote a change in attitude, increased self-confidence and self-esteem. Albert sees his main problem as being unemployed and with little opportunity to earn a good wage legally. My objectives are to reduce the risk of re-offending on release; enable the client to have access to training or employment opportunities; maintain his relationship with his partner and children through and beyond this sentence.*' Albert has those things which supposedly bring maturity and conformity: wife, children and home. Has he weighed the risks and found them acceptable?

It is not that having a child and family are less powerful as elements of a bond to conventional behaviour than traditional control theory has supposed, but that in the context of long-term economic blight and poor prospects where 'these jobs are going boys and they ain't coming back', too much is demanded of the family (from *My Home Town*, Springsteen, 1984, *Born in the USA*). At a time of changes in both the social division and demography of the institution of the family, the personal relationships which it embodies are asked, by some analysts (Dennis, 1993, ch.1), to carry increasing burdens of socialisation and bonding to support attachment, commitment, involvement and belief in conventional society (Hirschi, 1969) in the teeth of massive economic restructuring and long-term deprivation. Dennis denies the existence of the latter points, preferring to see the causes of social problems in the new father (strictly absentee); he blames the 'conformist intellectuals' for propagating myths such as 'crime is not really increasing'; he sees the remedy as being attachment to traditional family values (Dennis, 1993, ch.7). To use the Rightists' own imagery, money can be made to work only just so hard in the market place to reproduce capital. Social institutions too have a breaking-point at which they collapse under the burden of front-loading.

On the other hand, we wish to avoid generalising out of existence a person's own choice of behaviour and individual explanations for offending. The probation officer supervising **Liam's** throughcare, in prison for robbery, theft and fraud — his second custodial sentence out of five court appearances since he was 14 — does not think he can work with him: '*Moans about lack of opportunity but refuses to help himself legitimately — doesn't like working so offends to get money*'. Liam has a 3-month-old baby living with his girlfriend in Avon. Before custody he was in trouble with the DSS: '*Benefit refused as he makes himself unavailable for work*', so a throughcare objective was to '*get him back on benefit and on to a training course*'. The probation officer was unsympathetic about the back problem which Liam said affected his ability to work; '*probably has a bone in it!*'. Overall the probation officer concluded: '*Liam has an attitude problem — arrogant, which will be difficult to overcome. Also feels the world owes him a living . . . I don't know that I can work with him.*' Perhaps that was realistic. **Jamie**, 20, in prison for commercial burglary, had also '*never been employed*' since leaving school at 15. He had one child of 2 years and a baby of 3 months living with their mother in a Middlesbrough council tenancy. Since he was 15 he had appeared seventeen times before the courts for burglary and theft and served five previous prison sentences. The circumstances of Jamie and Liam were very similar and although the probation officer supervising Jamie's throughcare attributed the actual offences to the avarice of a style warrior, the social background was held to be a significant one, '*of material deprivation, where jobs are hard to obtain and the pressure from friends to offend is overwhelming*'. Unlike the case of Liam, the probation officer had practice objectives: '*My objectives have been to try and get Jamie to take a realistic attitude to his life-style and family responsibilities. My client's major problem is that he knows that he cannot live on benefits or on the wages he could expect from suitable work.*' Whatever moral stance one takes, in that comment lies the essence of Professional offending. Jamie's attitude is one which, in the current economic circumstances of the north east of England, is very difficult to counter with the personal problem solving model of probation.

One must avoid the trap of suggesting that material deprivation in an offender's past life is a necessary condition for current crime. Remaining in the undoubtedly depressed north east, **Duncan** had a secure base in his parents' hotel from which to conduct burglary and theft. *'He is an intelligent young man who has chosen to use his brains to illegitimate ends. He wants a standard of living unobtainable on DSS. If he put the effort he expends on offending into working I have no doubt he would be successful. He always wants more money than he has so generally his thefts have resulted from greed rather than need.'* Since leaving school at 16 without qualifications Duncan had done about eleven months regular work out of four years in building, re covering snooker tables, as a security guard and a pipe fitter's mate — not counting ninety days in YOI. A worrying problem with Duncan was that he seemed to be trying to improve at criminal activities and, as with Liam: *'Major issues with Duncan are his arrogant and chauvinist attitude — the world owes him a living. He learns from his mistakes. He was caught for thefts so gave that up. Bought and sold dodgy cars to make money and is now at court for road traffic offences, so says he's given that up.'* It is what he might move on to that causes concern, but then again he might settle down. His girlfriend was pregnant.

On the other hand the material circumstances and social background of **Neale** were unpromising: *'Lack of direction and discipline in the home and possibly, influence of his older brother who is an established offender are factors. It was the latter he left home to live with* [in Durham] *and he is currently, or has been, re-offending at an alarming rate (the client that is).'* Neale was on a probation order, but at the time of the survey actually on remand for more motoring offences. As an unemployed 17-year-old and not on a YTS he received no legitimate income, but Neale was, according to the probation officer, doing rather more than survive: *'His brothers are both offending, and it is my impression that Neale is making money out of, mainly motor-related theft, as he always has money in his pocket which he does not obtain from his parents. He has twice been remanded into custody since his order began — this is where he is now and new offences are still coming to light, committed while on bail.'* Neale's constant moving around had prevented his probation officer from doing constructive work. The probation officer wanted to establish regular contact and help Neale obtain training, *'also to do intensive work on his offending behaviour as he is of some intelligence and could grasp concepts without difficulty. This may be academic as he is becoming more at risk of custody and his motivation is gravely in doubt.'* Neal's very different explanation for offending blamed his girlfriend: *'Whilst he says he wouldn't offend if he had a job, he also explains his offending as triggered by his girlfriend having an abortion, which devastated him. He has*

shown no signs of any effort to do anything about this situation.'
Neale could have stayed with his mother who had 'subsidised'
him anyway several times, *'to the extent of board and lodging'*,
resisted his brother's lure to offend and coped with his relationship
problem. The probation officer was definitely implying a 'greed'
argument and suggesting that only prison would be likely to change
young Neale.

These cases demonstrate that entrenched offenders tended to
be older and had spent time in prison. Motivation to change was
generally absent. Personal relationship issues were present, but at
nothing like the intensity, or receiving nowhere near the attention,
of those of Self-expressive offenders. Residential child care had
often been significant as an apprenticeship, though these offenders
were described as having come through all that with a kind of
self-assertive stance of wanting to be what they were.

Prison shall not change them

It is argued that in their early twenties, after several arrests and a
taste of prison, opportunistic Social Activity offenders change from
risk-takers who understand those risks only vaguely, to young men
who weigh the costs more carefully. They develop a calculus of the
costs of their offending, and it has to start looking more profitable
than it did when they were just 'juvenile delinquents' (Zimring,
1981; Light et al., 1993). One of those costs would be prison
sentences, but others could be loss of job, friends and family life. As
we have illustrated, probation officers point out these disincentives
at length. We should remember that, whilst the process of criminal
maturation is occuring within the more committed and relatively
successful young offenders, a majority of youthful law-breakers do
stop offending. In our survey, most of the 23-year-old offenders are
those who have not stopped, although it must be remembered that
in each of our age bands there were some offenders just starting and
also a few for whom their probation officers believed the current
offence was definitely the last.

As age increases, two disparate sets of rational factors in the
calculus of risk vie for ascendancy in criminal motivation. First,
even though one has got away with it many times, the next prison
sentence may blow apart whatever has been achieved in one's life,
so that risk has to be balanced with the financial reward. On the
other hand, the committed offender may already have stolen so
much which has gone undetected and unpunished that he may
calculate that the criminal justice system could never deliver his
just deserts, homicide in the furtherance of property crime apart.
To be convinced by the second account one would have to be a

pretty successful thief, or, in the case of most of our probationers,
self-deceiving.

Lloyd was 23-years-old, a private tenant living in London
with his partner (no children). He left the parental home at 17,
when he also left school with six qualifications. He had been:
'Self-employed in various trades usually as a cover for crime' and
although unemployed Lloyd had never claimed social security.
There had been three custodial sentences out of his ten court
appearances for fraud, theft, handing, burglary and forgery since
Lloyd was 16. The probation officer supervising Lloyd's parole
licence judged him to be a: *'Professional criminal. Surveillance and
control by use of parole licence. No social work possible with this
professional criminal.'* The only objective was to *'get him through
the parole'*. With **Lionel** the same intransigence had led to breach:
*'Lionel is not co-operating with this probation order and I have breached
him. I will ask for the order to be revoked. Lionel is not the kind of
lad who responds to non-custodial sentences. He has a long history
of custody and he has a hard 'professional' attitude to crime.'* He
was from a family of offenders in North Shields, had been in
residential child care from 14 and currently, aged 20, lived with
a friend. The social background was: *'Inappropriate parenting skills
— violence and disorder. Early SSD intervention required. Long history
of care where crime developed. It is his social experience.'* A spell in a
secure unit for children was followed by three custodial sentences.
Lionel now *'sees himself as a smart offender'*, despite prison and over
ten court appearances. He must have been getting away with a great
deal to make it worthwhile. The probation officer who had been
supervising **Roy's** YOI licence, until he was remanded in custody,
suspected the same: *'Offends with a regular group away from home
(in Cumbria, Yorkshire and Humberside); offences of a planned nature.
He "gets away" with a lot more than he's caught for and makes
a lucrative "living" apparently accepting custody as an occupational
hazard. Roy says lack of finance is his problem, but he'd have to
be earning a "hell of a lot" to take employment.'* This 20-year-old
hard man was *'not frightened of custody'* which was just as well,
since he had served four sentences totalling nearly three years.

The cost of continual theft is usually prison and **Edmund**, a
23-year-old inside for dwelling and commercial burglaries, accepted
it. Since the age of 14 there had been nine court appearances for
handling, burglary, theft and twoc with three previous custodial
sentences totaling four years: *'He has no desire to change and to
date accepts custody as inevitable'*. Edmund left school at 15. *'He
has never worked nor accepted government training schemes. He does
not claim benefit either. . . . Edmund offends together with others to
finance his life-style and provide himself with an income as he has no*

other.' He does have somewhere to live. When discharged from prison, Edmund will return to his sister's home in Gateshead, to live with her baby and their brother. The probation officer supervising Edmund's throughcare was trying to impress the risks of offending on him, but Edmund saw his problem *'as the inability to earn enough money to finance his life-style without stealing'.*

If the twocers of Social Activity persist through adolescence learning the illicit motor trade they may move into the premier league, with their bravado intact. For example, 'Reality' was the issue with **Rigby**, a 20-year-old Londoner who lived either with his mother or his girlfriend and their 6-month-old baby. He worked, on and off, at car exhaust fitting, although he had failed to complete his City and Guilds in car mechanics. There had been fifteen court appearances since Rigby was 16 and he had been to prison five times. All his offences were with motor vehicles: *'Suspected "professional" car thief for local ringer?'* Rigby did not claim social security as he made sufficient from stealing *'expensive prestige cars'.* He was on a probation order with a day centre attendance condition and a community service order for theft of a briefcase, though at the time of the study Rigby was actually in custody on remand. The issues for Rigby's probation officer were: *'Attempting to overcome client's denial of offending. He is apparently concerned about housing, baby, girlfriend and lack of money'.* In order to achieve an acceptance of the offending the probation officer was: *'Attempting to find a means for this client to deal with reality',* but probation work was ruled out by the plethora of current re-offending. And Rigby just had to keep showing-off: *'Client took stolen sports car to the day centre and was caught by the senior probation officer.'* 'Professional' does not imply 'sensible'.

Important features have emerged concerning the calculus of risks operated by the Professional offenders in our study. Besides an acceptance of prison, we have identified the rejection of both regular employment and social security benefits as providing an adequate income. The wages which they could make if there were work would be less than the money available through crime. If that is so, it goes without saying that social security would have to be supplemented, though we have noted that many men would not claim. Presumably their reluctance to claim had nothing to do with moral rectitude and everything to do with avoiding detection. **Lon** is a classic in all these respects. He was 20, would be released from prison to live with his mother and step-sister in Bristol; was expelled from school at 15. *'Lon had previously had a variety of unskilled jobs in the building trade which he enjoyed, but such work is becoming increasingly limited and he is now expressing* *concern at his inability to get employment. He has never claimed benefit between jobs — calls it "charity".'* Despite all that: *'Lon has not been arrested for most of his offending. Involved in a large network of predominantly burglaries. He enjoys the easy money. He attributes it to the lack of a father, claiming most of his friends are steeped in crime and without fathers.'* The objectives for the probation officer supervising Lon's throughcare were first to get him to claim social security on release as he *'previously refused to do so, resorting to crime to provide an income'.* Lon would be encouraged to be realistic about employment and the probation officer proposed: *'Ongoing discussion re: advantages and disadvantages of legitimate as opposed to criminal life-style, strategies for dealing with peer group pressures, counselling re: family circumstances and childhood experiences. All above issues raised by client.'* Although such admissions and explanations were unusual from our offenders, this self-awareness has at least been noted in fictional musicals: 'Gee officer Krupke' in *West Side Story* (Sondheim and Bernstein, 1957).

Prostitution

We have established that Professional offenders tend to reject probation help, from which probation officers have drawn the conclusion that these offenders are not going to change; hence supervison would be better directed elsewhere. However the circumstances of rejecting probation and remaining committed to offending are not necessarily the same. **Ann**, for instance, was not so much committed to the offending as to the way of life she followed and the income it provided, which were not of themselves actually illegal. She was 20, living with her uncle in Avon, to whom she had recently returned. She had made six court appearances since her first at 17 for just one offence, *'loitering in connection with work as a prostitute'.* The probation officer was preparing the pre-sentence report and the *'recommendation was not for probation. Ann considered it inappropriate and did not consent'.* The way of life to which she was thoroughly committed was in some respects similar to aspects of the homeless Life-style we have described, as most prostitution too involves unavoidable street offences (plus occupational hazards: *'Ann has been the victim of severe violence at times'*). Ann did not want to change: *'She denies any connection* [between offending and her social background] *and was not willing to discuss it at any length for the purposes of the SIR* [pre-sentence report]. *Attributes offending to prostitution being the only viable work to offer the income she requires.'* Ann's position reads as a calculated commitment, fines for loitering being a 'tax' on her chosen trade. Probation is rejected because it cannot suggest a way of improving her material circumstances, alter the law or help her avoid the unlooked for consequences of what she does.

In sharp distinction from the very different moral view taken of other Professional offenders, the officers supervising the probation orders of prostitutes tended to regard it as a trade which had certain legal problems. That is, if the women could be advised how to avoid contact with the courts they could carry on trading and not bother the probation service. But as we have commented, the circumstances of prostitution make avoidance of offending extremely unlikely, certainly at the lower end of the market. There was one element of consistency amongst these cases: like Ann, none of the women wanted to quit. **Enda** was 20, living with a pimp in Bristol. She started prostitution when she was 13, left school at 15, and had never done anything else. There had been about twenty court appearances for soliciting, with various fines for which she was £360 in debt. There were also debts of rent, poll tax, electricity, gas and catalogue. She had a child and was claiming Income Support of £49.25 per week with rent direct. The probation officer's objectives were: *'To get her re-housed away from her pimp. To stop the courts fining her for her job. To negotiate with agencies to which she owes money.'* The reason for offending was *'to earn money to pay-off her pimp and support her child'*. **Joanna** had a grander objective in mind: *'Client feels that her most useful attribute is her body and she intends to use it to make money and then "retire" at the age of 21. Has no credible alternative at the moment. The majority of Joanne's friends are prostitutes and she was given assistance by a friend to learn the ropes when she was 16.'* Joanne was still only 17, but had three court appearances for soliciting. The probation officer intended to, *'gain Joanna's trust in order that we can begin to look at issues such as self-worth; health; assertiveness'*. A root cause was held to be an unstable home life and so Joanna's relationship with her mother was to be analysed. She did have two school qualifications and had worked as a care assistant in a residential home for old people. Unlike Ann and Enda, Joanna had not as yet experienced the hazards of her trade.

Trying to quit

Even within the Professional type there were cases in which the offender appeared to have responded to supervision, or despite a Professional stance to offending the probation officer believed addressing offending made sense. The prospect of change, however, rarely seemed to rest on the 'valued' personal relationbships associated with desistance among less commited offenders. **Curtly** lived alone, a council tenant in the St Paul's district of Bristol. He had been received into residential child care at the age of 13 after his: *'mother left home — he went to grandparents who couldn't cope with disturbed behaviour'*. Curtly was moving away from stealing for gain, but that was not because at 20 he had met a particular partner, enjoyed fatherhood, or even got a job; what he had got was a council flat. He had done several temporary jobs such as radio control for a taxi firm, but only for a few months each. The current conviction for lesser assault and criminal damage resulted from frustration with the DSS following his last lay-off: *'Well-known to me in past for more serious offences of dishonesty. Had been doing well — we both saw these offences as "one offs" caused by frustration with DSS. Recently given council accommodation — helping him to get on his feet as I don't think he will now re-offend if stable'*. His offences had been motoring, developing into more serious and committed theft with one 21-month-period in prison. Curtly's adolescence followed a well-established pattern of residential child care followed by offending, but he was breaking free with probation support, accommodation help, encouragement into work, and an understanding of how he arrived at his current state: *'Totally chaotic childhood — no stability in family and final reception into care. He was a very disturbed teenager and carried a lot of frustration and anger. Underneath was an intelligent and charming young man.'*

It was **Larry's** third spell in prison at age 20. The probation officer supervising his throughcare was trying to *'convince Larry to stop offending'*. In a custodial setting the probation officer addressed an accumulation of at least seven years offending which his family had supported. *'This young man has been in trouble on a number of occasions and seems to accept his punishment in a light-hearted manner. My main involvement with him is to address his offending behaviour and to offer support during his sentence. Much of our time together is taken up with discussing offences — reasons and arguments for and against. I think Larry is ambivalent regarding his circumstances and considers getting caught as an occupational hazard.'* He had no partner or children to weigh in the balance at that time. Larry would have to resist that very powerful source social pressure, the family itself. Nor was it an uncommon situation. **Ted** had a family with two children of 4 and 13-months living in a Birmingham council tenancy. What is more, he worked full-time, self-employed as a scaffolding erector. Yet despite this the power of Ted's original family was considerable: *'Whole family known to Service — mother encourages other members to offend with her or on her behalf. Children appear to feel guilty and unable to resist mother.'* From the age of 12 Ted had appeared before the courts about twenty times, served four prison sentences, and was at the time of the study on remand for another motoring offence.

What we have elsewhere described as 'shop-lift suppliers' (Stewart and Stewart, 1993a, pp.69–70) operate all over the country. They steal from shops after having collected orders from their 'customers' or sell what they have already stolen door-to-door around estates. The shop-lifters learn their thieving trade as a peer group activity often within a gang. A subcultural context helps to explain this Social Activity, but in its intrumentality such organised shop-lifting is Professional. *Ava* who lived in London had in her twentieth year accumulated four convictions for shop-lifting, including her first, all disposed of by fines. But also in that short time she had changed her attitude to offending. *'Ava used to mix with a group known to me who are professional shop-lifters, supplementing their state benefit. Shop-lifting was common in her peer group a year ago and easier than working in her view. She has realised* [I hope] *that a custodial sentence is just round the corner and has obtained a* [clerical] *job* [at £500 per month take-home pay]. *There has been no collusion over offending from her family and there is good support in childminding while she works.'* She had a child when she was 18 after leaving school at 17 with two 'O' level passes and then took courses in computing and commercial skills. She had never left the parental home, although her supervising probation officer wrote: *'She is anxious to leave home to set-up her own place with her daughter'.* The shift from subcultural Social Activity to Professional can be seen in the probation officer's remark that: *'She was mixing with a group of young women shop-lifters and learned the tricks of the trade'.* The probation officer was negotiating with Lewisham housing department for a flat.

Difficult though change may be, it is not necessarily impossible. The outlook for Ava was relatively bright as she had just obtained a job and was being supported in her search for independent accommodation. However, the type of crime in which she had been engaged was widespread, cropping up several times in our survey.

Some probation officers certainly expected their clients to stop offending once they had family responsibilities. *Digby's* probation officer was of that opinion: *'Nothing seems to affect his offending (i.e. doesn't think about stopping because of his girlfriend and child). Has no intention of stopping. Digby has been offending since 12-years-old, a combination of burglaries, twocs and other RTAs.'* Digby left the parental home when he was 17 to live with his girlfriend on an outer Newcastle estate. At the time of the study their child was 3 and Digby was 20. Offending was deeply ingrained: *'Hasn't known anything else, always offended.'* Probation work was very limited as *'there were no obvious reasons why he offended. He just "did it".* *Digby had no intention of stopping offending so this couldn't really be worked on'.*

Tam was moving away from more serious offending and his probation officer related this change to a stable partnership and housing association tenancy, though as yet they had no children. There were other influences too. Tam had been able to resist peer group pressure. *'In the last four years he has moved from quite serious domestic burglaries to minor thefts. Offending began after he was released from residential child care. An isolated and very guarded young man — not integrated in any social group. At present he is in a settled relationship and hence the frequency and gravity of his offences are reduced.'* However, the couple were in quite serious financial difficulties with only £62 per week sickness benefit and rent, electricity and gas direct; a Social Fund loan repayment; poll tax arrears. A settled relationship may lead to a reduction in the frequency and gravity of offences, but as we have seen Professional offending can often persist when the offender has an apparently settled relationship. That observation may prompt one to consider the paradox of whether, in certain circumstances, having a family increases the likelihood of offending to attain a 'decent standard of living' by less predatory, 'victimless' offending such as shop-lifting from chain-stores.

The offending might, however, become less serious, perhaps all that can be expected of entrenched Professionals. **Alistair** lived with his girlfriend and chilren of 1 and 2 on an estate in Stockton. He moved in when he was 18. Offending had first come before the courts when he was 16 and consisted of thefts and currently domestic burglary: *'Willingly dishonest when out-of-work.'* He had a fair income from social security and about £100 a week tent erecting, *'on the fiddle'.* *'The main thrust of work with Alistair during the past 22 months has centred on the offending behaviour and his problems in coping with responsibilities as a partner and parent — original problems were caused by poor quality of care by his own parents. He has always accepted the above problems and has stated that additionally he has always found budgeting extremely difficult, despite the fact that there is quite a considerable income available to him and his partner. He is not available for the [probation] budgeting course because the course is during his working hours.'* The order was drawing to a close, perhaps successfully, though not of course from the point of view of the Secretary of State for Social Security.

Conclusion

The theme of the criminological literature seeks to establish a progression for some males into Professional offending. Whilst that progression is occurring, the presence of social bonds which normally protect people from criminality cannot be guaranteed because of individual material circumstances and the economic climate in which they are located. We have shown that changes are not always for the worse. Neither probation officers nor the service in general can change economic prospects, but through community development work the service can have an impact. If it does not, the probation service remains a corrections agency. The probation service can add the dimensions of personal experiences and their social contexts which we have demonstrated in these chapters to inter-agency crime prevention led by the local authority. Of course, each agency has its own interests to promote in crime prevention, but it should be more than just an opportunity for crime reduction. The probation service needs to be concerned with family support, leisure — things that are exciting, in order to promote an interest in the needs of neighbourhoods lacking 'community'.

9 Policy and management implications

Cedric Fullwood, Chief Probation Officer, Greater Manchester Probation Service

The author is grateful for the contribution of Mary Fielder, now with the Home Office Inspectorate of Probation, and Hilary Thompson, Assistant Chief Probation Officer, in Greater Manchester Probation Service.

The profile of offenders included in the Lancaster Study has been well documented elsewhere. The NAPO study (May 1993) of the financial circumstances of 1,331 offenders on probation supervision revealed that 64 per cent (a figure that went up to 80 per cent for inner cities) had been unemployed for twelve months or were in receipt of sickness benefit. 79 per cent were solely dependent on means tested benefits. The statistics in Figure 9.1 from a University of Southampton survey of Dorset and Hampshire Probation Area's workload confirm the complex and multi-faceted features of offenders' problems.

As commentators on that study have emphasised, no agency other than the Probation Service has this type of profile of individuals on its workload, with the responsibility of providing them with control and help through very destructive phases of their lives.

Staff working in such an organisation as the probation service must have a range of skills and knowledge together with supervision and support structures. They must feel to a considerable degree, whether they articulate it or not, that the organisation is investing in people, both staff and 'clients'. They must feel that the organisation

Some problems of Dorset and Hampshire probationers

33% had been in care
40% had served a custodial sentence
28% had chronic housing problems
75% were unemployed
10% had attempted suicide
15% were HIV positive
15% had mental illness problems
35% and 46% had drug and drink problems

(Pritchard, 1992)

Figure 9.1

is prepared to stand up for fundamental principles of justice and dignity and a commitment to change and progress, to build on everyone's strengths. They must also feel that the organisation is able to tap the rich sources of available knowledge about its clientele, its working methods, and the personal and social circumstances of those with whom it works in a way that informs the agendas of other criminal justice agencies and the policy developments of Government departments, whether central or local.

As the 1990s began, it could be said that a grave lacuna opened up between social justice research and criminal justice policy and legislative developments. The Lancaster University Study was being undertaken in 1991 and parts of it were published in the early months of 1992. This was the very period when consultation of a most radical kind was taking place on the Criminal Justice Act 1991 and the training and preparation for its implementation in 1992 was under-way. The report *Social Circumstances of Younger Offenders Under Supervision* was finally published in February 1993 just when the Lord Chief Justice and the then Home Secretary were sending the 1991 Criminal Justice Act into a tailspin. The year that then followed included new, or revisited, statements that 'prison works', and from many Government Ministers an outright assertion that there was no link between poverty and crime, between unemployment and offending. In this legislative and policy turmoil it is not surprising that the probation service nationally and probation areas locally have yet to come fully to grips with the implications of the social policy research for probation practice and criminal justice strategies.

The years 1993 and 1994 saw a range of initiatives affecting the probation service and the wider public sector within which context any consideration of the management response to the research on social circumstances of offenders must be set. The partnership clause in the 1991 Act enables probation committees to make grants to the voluntary and independent sector as well as the private sector. Eventually at least 5 per cent of an area's budget will be spent on buying services from the independent and private sector to set alongside the work of the probation service. This was seen as one of a number of strands which were breaking down the monopoly position of the probation service and developing a notion in the Government's mind of a more pluralist range of providers — by its very nature seen as a good development. The first circular from the Home Office to probation services asking them to consider competitive tendering of a range of critical support services was issued in February 1994. Some probation services were having to subject their prison social work services to market testing. The role of the private sector in community penalties and the provision of information to courts was clear to see in the announcement that further initiatives would take place in respect of electronic monitoring (tagging) for sentenced offenders in the community. The development of agency status for the prison service and the announcement that agency status would apply to the court administration signalled behaviour which made those involved in Next Steps agencies much more inward looking than outward. The purchaser and provider fragmentation within the Social Services and the Health Service was clearly hinted at in various developments affecting the probation service. A number of probation areas had for several years been attempting to ensure that their crime prevention work impacted on local strategies for urban regeneration and multi-agency approaches to crime reduction. The announcement of the establishment of co-ordinating Central Government regional departments overseeing Single Regeneration Budgets in 1993/94 produced demands on probation service management in responding to further funding and organisational upheaval at local and regional government level. These are but some of the public policy developments bearing down on probation service management.

As the vivid case examples in this book eloquently testify, responding to offenders in crisis demands an individualised response on the part of probation staff as well as a variety of networks in the community. That basically individualised act, individualised in a similar way to the act of sentencing and thus a common denominator with sentencers, must however be linked to the wider social context and public policy developments referred to above. We have probably not stressed enough that a common characteristic of probation officers' activity in both supervising offenders and the probation manager's activity in leading and developing probation organisations is in the interface work of both within the criminal and

social justice arena and within local communities where offenders
and victims merge, where concerns and anxieties about law and
order and its destructive potential affect all, including offenders as
victims — unpopular though this notion is.

The widespread nature of disadvantage, underachievement and
hopelessness experienced by the majority of those interviewed for
the Lancaster study is evidenced in the statistics of 64 per cent
being unemployed, 68 per cent with a weekly income below £40,
27 per cent already being parents and 22 per cent classified as
incapacitated. The impoverished life of so many young offenders
was clearly illustrated in their experience of education where the
majority not only trailed behind the average achievement of their
contemporaries but reflected a yawning gulf. Despite these figures,
material issues appeared to have been given a low rating by
supervising officers in their actual practice although unemployment
and housing were often seen as high priority issues in the intention
of current supervision. There is a historical and sociological chapter
to be written as to why the management of the service had not
assessed in any substantive way the gap between the clear and
often perceived needs of young offenders and the supervising
practices of staff. What is clear is that, if supervising offenders
in the community is to have any chance of being effective, priority
must be given to alleviating practical problems. This is not to say
that such an approach should be an alternative to other strategies
for intervention such as offence focused work, nor does it deny the
necessity of emotional support and counselling. But what is clear
is that the practical problems of housing, debt, unemployment and
addiction are so dominant in the experience of offenders that they
are likely to negate all other efforts unless tackled. What is also
clear is that these problems do not generally appear as a single
issue, but the majority of young offenders experience very many
of them, and thus what is required is a comprehensive approach to
the planning and delivery of supervision. Giving priority attention
to issues of material deprivation and restricted opportunity clearly
means a significant change of focus in the practice of probation staff.
Clearly the macro issues which are causative of the social exclusion
of offenders affect many others also and require action at the highest
level. This is not within the direct influence of the probation service.
However, this should not mean that the probation service therefore
assumes a position of fatalistic acceptance. To do so would be
irresponsible to those for whom we have continuing responsibility
to advise, assist and befriend as well as to supervise and control.

There is at present little managerial direction about the required
focus for attention in supervision, especially bearing in mind social
circumstances as described in this book. National Standards

promulgated by the Home Office lay down expectations about the structure of supervision, and various guidelines/policies advise or define the action to be taken in particular circumstances, e.g. where suspected child abuse is identified. However, there is no requirement about the weight of attention to be given to problems such as unemployment and poverty, despite their importance and prevalence.

The task to be tackled in achieving a shift of focus should not be underestimated. It will mean challenging and overcoming 'political' positions articulated by some members of probation staff to justify failure to engage in, for example, employment issues. It will raise questions about the skills needed by staff and therefore, perhaps, about the nature and qualifications of staff required to undertake the necessary work. The overlap with the partnership considerations is probably obvious. These matters will inevitably mean a review of the deployment of resources. If the focus of practice is to be more clearly stated, what is required of management is:

— a specific statement of expectation
— a strategy for achievement
— a review of the resources implications.

Statements of intent and broad strategies have characterised much policy in the public sector field generally and probation policy in particular over the past ten years. If these often grandiose and jargon-ridden statements are to have any impact, they must be relevant to the working practices of probation staff and the lives and communities of offenders. Failure to address this in an effective way will simply deepen the breach between managers and practitioners just at a time when the service needs an integrated and well-directed workforce.

Government policies and Home Office National Standards/ Guidelines for the Probation Service concentrate our efforts on tasks derived from criminal justice issues. We are expected to come to (some) social policy aspects of offenders' lives through offending or the judicial response to it of a court order that has to be assiduously overseen in the community. Some social issues, for example drug and alcohol problem, are easier for the central policies and guidelines to target. Others, such as employment, poverty[1] and homelessness are much more sensitive for Home Office attention. To openly encourage the Probation Service to prioritise its work on such factors in offenders' lives runs the risk of admitting or exposing the flaws in Government policies over the past fifteen years. This makes it critically important that national bodies, such as the Association of Chief Officers of Probation, give guidance and attention to these complexities.   Similarly, it is vital for local service management to include these problem areas in their strategies and deployment of resources.

Most services have been characterised by an incremental growth of specialists concentrating on one or other of these social policy developments. In the 1980s some services appointed Welfare Benefits Advisers. However, as research and practice demonstrate, no one social issue exists in isolation when it comes to the complex lives of offenders. Substance misuse issues particularly require attention to accommodation, employment and community context for stabilising solutions. Accommodation move-on projects are unlikely to work if collaborative employment/income generation projects and work on substance misuse problems are not put in context. An employment worker will not achieve good results without collaboration with substance misuse workers, since 40 per cent of his or her target group will have substance misuse problems. Poverty underpins many, if not all, of these other characteristics. External consultants to the probation service are already indicating the need for linkages between the different approaches and the need to give priority to half a dozen core elements of practice. Management needs to be bold in forming new alliances alongside practitioners both internal and external to the probation service. Traditional team structures and narrow, possessive and inward-looking approaches must be broken down by true 'partnership'.

There are also core elements to the strategic development. Half a dozen such elements are always identified:

- practice issues, guidelines and assessment
- information strategy
- funding strategy
- training strategy
- special project approach
- partnership contributions.

At the end of the day the matrices of intervention are complex but worth engaging with and will give credibility to the substance and authority of the service's voice and contribution to the problems of crime and breakdown in communities. Implicit in this last statement is the need for a public relations strategy to explain the nuances of the service's approach to these matters.

The Lancaster studies were commissioned by the Association of Chief Officers of Probation. What has taken place nationally and locally since their publication? The relevant Committee of ACOP, the newly named Social Policy and Employment Committee, met in January 1993 and agreed to oversee the taking forward of work connected with the studies. Over the past eighteen months, five subcommittees have been formed to respond to the reports' findings. These subcommittees of the Social Policy and Employment Committee are:

1. Employment (linked to the National Offender Forum which brings together ACOP and voluntary agencies, and meets with representatives of the Probation Service Division of the Home Office)
2. Poverty and Benefits (a Group that has links with and advice from the Welfare Benefits Advisers who work in the Probation Service)
3. Alcohol
4. Addictions
5. HIV and health issues.

The work of these various subgroups is monitored and supported through twice-yearly meetings of the full Social Policy and Employment Committee. Space does not allow for a full coverage of all the activities of these groups, but reference by way of example can be made to the Employment Group and the Poverty and Benefits Group. On the employment front, initiatives have been taken to develop policy and practice guidelines for Probation Services and this has involved the Service and its partners in the voluntary sector (APEX, NACRO, etc), as well as making representations to the Home Office. It is not insignificant that, at a time when Home Office Ministers have been protesting that there is no link between unemployment and crime, this work has not only been progressed, but the Home Office, with Ministerial support, have issued circular guidance in May 1994 to all Probation Services asking them to take measured and significant steps to ensure that supervision of offenders attends to the problem of unemployment and the opportunities for training and pre-employment training.

The Poverty and Benefits Group has been similarly active. It has made contact with the Independent Commission for Social Justice established by the Labour Party and chaired by Sir Gordon Borrie, and also with NACRO's working group on Social Policy and Crime Prevention, chaired by Professor David Donnison (due to report in the summer of 1994). The Group has had meetings with and made representations to the Home Office to encourage a more co-ordinated approach to Government policy developments overall, and to the Social Security Advisory Committee, and the Association of Directors of Social Service. In respect of the Social Security Advisory Committee, the meeting which took place between ACOP representatives and the Committee in February 1994 covered presentations on:

• discharge grants to prisoners
• lack of benefits for young people under 18 years

- housing benefit allowances for persons residing at approved hostels
- Social Fund issues.

The meetings with the Association of Directors of Social Service have covered residential issues, community care assessments, work with mentally disordered offenders, and juvenile/young offenders.

The Poverty and Benefits Subgroup has attended and participated in the Social Security Consortium and made formal responses to Social Security and Housing legislation and regulations. It prepared a workshop at the ACOP Conference in Newcastle in April 1994, entitled 'Towards a Poverty Strategy'. The subgroup in 1993 devised a three-part plan to respond to the Lancaster research based on a general principle of developing advice for practice, and aiming to:

- identify those areas of social policy which required probation areas to develop policies to meet the identified need, and strategies to implement those policies
- monitor and respond to developments/changes in relevant regulations and legislation which will affect directly the lives of offenders and the work of the Probation Service
- develop links and liaison with other relevant groups in ACOP and elsewhere to inform the work of the Probation Service in its work with offenders and the wider criminal justice system — these links to include the European dimension.

At a local probation area level, a number of management groups have established initiatives to prepare reports and receive papers on the implications of the Lancaster reports and related developments. Such major reports from individuals or task groups were received in Greater Manchester (October 1993) and Inner London and Northumbria (in November 1993). These and developments in other probation areas in England and Wales have required the establishment of co-ordinating groups to bring together the diverse activities of staff dealing with social policy issues and practical problems. Some areas, like Inner London, have recommended the deployment of specialist staff (twelve money advice worker posts, together with a co-ordinator).

It is not only the probation service though that is taking initiatives in this area. As long ago as the late 1970s, Strathclyde Social Work Department were establishing officer/ member groups to look at the problems of poverty and the need for co-ordinated strategies and intervention to maximise the benefits received, as well as to provide specialist facilities for drug and alcohol problems. More recently the North West Legal Services Committee, which is now working to the Legal Aid Board is developing its services along with others in the community (welfare rights and CAB) to maximise the help it provides on a range of fronts, such as debt and housing law. The North West Legal Services Committee has access to national data on poverty and social need in local areas. These are identified on maps which are then shared with solicitors locally, who provide their knowledge to target the advice. This approach is used by solicitors in both inner city areas and rural situations. Its aim is to ensure that clients reach the most appropriate source of help for their needs and to encourage firms of solicitors and agencies to work together in formal schemes.

It is critical, however, that the work of Probation Services and the initiatives from other sources, such as legal advice, are anchored in related work of both local authorities and the new regional single regeneration departments of central government. Some local authorities are making real efforts to co-ordinate departments of social services, housing and voluntary organisations *'to ensure that the bewildered 16-year-old is not bounced backwards and forwards between officials'*. There are still too many developments which can be characterised by the following:

> One Government Department cuts benefits to save money and several others are then forced to come up with partial solutions to patch up the resulting mess.   This is an issue which entangles almost every department: it is about education, health, training, homelessness, benefits and crime. The reason why there has been no co-ordinated strategy is because it would open a can of worms over the ideology of family life and parental authority — issues which have now become highly criticised. (Madeleine Bunting, *Guardian* 1 June 1994).

'The fragility of hope' is the first casualty in the complex web of social policy and family and individual lives represented in the Lancaster studies. We must not abandon that hope and the probation service's response to date, together with the advice and guidance given in this book, hopefully will shore up our commitment and determination.

Note

1. The new Rule 41A implementing clause 97 of the Criminal Justice Act 1991 allowing Probation Committees/Boards to grant-aid the independent and private sector states that these grants can be for the provision of services concerned, *inter alia*, with employment, various substance abuse problems and financial advice.

Index of names of cases by probation area and typology

Name	Probation Area	Typology	Pages
Joe	Avon	Social Norm	90
Karl	Avon	Life-style	129
Keir	Avon	Life-style	137
Leo	Avon	Life-style	127
Les	Avon	Self-expression	47
Liam	Avon	Professional	155
Lon	Avon	Professional	159
Mandy	Avon	Self-expression	33
Marianne	Avon	Life-style	134
Matt	Avon	Life-style	126
Max	Avon	Life-style	139
Nev	Avon	Social Activity	72
Niall	Avon	Coping	112
Pat(ricia)	Avon	Self-expression	42
Pete	Avon	Social Activity	60
Phil	Avon	Social Activity	67
Ray	Avon	Social Norm	90
		Coping	117
Rob	Avon	Self-expression	46
		Coping	116
Ron	Avon	Social Activity	59
Russell	Avon	Self-expression	38
Stephan	Avon	Social Norm	81
Alan	Cleveland	Self-expression	32
Alistair	Cleveland	Professional	164
Andy	Cleveland	Social Norm	86
Bicky	Cleveland	Coping	105
Bill	Cleveland	Social Activity	69
Don	Cleveland	Life-style	132
Duncan	Cleveland	Professional	156
Gordon	Cleveland	Social Norm	84
Greg	Cleveland	Social Norm	87
Guy	Cleveland	Professional	149
Jake	Cleveland	Life-style	130
Jamie	Cleveland	Professional	155
Jenny	Cleveland	Self-expression	51
Jonathan	Cleveland	Coping	115
Kevin	Cleveland	Coping	104
Lee	Cleveland	Self-expression	40
Mark	Cleveland	Social Activity	58
Ruby	Cleveland	Social Norm	87

Name	Probation Area	Typology	Pages
Priti	ILPS	Life-style	130
Ralph	ILPS	Life-style	136
Rigby	ILPS	Professional	159
Ryan	ILPS	Professional	147
Sarah	ILPS	Life-style	138
Sid	ILPS	Social Activity	64
Spider	ILPS	Life-style	126
Steve	ILPS	Self-expression	49
Walt	ILPS	Self-expression	48
Albert	North'b	Professional	154
Alec	North'b	Social Activity	67
Amanda	North'b	Life-style	123
Bert	North'b	Self-expression	31
Callum	North'b	Professional	153
Camilla	North'b	Social Norm	82
Dean	North'b	Professional	151
Dick	North'b	Social Activity	71
		Social Norm	85
		Life-style	130
Digby	North'b	Professional	163
Edmund	North'b	Professional	158
Erol	North'b	Professional	148
Gaz	North'b	Social Activity	57
Griff	North'b	Life-style	127
Howard	North'b	Professional	147
Jill	North'b	Self-expression	34
Keith	North'b	Self-expression	43
Kurt	North'b	Social Activity	62
Lance	North'b	Self-expression	50
Lawrence	North'b	Coping	103
Lionel	North'b	Professional	158
Martin	North'b	Social Norm	81
Mike	North'b	Social Activity	64
		Life-style	129
Morris	North'b	Social Norm	87
Nigel	North'b	Social Activity	71
Oscar	North'b	Life-style	133
Owen	North'b	Coping	111
Rebecca	North'b	Coping	107
Roy	North'b	Professional	158

Name	Probation Area	Typology	Pages
Larry	West Mid.	Professional	162
Mo	West Mid.	Self-expression	37
Ned	West Mid.	Self-expression	45
Richard	West Mid.	Social Norm	80
		Life-style	129
Rik	West Mid.	Coping	114
Roger	West Mid.	Life-style	133
Rosemary	West Mid.	Life-style	136
Sharon	West Mid.	Coping	114
Ted	West Mid.	Professional	162
Tim	West Mid.	Self-expression	42
Tristan	West Mid.	Self-expression	32
Viny	West Mid.	Social Norm	89
Wayne	West Mid.	Life-style	132
Zac	West Mid.	Social Norm	89

Bibliography and index of author citation

The page numbers after each entry in parenthesis refer to the places in this book where the references are cited.

Agnew, R. (1985) 'A revised strain theory of delinquency', *Social Forces*, **64**, pp.151–167. (p. 25, 30)

Banks, M., Bates, I., Breakwell, G., Bynner, J., Emler, N., Jamieson, L. and Roberts, K. (1992) *Careers and Identities*, Milton Keynes, Open University Press. (p. 53, 54)

Barclay, G. C. (ed.) (1993) *Digest 2: Information on the Criminal Justice System in England and Wales*, London, Home Office. (p. 10)

Barke, M. and Turnbull, G. (1992) *Meadowell: the biography of an estate with problems*, Aldershot, Avebury. (p. 76, 77)

Bennett, T. and Wright, R. (1984) *Burglars on Burglary*, Aldershot, Gower. (p. 5)

Birmingham Settlement (1993) *The Hidden Disconnected: an investigation of consumer fuel companies and agency responses to pre-payment meters and fuel direct*, Birmingham, Birmingham Settlement Research Unit. (p. 116)

Blagg, H., Pearson, G., Sampson, A., Smith, D. and Stubbs, P. (1988) 'Inter-agency co-ordination: rhetoric and reality' in Hope, T. and Shaw, M. (eds.) *Communities and Crime Reduction*, London, HMSO. (p. 77)

Blagg, H. and Smith, D. (1989) *Crime, Penal Policy and Social Work*, Harlow, Longman. (p. 3, 7)

Bonnerjea, L. and Lawton, J. (1987) *Homelessness in Brent*, London, Policy Studies Institute. (p. 77)

Bottoms, A. E. and McWilliams, W. (1979) 'A non-treatment paradigm for probation practice', *British Journal of Social Work*, **9**, pp.159–202. (p. 4)

Bottoms, A. E., Mawby, R. I. and Xanthos, P. (1986) 'A tale of two estates' in Downes, D. (ed.) *Crime and the City: essays in memory of John Barron Mays*, London, Macmillan. (p. 74)

Box, S. (1981) *Deviance, Reality and Society*, London, Holt, Rinehart and Winston. (p. 28, 29)

Braithwaite, J. (1989) *Crime, Shame and Reintegration*, Cambridge, Cambridge University Press. (p. 5, 6, 16, 17, 18, 20, 23, 24, 25, 29, 30, 55, 56, 62)

Braithwaite, J. and Pettit, P. (1990) *Not Just Deserts*, Oxford, Oxford University Press. (p. 11)

Brody, S. and Tarling, R. (1980) *Taking Offenders out of Circulation* (Home Office Research Study 64), London, HMSO. (p. 10)

Brown, A. and Caddick, B. (eds.) (1993) *Groupwork with Offenders*, London, Whiting and Birch. (p. 72)

Campbell, B. (1993) *Goliath: Britain's dangerous places*, London, Methuen. (p. 16, 39, 77, 112)

Cavadino, M. and Dignan, J. (1992) *The Penal System: an introduction*, London, Sage. (p. 3, 10)

Cleckley, H. (1964) *The Mask of Sanity*, St Louis, Missouri, C. V. Mosby. (p. 151)

Cloward, R. A. and Ohlin, L. E. (1960) *Delinquency and Opportunity: a theory of delinquent gangs*, Glencoe, Ill., Free Press. (p. 30, 56, 62, 64, 131, 133)

Coates, K. and Silburn, R. (1973) *Poverty: the forgotten Englishmen*, Harmondsworth, Pelican. (p. 77, 81)

Cocket, M. and Tripp, J. (1994 forthcoming) *Exeter Family Study*, London, Family Policy Studies Centre. (p. 28)

Coleman, A. (1985) *Utopia on Trial*, London, Shipman. (p. 76)

Cornish, D. B. and Clarke, R. V. G. (eds.) (1986) *The Reasoning Criminal*, Berlin, Springer-Verlag. (p. 5, 145)

Corrigan, P. (1978) *Schooling the Smash Street Kids*, London, Macmillan. (p. 65)

Damer, S. (1989) *From Moorepark to 'Wine Alley': the rise and fall of a Glasgow housing scheme*, Edinburgh, Edinburgh University Press. (p. 75)

Davies, M. (1969) *Probationers in Their Social Environment: a study of male probationers aged 17–20*, London, Home Office Research Studies, HMSO. (p. 13, 99, 124)

Dell, S. et al. (1991) *Mentally Disordered Offenders*, summary of a report to the Home Office by the Cambridge Institute of Criminology. (p. 49)

Denman, G. (1982) *Intensive Intermediate Treatment with Juvenile Offenders: a handbook of assessment and groupwork practice*, Lancaster, Centre for Youth, Crime and Community, Lancaster University. (p. 4)

Dennis, N. (1993) *Rising Crime and the Dismembered Family*, London, Institute of Economic Affairs. (p. 154, 155)

Dickinson, D. (1993) *Crime and Unemployment*, Cambridge, Department of Applied Economics, University of Cambridge. (p. 102)

Dimmock, B. (1993) *Working with Troubled and Troublesome Young People in Residential Settings*, Milton Keynes, Open University Press. (p. 142)

Dodd, T. and Hunter, P. (1992) *The National Prison Survey 1991*, London, HMSO. (p. 13)

Downes, D. (1966) *The Delinquent Solution*, London, Routledge & Kegan Paul. (p. 30)

Downes, D. (1993) *Employment Opportunities for Offenders*, London, Home Office. (p. 6, 14, 24, 94)

Downes, D. (1994) '"Hostages to fortune"? The politics of law and order in post-war Britain' in Maguire, M., Morgan, R. and Reiner, R. (eds.) *The Oxford Handbook of Criminology*, Oxford, Clarendon Press. (p. 2)

Downes, D. and Rock, P. (1988) *Understanding Deviance*, Oxford, Oxford University Press. (p. 55)

Emler, N., Reider, S. and Ross, A. (1987) 'The social context of delinquent conduct', *Journal of Child Psychology and Psychiatry*, 27, pp.99–109. (p. 54)

Evans, D., Fyfe, N. and Herbert, D. (eds.) (1992) *Crime, Policing and Place: essays in environmental criminology*, London, Routledge. (p. 74)

Fagin, L. and Little, M. (1984) *The Forsaken Families*, Harmondsworth, Penguin. (p. 39)

Farrington, D. P. (1990) 'Implications of career research for the prevention of offending', *Journal of Adolescence*, 13, pp.93–113. (p. 16, 31, 78)

Faulkner, D. E. R. (1993) 'All flaws and disorder', *The Guardian*, 11 November. (p. 10)

Feaver, N. and Smith, D. (1994) 'Editorial introduction', *British Journal of Social Work*, **24**, 4, pp.379–386. (p. 9)

Field, S. (1990) *Trends in Crime and Their Interpretation: a study of recorded crime in post-war England and Wales* (Home Office Research Study 119), London, HMSO. (p. 6, 94)

Finkelhor, D. (1984) *Child Sexual Abuse: new theory and research*, New York, The Free Press. (p. 20)

Fitzwilliam-Pipe, A. J. (1992) *The Use of a Computer Expert System to Enhance the Professional Decision Making of the Probation Service*, Lancaster, unpublished MPhil. thesis, Lancaster University. (p. 121)

Ford, J. (1991) *Consuming Credit: debt and poverty in the UK*, London, Child Poverty Action Group. (p. 116)

Foster, J. (1990) *Villains: crime and community in the inner city*, London, Routledge. (p. 18, 56, 73, 74, 75, 91, 142)

Foster, J. and Hope, T. (1993) *Housing, Community and Crime: the impact of the Priority Estates Project*, London, Home Office Research and Planning Unit Report 131, HMSO. (p. 18, 74, 76, 78)

Gelsthorpe, L. R. (1989) *Sexism and the Female Offender*, Aldershot, Gower. (p. 21)

Geraghty, J. (1991) *Probation Practice in Crime Prevention* (Crime Prevention Unit Paper 24), London, Home Office. (p. 19)

Gifford, Lord (chair) (1986) *The Broadwater Farm Inquiry*, London: Karia Press. (p. 77)

Gill, O. (1977) *Luke Street: housing policy, conflict and the creation of a delinquent area*, London, Macmillan. (p. 75)

Glaser, D. (1980) 'The interplay of theory, issues and data' in Klein, M. and Teilmann, K. (eds.) *Handbook of Criminal Justice Evaluation*, Beverley Hills Cal., Sage. (p. 145)

Goodman, A. and Webb, S. (1994) *For Richer, for Poorer: the changing distribution of Income in the UK, 1961–91*, London, Institute for Fiscal Studies. (p. 100)

Hagell, A. and Newburn, T. (1994) *Persistent Young Offenders*, London, Policy Studies Institute. (p. 142)

Haines, K. (1990) *After-care for Released Prisoners: a review of the literature*, Cambridge, Institute of Criminology. (p. 6, 150)

Hall, S. and Jefferson, T. (eds.) (1976) *Resistance Through Rituals: youth sub-culture in post-war Britain*, London, Hutchinson. (p. 56)

Hammersley, R., Morrison, V., Davies, J. B. and Forsyth, A. (1989) *Heroin Use and Crime: a comparison of heroin users and non-users in and out of prison* (Report to the Criminology and Law Research Group), Edinburgh, Scottish Home and Health Department. (p. 120)

Heidensohn, F. (1988) *Crime and Society*, Basingstoke, Macmillan. (p. 21)

Hirschi, T. (1969) *Causes of Delinquency*, Berkeley Cal., University of California Press. (p. 16, 23, 28, 154)

Home Office (1984) *Statement of National Objectives and Priorities*, London, HMSO. (p. 2)

Home Office (1988a) *Punishment, Custody and the Community* (Cm. 424), London, HMSO. (p. 3, 7, 122)

Home Office (1988b) *Tackling Offending: an action plan*, London, Home Office. (p. 3, 7)

Home Office (1990a) *Crime, Justice and Protecting the Public* (Cm. 965), London, HMSO. (p. 6, 7)

Home Office (1990b) *Supervision and Punishment in the Community* (Cm. 966), London, HMSO. (p. 7, 122)

Home Office (1990c) *Partnership in Dealing with Offenders in the Community*, London, Home Office. (p. 7)

Home Office (1993) *Monitoring of the Criminal Justice Act 1991: data from a special data collection exercise* (Statistical Bulletin 25/93), London, Home Office. (p. 9)

Hood, R. (1992) *Race and Sentencing: a study in the Crown Court*, Oxford, Clarendon Press. (p. 22)

House of Commons Home Affairs Committee (1986) *Racial Attacks and Harassment* (3rd. report, session 1985–86, HCP 409), London, HMSO. (p. 77)

Humphrey, C. and Pease, K. (1992) 'Effectiveness measurement in the probation service: a view from the troops', *Howard Journal of Criminal Justice*, **31**, 1, pp.31–52. (p. 3)

Jarvis, G. and Parker, H. (1989) 'Young heroin users and crime: how do the new users finance their habits?', *British Journal of Criminology*, **29**, pp.175–185. (p. 120)

Jones, G. (1987) 'Leaving the parental home: an analysis of early housing careers', *Journal of Social Policy*, **16**, pp.49–74. (p. 27)

Light, R., Nee, C. and Ingham, H. (1993) *Car Theft: the offender's perspective* (Home Office Research Study 130), London, HMSO. (p. 10, 56, 142, 157)

Limehouse Fields Tenants',Association (1987) *Tenants Tackle Racism*, London, Dame Colet House. (p. 77)

Lloyd, P. (1989) 'In defence of the Social Fund', *Social Work Tody*, 19 January p.12. (p. 94)

Macdonald, G. (1994) 'Developing empirically-based practice in probation', *British Journal of Social Work*, **24**, 4, pp.405–427. (p. 21)

McGillivray, M. (1993) *Putting the Brakes on Car Crime: a local study of auto-related crime among young people*, London, The Children's Society. (p. 59)

McIvor, G. (1990) *Sanctions for Serious or Persistent Offenders: a review of the literature*, Stirling, Social Work Research Centre, University of Stirling. (p. 8)

McWilliams, W. and Pease, K. (1990) 'Probation practice and an end to punishment', *Howard Journal of Criminal Justice* **29**, pp. 311–327 (p. 68)

Maden, A., Swinton, M. and Gunn, J. (1992) 'A survey of pre-arrest drug use in sentenced prisoners', *British Journal of Addiction*, **87**, pp.27–33. (p. 121)

Matza, D. (1964) *Delinquency and Drift*, New York, John Wiley. (p. 66)

Mayhew, P., Clarke, R. V. G., Sturman, A. and Hough, J. M. (1976) *Crime as Opportunity* (Home Office Research Study 34), London, HMSO. (p. 4)

Maynard, M. (1985) 'The response of social workers to domestic violence' in Pahl, J. (ed.) *Private Violence and Public Policy*, London, Routledge. (p. 59)

Merton, R. K. (1957) *Social Theory and Social Structure*, Glencoe Ill., Free Press. (p. 29, 153)

MORI (1991) *A Survey of 16 and 17 Year Old Applicants for Severe Hardship Payments*, London, MORI for the Department of Social Security. (p. 97)

Morrison, T. (1978) *Song of Solomon*, London, Picador. (p. 29)

National Association of Probation Officers (1993) *Probation Caseload: income and employment — a study of the financial circumstances of 1331 offenders on probation supervision*, London, NAPO. (p. 97, 98, 101, 166)

Office of Population Censuses and Surveys (1992) *Labour Force Survey 1990 and 1991* (series LFS no. 9), London, HMSO. (p. 101)

O'Higgins, M. and Jenkins, S. (1990) 'Poverty in the EC: estimates for 1975, 1980 and 1985' in Terekens, R. and Van Praag, B. (eds.) *Analysing Poverty in the European Community*, Luxembourg, Eurostat News Special Edition. (p. 99)

Parker, H., Bakx, K. and Newcombe, R. (1988) *Living with Heroin: the impact of a drugs 'epidemic' on an English community*, Milton Keynes, Open University Press. (p. 120)

Paylor, I. (1992) *Homelessness and Ex-offenders: a case for reform*, Norwich, University of East Anglia. (p. 2)

Paylor, I. and Smith, D. B. (1994) 'Who are prisoners' families?', *Journal of Social Welfare and Family Law*, **16**, 2, pp.131–144. (p. 6)

Pearson, G. (1987) *The New Heroin Users*, Oxford, Blackwell. (p. 24, 120, 130)

Peelo, M., Stewart, J., Stewart, G. and Prior, A. (1991) 'Women partners of prisoners', *Howard Journal of Criminal Justice*, **30**, 4, pp.311–327. (p. 6, 118)

Peelo, M., Stewart, J., Stewart, G. and Prior, A. (1992) *A Sense of Justice: offenders as victims of crime*, London, Association of Chief Officers of Probation. (p. 20, 91)

Philp, M. (1979) 'Notes on the form of knowledge in social work', *Sociological Review*, **27**, 1, pp.83–111. (p. 5, 52)

Pitts, J. (1988) *The Politics of Juvenile Crime*, London, Sage. (p. 4)

Priestley, P. and McGuire, J. (1985) *Offending Behaviour: skills and stratagems for going straight*, London, Sage. (p. 4, 72)

Raffe, D. and Smith, P. (1987) 'Young people's attitudes to YTS: the first two years', *British Educational Research Journal*, **13**, pp.241–260. (p. 54)

Rainwater, L. (1971) *Behind Ghetto Walls: black families in a Federal slum*, London, Allen Lane. (p. 74)

Raynor, P. (1980) 'Is there any sense in social inquiry reports?', *Probation Journal*, **27**, 2, pp.78–84. (p. 5)

Raynor, P. (1988) *Probation as an Alternative to Custody*, Aldershot, Avebury. (p. 8)

Raynor, P., Smith, D. and Vanstone, M. (1994) *Effective Probation Practice*, Basingstoke, Macmillan. (p. 4, 9, 11, 122)

Rex, J. and Moore, R. (1967) *Race, Community and Conflict: a study of Sparkbrook*, Oxford, Oxford University Press. (p. 75)

Reynolds, F. (1986) *The Problem Housing Estate*, Aldershot, Gower. (p. 75)

Riley, D. and Shaw, M. (1985) *Parental Supervision and Juvenile Delinquency* (Home Office Research Study no. 83), London, HMSO. (p. 54)

Roberts, C. H. (1989) *First Evaluation Report, Young Offenders Project*, Worcester, Hereford and Worcester Probation Service. (p. 8)

Rock, P. (1988) 'Crime reduction initiatives on problem estates' in Hope, T. and Shaw, M. (eds.) *Communities and Crime Reduction*, London, HMSO. (p. 77)

Roll, J. (1990) *Young People Growing up in the Welfare State*, London, Family Policy Studies Centre. (p. 27)

Shaw, C. and McKay, H. (1971) in Short, J. (ed.) *The Social Fabric of the Metropolis*, Chicago, University of Chicago Press. (p. 75)

Shover, N. (1985) *Aging Criminals*, London, Sage. (p. 143, 144, 145, 146, 147)

Smith, D. (1987) 'The limits of positivism in social work research', *British Journal of Social Work*, **17**, 4, pp.401–416. (p. 9)

Smith, D. (1994) *The Home Office Regional Criminal Justice Conferences May 1990–March 1993*, Liverpool, Home Office Special Conferences Unit. (p. 2)

Smith, D., Paylor, I. and Mitchell, P. (1993) 'Partnership between the independent sector and the probation service', *Howard Journal of Criminal Justice*, **32**, 1, pp.25–39. (p. 9, 118, 122)

Smith, L. F. J. (1989) *Domestic Violence* (Home Office Research Study), London, HMSO. (p. 20)

Stewart, G. and Stewart, J. (1986) *Boundary Changes: social work and social security* (Poverty Pamphlet 70), London, Child Poverty Action Group. (p. 94)

Stewart, G. and Stewart, J. (1991) *Relieving Poverty? Use of the Social Fund by social work clients and other agencies*, London, Association of Metropolitan Authorities. (p. 37, 122)

Stewart, G. and Stewart, J. (1993a) *Social Circumstances of Younger Offenders Under*

Supervision, London, Association of Chief Officers of Probation. (p. 12, 14, 19, 29, 124, 163, 167)

Stewart, G. and Stewart, J. (1993b) *Social Work and Housing*, Basingstoke, Macmillan. (p. 27, 49, 109)

Stewart, G. and Stewart, J. (1993c) 'The politics of the Social Fund: social security policy as an issue in central-local government relations', *Local Government Studies*, **19**, 3, pp.408–430. (p. 94)

Stewart, G., Lee, R. and Stewart, J. (1986) 'The right approach to social security: the case of the Board and Lodging Regulations', *Journal of Law and Society*, **13**, 3, pp.371–399. (p. 94)

Stewart, G., Stewart, J., Prior, A. and Peelo, M. (1989) *Surviving Poverty: probation work and benefits policy*, Wakefield, Association of Chief Officers of Probation. (p. 2, 118, 122)

Sykes, G and Matza, D. (1957) 'Techniques of neutralization: a theory of delinquency', *American Sociology Review*, **22**, pp.664–670. (p. 66, 70)

Thorpe, D. H., Smith, D., Green, C. J. and Paley, J. H/ (1980) *Out of Care: the community support of juvenile offenders*, London, Allen and Unwin. (p. 3)

Utting, D., Bright, J. and Henricson, C. (1993) *Crime and the Family: improving child-rearing and preventing delinquency*, London, Family Policy Studies Centre. (p. 28, 37)

Ware, V. (1988) *Women's Safety on Housing Estates*, London, Women's Design Services. (p. 77)

Waters, R. (1988) 'Race and the criminal justice process', *British Journal of Criminology*, **28**, 1, pp.82–94. (p. 82)

Willis, P. (1977) *Learning to Labour*, Aldershot, Gower. (p. 30, 39)

Wilson, H. (1980) 'Parental supervision a neglected aspect of delinquency', *British Journal of Criminology*, **20**, pp.203–235. (p. 90)

Wilson, J. Q. and Herrnstein, R. (1985) *Crime and Human Nature*, New York, Simon and Schuster. (p. 28)

Wootton, B. (1959) *Social Science and Social Pathology*, London, Allen and Unwin. (p. 146)

Yablonsky, L. (1967) *The Violent Gang*, Harmondsworth, Penguin. (p. 55)

Zimring, F. E. (1981) 'Kids, groups and crime', *Journal of Criminal Law and Criminology*, **72**, pp.867–885. (p. 157)

Index

An index of author citations can be found in the bibliography.